Abortion Politics

Abortion Politics

DAVID MARSH AND JOANNA CHAMBERS

JUNCTION BOOKS/LONDON

First published in Great Britain by
Junction Books Ltd
33 Ivor Place
London NW1

ISBN: 0 86245 016 0 (hard)
0 86245 017 9 (paper)

Printed in Great Britain by Nene Litho, Earls Barton, Northants.
Bound by Weatherby Woolnough, Wellingborough, Northants.
Typesetting by Photo-Graphics, Yarcombe, Nr. Honiton, Devon.

Contents

List of Tables

Preface

Abortion is a controversial issue on which it is almost impossible not to hold strong opinions, or to prevent those opinions influencing what one writes. Here we state our views on abortion so that the reader can judge the book and our conclusions in the light of our position. We both believe that up to the stage when the foetus becomes viable the choice on abortion should be left to the woman concerned, after consultation with her doctor. Our opinion on the issue is reflected throughout the book if only in the terminology we use. We have used the term 'foetus' whereas a strong anti-abortionist would talk of the 'baby' from conception onwards. Similarly we discuss positions which we describe as 'pro-abortion' and 'anti-abortion', although anti-abortionists would probably describe their position as 'pro-life'. We have adopted what appears to us to be the more common usage in both cases but we are aware that not all our readers will agree.

In fact this book does not directly discuss the political or moral issues involved in abortion; rather we are interested in describing and explaining parliamentary events. This probably enables us to be less polemical than most people who write on the subject. At the same time, in order to ensure balance, we talked to most of the MPs directly involved in the issue since the 1960s and with all the major campaigning interest groups. Everyone co-operated with us and supplied us with material which has helped to build up a complete picture. Essentially, then, this is intended as an academic study of the abortion issue in Parliament. We have tried, as far as possible, to divorce our views on abortion from the analysis. The book is severely weakened if we have failed to do so to any great extent.

We have an additional and related problem. Joanna Chambers was Co-ordinator of the Co-ordinating Committee in Defence of the 1967 Abortion Act throughout the passage of the Corrie Bill and was, therefore, an important activist in the pro-abortion lobby. Obviously this gives us privileged access to information about that lobby and is a major asset. However, it does mean that at the start of our research we had considerably better access to the opponents of the Corrie Bill than to its supporters. We have tried to remedy this by interviewing individuals within the anti-abortion lobby from whom we received an enormous amount of co-operation. In particular David Marsh talked to: John Smeaton (general secretary) and Phyllis Bowman (director) of the Society for the Protection of the Unborn Child (on three separate occasions and for a total of five hours); Professor Scarisbrick (national chairman) of LIFE; John Corrie (interviewed twice); and most of the other major parliamentary opponents of abortion. We have, therefore, done as much as possible to prevent the differential access which we had at the outset from influencing our analyses.

The expense of interviewing MPs and interest group activists, and of collecting much of the quantitative material was greatly facilitated by a grant to David Marsh from the Nuffield Foundation. In addition a small amount of money was kindly made available by the University of Essex for the collection of material on the voting behaviour of MPs on capital punishment and homosexuality. We would like to thank both of these institutions for their financial help.

A number of people have aided us in the preparation of this book. Melvyn Read and Maria Lenn were responsible for the collection of much of the data used, while Gillie Burrell and Brenda Woolton undertook most of the typing. We are extremely grateful to them for their assistance. We would also like to thank David Sanders who advised on the computing and statistical elements in the book. Our greatest debt is to all those MPs and interest group activists who talked to us and gave us so much information. Without their help this book could not have been written.

Introduction

In the last decade and a half the abortion issue has become a parliamentary saga. In fact it has proved to be one of the most contentious and least reconcilable private members' issues in the entire history of Parliament. Since David Steel's private members' Bill was passed as the Abortion Act in 1967 there have been nine parliamentary attempts to amend it, culminating in John Corrie's Abortion (Amendment) Bill in the 1979-80 session. What is more, whenever abortion is discussed in the House of Commons the Chamber takes on a particular atmosphere. It is well filled, which itself is uncommon, the debates are emotionally charged and personal attacks are frequent. In addition there is uncertainty in the air because in the absence of the whips the result of any vote is in doubt.

Of course there are other social and moral issues which have been the subject of frequent debates in Parliament, the most notable being capital punishment. However, none of these has generated anything like as much interest and activity in and around the Chamber as abortion. The matter is a major interest for a significant number of MPs, and few other backbench Members have been able to avoid it, if only because they are subjected to considerable pressure from their constituencies on the issue. This concern is reflected not only in the high turnouts in debates and on votes but also in the fact that when an abortion bill is introduced the Parliamentary Bills Office runs out of copies within hours. At the same time the interest group activity on abortion is unparalleled. There are more interest groups concerned with this topic, and they are more politicized, than on any other social issue.

One story will amply illustrate the intensity of the feeling, activity and pressure on the issue. On the day of the anti-abortion lobby on the Corrie Bill, David Steel had arranged to meet a group from his constituency to discuss the issue. His personal assistant came down into the Central Lobby and announced the name of the leader of the group, asking him and his group to come to the desk to be taken to see David Steel in his room. There was no response so the assistant asked if anyone from the group would come to the desk. Again there was no response but the assistant made one last attempt. He asked if there was anyone who wished to see David Steel. Immediately a large number of people rushed at the desk shouting 'Murderer, Murderer'. The assistant retreated somewhat chastened.

Until the Corrie Bill none of the amending bills reached the Report Stage so that the House was confined to debates on Second Reading. On this occasion, however, for reasons which will become clear later, there was a Report Stage debate which spread over four days and a total of 13¾ hours. This is unprecedented. No other private member's bill we can trace, which did not receive government time, had more than two days on Report, and even two days is very unusual. Even hardened parliamentarians were surprised by the atmosphere generated during those four days and many of the MPs who had been newly elected in May 1979 were stunned by the level of interest in, and rancour about, the issue shown by the media, their constituents and fellow MPs. Indeed the debates and the lobbying associated with the Bill provided a very rapid politicizing experience for most of these new MPs.

The issue is unusual, perhaps even unique, in contemporary British politics, and as such is worthy of study. The main aim of this book is to examine the evolution, progress and defeat of the Corrie Bill against the background of the parliamentary history of the abortion issue. Why did the Bill progress further than previous amending bills? Why did it fail in the end? Is a similar future bill likely to succeed? However, in addition to raising and answering such specific questions, an analysis of the Corrie Bill also throws light on some wider questions of interest to observers of British politics.

First, as abortion bills are always raised under private members' business, a study of the issue, and of the Corrie Bill in particular, gives us an opportunity to examine the appropriateness of that process for dealing with highly controversial issues. Secondly, because the issue is unwhipped it provides an excellent chance to examine the factors which influence MPs' voting when they are not subject to party discipline. How important are party and constituency pressures in affecting these votes? Thirdly, because this is a private members' issue, and because the interest groups are so well developed and fairly evenly balanced, it provides an excellent case study of the tactics and strategies used, and the potential influence of parliamentary, as distinct from Whitehall, lobbying. Lastly, this case study offers an opportunity to assess the influence of feminism in British politics. Feminists have been directly involved in lobbying on this issue both inside and outside Parliament, and indeed the 'woman's right to choose' has become a major rallying call for the feminist movement. How successful have these efforts been?

This book, therefore, is largely, although not exclusively, concerned to describe and explain the various events during the passage of the Corrie Bill. The structure of the book is mainly chronological. The first chapter looks at the parliamentary history of the issue in order to provide the background which is essential for any analysis of the Corrie Bill. For the same reason Chapter 2 discusses the development and growth of the abortion lobby up to 1979. The following three chapters examine the various parliamentary stages of the Bill. Chapter 3 looks at its origins and Second Reading, Chapter 4 at the Committee Stage and Chapter 5 at the Report Stage. In the light of this analysis Chapter 6 attempts to identify the reasons for the failure of the Corrie Bill. The final chapter broadens the perspective to examine what this case study tells us about the usefulness of private members' business, the factors which influence MPs' voting on unwhipped issues; the strategy and tactics of parliamentary interest groups; and the role of feminism in British politics.

The Data Sources used in this Study

As we intend to explain as well as describe the fate of the Corrie Bill it is essential to identify our data sources before we continue. We have a number of major sources of data.

MPs' Voting Records

The voting records of MPs on abortion are taken from Hansard. We are dealing, prior to the Corrie Bill, with the votes on the following: the Second Reading of the Steel Bill in 1966; the Third Reading of the Steel Bill in 1967; the St John-Stevas ten-minute rule bill in 1969; the Second Reading of James White's Bill in 1975; the Second Reading of William Benyon's Bill in 1977; and Sir Bernard Braine's ten-minute rule bill in 1978.[1] On the Corrie Bill we consider the vote on the Second Reading in 1979 and the four most important votes taken by the House at the Report Stage. The context and nature of these votes are dealt with at length below.[2]

In examining the votes we are making one assumption throughout. We are concerned, among other things, with the patterns of consistency and change in parliamentary voting on the abortion issue. To this end, we have defined voting for the original Act and against all amendments as a consistent pro-abortion stance. Obviously this does not mean that we believe that anyone who voted for the bills to amend the 1967 Act was necessarily against all abortion. It is evident that some MPs who voted for these bills were indeed, on religious and moral grounds, opposed to all abortion; but most MPs who voted for them did favour abortion under certain circumstances. Our argument here is merely that a vote for the St John-Stevas Bill, the White Bill, the Benyon Bill, the Braine Bill or the Corrie Bill represented a vote to amend the Act in such a way as to make abortions less readily available. As such, these votes reflect a less liberal attitude towards abortion, if not necessarily a totally anti-abortion stance.

Even so some readers might argue that the changes we identify are a product of our definition of change; that MPs' attitudes have not really changed, rather subsequent amending legislation has more accurately reflected Parliament's real view than did the original 1967 Act. Such a position, although plausible, seems to be significantly weakened when one appreciates that the biggest parliamentary support has been for the more radical amending Bills proposed by White and Corrie. If MPs' attitudes had only been slightly less pro-abortion than the 1967 vote appeared to indicate one would have expected larger votes in favour of the St John-Stevas, Benyon or Braine Bills which would have had a much less radical effect. Our view is, therefore, that important changes have occurred which need to be explained.

In the final chapter we also examine the voting patterns of MPs on capital punishment and homosexuality reform. We are dealing with six votes on capital punishment and two votes on homosexuality reform. These votes are also taken from Hansard and are discussed in more detail below.[3]

MPs Background Characteristics

In explaining the patterns of parliamentary voting both quantitative and qualitative material are used. We employ three sets of factors in the quantitative analysis; the party identification/ideological position of the MPs; the personal background characteristics of MPs; and the characteristics of the MPs' constituency. The information on which this analysis is based is drawn mainly from *The Times Guide to the House of Commons* which is published by Times Books after each election. However, in some cases additional information has been added from other sources and details of such sources are given at the appropriate position in the text. As an example, while *The Times Guide to the House of Commons* contains information about the religious affiliation of MPs this information is far from complete. Additional information on Roman Catholic MPs was collected from the *Catholic Directory,*[4] and on Jewish MPs from the *Jewish Chronicle.*[5]

Interviews with, and Letters from, MPs

This book examines both the failure of the Corrie Bill in particular and parliamentary voting patterns on abortion in general. Our statistical analysis of the relationships between voting and certain of the political and demographic characteristics of MPs helps in understanding these problems, as does an examination of the parliamentary debates and the media coverage of the issue. However, such an approach offers only a partial picture.

It is impossible to understand what was happening in Parliament solely from the outside. Therefore, in order to supplement the quantitative material three other data sources were used. First, in 1978 after the vote on the Braine Bill, but before the tabling of the Corrie Bill, we wrote to all those MPs who at any stage had changed their vote on abortion — that is from a liberal to a conservative position or vice versa — asking them for an explanation of that change. In total we wrote to 53 MPs, 27 MPs who had changed their votes between 1967 and 1975, and 26 MPs who had changed their votes between 1975 and 1979. We received 27 usable replies. In fact this is a minor source of data in the context of the book as it does not relate to the Corrie Bill, but it will be used to reinforce the quantitative material in Chapter 1. Our second additional source of data on MPs' views is much more important. One cannot understand the passage of the Corrie Bill without appreciating what went on in Parliament, that is in the Committee Room, the Chamber and in the lobbies. This necessitated a series of interviews with MPs about the Corrie Bill and particularly the strategy and tactics involved inside and outside Parliament. In total we have interviewed 32 MPs. They do not comprise a representative sample of the House of Commons as most were chosen because of their interest in, knowledge about, or involvement with, the issue. As such we interviewed 12 of the 17 members of the Standing Committee on the Corrie Bill, including Mr Corrie and Dr Vaughan. However, we were also concerned to obtain the impressions of MPs who were less involved in the issue and for this reason we interviewed 9 MPs who were newly elected in May 1979, and who voted on the Corrie Bill. Overall, of the MPs interviewed, 14 were Conservatives, 15 Labour and 3 Liberals, while 17 had supported the Corrie Bill at Second Reading and 15 had opposed it. Therefore, while our interview data does not offer a representative sample it does provide a cross-section of views and experience on the issue, and adds a great deal to our knowledge and understanding of the Corrie Bill. We have attributed material from MPs where possible, but some MPs only talked to us on the understanding that we guaranteed anonymity. In such cases we report their comments with the date of the interview but without attributions.

Interviews with Interest Groups and Professional Associations

Our third source of data allowed us to approach the same problems from another perspective. We interviewed representatives of all the major interest groups and professional organizations interested in the issue. The interest groups were LIFE and the Society for the Protection of the Unborn Child on the anti-abortion side; and the Abortion Law Reform Association, Christians for Free Choice, Doctors in Defence of the 1967 Abortion Act, Doctors and Overpopulation Group, Doctors for a Woman's Choice on Abortion, Labour Abortion Rights Campaign, National Abortion Campaign and Tories for Free Choice on the pro-abortion side. The professional organizations interviewed were the British Medical Association, the Royal College of Obstetrics and Gynaecology and the Royal College of Nursing. All these organizations talked openly and fully to us; this provided a crucial source material which is drawn on heavily in our analysis.

A Note on the Statistical Analysis Used

In a number of sections of this book we are dealing with quantitative evidence about MPs' voting on abortion, capital punishment and homosexuality reform and the relationship between their voting and a series of other variables. The votes are always our dependent variables which we attempt to explain by reference to a series of independent variables — party, religion, sex, age, occupation, education, etc. Much of the analysis is based upon summary statistics which simplify the presentation of a considerable amount of material.

Most statistical analysis is concerned with two aspects of a relationship between two or more variables, the strength of the relationship and the significance of the relationship. If a relationship is strong it means that a knowledge of an MP's score on an independent variable, say party, is a good basis on which to predict his or her score on the dependent variable, in this case on parliamentary divisions. If a relationship is 'significant' it means that there is little if any possibility that the given relationship occurred by chance. There is no necessary association between the strength of a relationship and its significance, although strong relationships will normally be significant if they are based on a large number of cases. In contrast, weak relationships may well be significant and indeed throughout this book we will encounter a large number of relationships which are of this type — weak, or nonexistent, but significant.

As most of the data is nominal[6] our analysis is based upon cross-tabulations. The cross-tabulations we report indicate what percentage of those who are in a particular category of the independent variable occur in each category of the dependent variable. It is perhaps worth presenting a couple of examples in order to help readers who are not used to reading such tables.

Table I.1: Relationship between Voting and Party on the Second Reading of the Corrie Bill (Labour and Conservative MPs only)

	Labour %	Conservative %
Voted for	39	93
Voted against	61	7
Total	100	100

Table I.1 indicates the relationship between party and voting on the Second Reading of the Corrie Bill. It reveals that 39 per cent of Labour MPs supported the Corrie Bill on the Second Reading and 61 per cent opposed it. In contrast 93 per cent of Conservative MPs supported it and only 7 per cent opposed it. The table indicates that there is a relationship between party and voting, a relationship which we shall discuss at length later.

Any analysis employing cross-tabulation can be made more sophisticated if we control for a third variable such as the marginality of constituency. In such circumstances we are interested in discovering if the relationship between party and voting is affected by the level of the MP's majority in his or her constituency. So if we distinguish between marginal and safe seats, control for marginality and re-examine the relationship between party and vote we are faced with two tables (I.2(a) and (b)).

These tables show that if we consider only those MPs in safe seats then 48 per cent of such Labour MPs voted for the Corrie Bill, and 52 per cent opposed it, while 92 per cent of such Conservative MPs voted for it, and 8 per cent opposed it. In contrast if we consider only MPs in marginal seats then 20 per cent of such Labour MPs voted for the Corrie Bill and 80 per cent opposed it, while 95 per cent of those Conservative MPs in this position voted for it, and only 5 per cent opposed it. It is clear from this

Table I.2: Relationship between Voting and Party on the Second Reading of the Corrie Bill

(a) Only MPs in Safe Seats

	Labour %	Conservative %
Voted for	48	95
Voted against	52	8
Total	100	100

(b) Only MPs in Marginal Seats

	Labour %	Conservative %
Voted for	20	95
Voted against	80	5
Total	100	100

table that marginality does have an effect on the relationship between voting and party. In particular Labour MPs in marginal constituencies were much more likely to oppose the Corrie Bill at Second Reading than were their colleagues in safe seats. Once again this pattern will be discussed in a later chapter.

So far we have only dealt with what are called the column percentages in cross-tabulations. However, there are a number of summary statistics which are derived from cross-tabulations and which provide a measure of the strength of the association between two variables. In this book in most cases *Lambda B* is used as our measure of the strength of the association between the independent and dependent variables. In effect *Lambda B* indicates how good a predictor of the dependent variable in each cross-tabulation, the independent variable is considered to be.[7] In a limited number of circumstances however *Lambda symmetrical* is employed as the measure of the strength of the association. This is used when we are interested in the association between two variables but have no basis at all on which to assume which variable is the causal one. In our analysis *Lambda symmetrical* is in fact used only when we are considering the relationship between various votes, for example, when considering MPs' voting on abortion and their voting on capital punishment or homosexuality reform.

Both *Lambda B* and *Lambda symmetrical* vary from 0.000 to 1.000. *A Lambda* of 0.750 for example indicates a very strong relationship whereas one of 0.010 indicates virtually no relationship. The closer the relationship between two variables the higher is the *Lambda.* It is usual to regard any *Lambda* in excess of 0.15 as worthy of further analysis, and of course a number of *Lambdas* can be compared in order to reveal which of a number of independent variables is the best predictor of a dependent variable.

Chi Square is used as a measure of significance in this book.[8] We report relationships which are significant at the 0.05 level which means there is only a one in twenty or 5 per cent chance of such a relationship occurring if there is no association. We also report relationships significant at the 0.001 level. This means there is only a one in a thousand chance of such a relationship being observed if there is no association between the variables. In addition there are some relationships which we report which it was not possible to compute Chi Square because there were a number of cells in the data matrix with no cases in them. This does not mean that the relationship concerned is not significant; rather it means that we have no way of knowing if it is significant.

Notes

1. See below p. 137.
2. See below pp. 147-54.
3. See below pp. 213-14.
4. The *Catholic Directory* is published annually by Associated Catholic Newspapers 1912 Ltd, and each edition contains a list of Roman Catholic MPs.
5. The *Jewish Chronicle* publishes a list of successful Jewish candidates in the edition immediately following each general election.
6. For a discussion of the difference between nominal, ordinal and interval data, and statistics appropriate to different levels of data see H. Blalock, *Social Statistics,* New York, McGraw Hill, 1972, ch. 2.
7. Ibid., pp. 302-3.
8. Ibid., ch. 15.

1
Parliament and the Abortion Issue

It is impossible fully to understand the origins and progress of the Corrie Bill without some knowledge of the parliamentary history of the abortion issue. The aim in this chapter is to examine the background to the 1967 Abortion Act, its content and passage and the subsequent attempts to amend it.

Before Steel

Abortion was common in primitive society and later approved of in Greece and Rome. In fact it was the development of Christianity and the belief in the existence of a soul capable of salvation through baptism which produced a fundamental change in attitudes to abortion. Traditionally, Christian theologians believed that when the foetus stirred in the womb — the period of quickening — it acquired a soul. Abortion after this stage destroyed life and caused the eternal damnation of the unbaptized soul.[1] Though present-day Christians are divided in their attitudes to abortion, the traditional theological position was the basis of English abortion law as enshrined in the Act of 1803, which made carrying out or attempting to procure an abortion, an offence at any stage of pregnancy, although the penalties were much harsher after 'quickening'. However it was the Offences Against the Person Act of 1861 which provided the statutory basis for the law on abortion until the passage of the 1967 Abortion Act. Section 58 of this Act appeared unequivocal.[2]

> Every woman, being with Child, who, with intent to procure her own Miscarriage shall unlawfully administer to herself any Poison or other noxious Thing, or shall unlawfully use any instrument or other Means whatsoever with like Intent and whosoever, with Intent to procure the Miscarriage of any woman; whether she be or be not with Child, shall unlawfully administer to her or cause to be taken by her any Poison or other noxious Thing, or shall unlawfully use any instrument or other means whatsoever with like Intent, shall be guilty of a felony.

While this remained the basis of abortion law for over a hundred years it was supplemented by the Infant Life (Preservation) Act of 1929, and by case law. The 1929 Act provided that abortion would not be an offence under that Act if 'such an act were done in good faith with the intention of saving the life of the mother'. However as the 1861 Act was not repealed or amended there appeared to be a contradiction between the two Acts. This contradiction was resolved in an interesting if somewhat dubious legal decision taken by Mr Justice MacNaughton in the case of R. v. Bourne, a decision which influenced the interpretation of abortion law until 1967.[3]

The case arose as a result of an abortion operation performed by Mr Aleck Bourne a consultant obstetrician at St Mary's Hospital, London, on a 14-year-old girl who had been raped by four soldiers. Mr Bourne accepted no fee and performed the operation because in his opinion, formed after consultation with colleagues, if the girl had had to continue with the pregnancy it would have severely damaged her mental health. The abortion therefore was carried out not to save the mother from immediate death but on therapeutic grounds. Bourne made no attempt to conceal the operation but rather reported the matter to the police so that it became a test case.

Justice MacNaughton's summing up presented a liberal interpretation of the Offences Against the Person Act which few lawyers would support. He argued that the repeated use of the word 'unlawful' in the Statute indicated that Parliament had conceived of some circumstances in which abortion might be legal. He went on to argue that what Parliament had meant was in fact enshrined in the 1929 Infant Life (Preservation Act) —

that is that an abortion could be legal if performed in good faith to protect the life of the mother. This view represented an ingenious if legally doubtful attempt to reconcile the two pieces of legislation. However the judge's interpretation had even more wide-ranging implications as he accepted the validity of therapeutic grounds for abortion, arguing that no clear distinction could be made between a threat to life and a threat to health. Despite the fact that this seems to represent a clear case of 'judge-made law' the decision definitely influenced subsequent judgements and, perhaps more significantly, medical practice for 30 years until the 1967 Abortion Act became law.

Nevertheless despite the Bourne judgement legal abortions were few, illegal abortions were common and legal and medical opinion was unsure of the law. As such it is perhaps not surprising that six attempts were made at abortion law reform before the Steel Bill was introduced. The first attempt was a private member's bill introduced by Joseph Reeve in 1953. It was a limited measure which would merely have given unquestioned legality to therapeutic abortion. The bill was hardly discussed at Second Reading as it was the third bill in that day's private members' business and was only just reached.[4] This was partly because of a filibuster on the first two bills by some Roman Catholic MPs. The second attempt at reform was also a private member's bill. This was introduced by Kenneth Robinson in 1961 and aimed to put on the statute book what was current medical practice. However once again this bill was never voted upon because it was 'talked out' by a group of Roman Catholic MPs.[5]

The next two bills introduced into the House of Commons were more radical in scope. This was partly because of the more liberal atmosphere which prevailed both in the country and in Parliament by the middle of the 1960s, but perhaps mainly because of the influence of the thalidomide tragedy, the impact of which on the public and press in Britain is difficult to exaggerate. The drug affected the foetus in a way which caused some children to be born with gross deformities. In consequence there was considerable demand for abortion to be made legal where there was a risk of a child being born badly deformed. As such both Renée Short's ten-minute rule bill introduced in June 1965[6] and Simon Wingfield Digby's private member's bill introduced in February

1966[7] contained a provision for abortion to be legal in such circumstances. Nevertheless neither bill progressed. The Short Bill was given an unopposed First Reading but was objected to on Second Reading. The Wingfield Digby Bill was talked out by two Labour Roman Catholic MPs, Simon and Peter Mahon, after one hour's debate at Second Reading. In fact then it was not until the Second Reading of the Steel Bill in 1966 that the House of Commons first voted on an abortion bill.

However one bill did make substantial parliamentary progress before the Steel Bill. This was the private member's bill introduced in the House of Lords by Lord Silkin in November 1965.[8] Silkin's Bill is interesting for two reasons. It was the first to pass through one of the Houses of Parliament receiving a Second Reading in the Lords by 67 votes to 8 and an unopposed Third Reading after being much amended at the Committee and Report Stages. The Bill was not introduced into the House of Commons because Parliament was dissolved and an election called in 1966. The Silkin Bill was also important however because, when originally introduced, it was the first abortion bill to contain a 'social clause'. Clause 1(c) stated that a pregnancy could be legally terminated

> in the belief that the health of the patient or the social conditions in which she is living (including the social conditions of her existing children) make her unsuitable to assume the legal and moral responsibility for caring for a child or another child as the case may be.

This clause was amended by Silkin after the Second Reading and defeated at Report Stage but, as we shall see later, discussions on a 'social clause' were to play a large part in the debates upon the Steel Bill.

Lord Silkin in fact reintroduced another bill in the next parliamentary session similar to the one which the Lords had approved[9] but he withdrew it when it became clear that David Steel, Liberal MP for Roxburgh, Selkirk and Peebles was going to sponsor a private member's bill on abortion in the House of Commons.

The Steel Bill

In the private members' ballot for the 1966-7 parliamentary session David Steel drew third place. He was approached by a number of interested parties but after some delay decided to introduce an abortion bill, which was duly published on 15 June 1966. In the original Bill[10] there were four legal grounds for abortion: if there was serious risk to the life of the mother, or grave risk to her physical or mental health or that of the child after birth; if there was substantial risk that a child would be born seriously handicapped; if there was reason to believe that the pregnant woman would be severely overstrained as a mother (the 'social clause'); or if the pregnancy was of a girl under sixteen, or had occurred as a result of rape. The Bill did not require one of the two doctors to be a consultant, and contained no specific provisions about a time limit, relying upon the provisions of the Infant Life (Preservation) Act 1929 which made all abortion an offence after 28 weeks.

The Medical Termination of Pregnancy Bill was debated at Second Reading for five hours on 22 July 1966.[11] This was the first full debate ever in the House of Commons on the issue and when a vote was taken the Bill was given a Second Reading by a majority of 223 votes to 29.[12] This vote was only a first step. David Steel received an enormous amount of advice and pressure before the Bill reached Standing Committee on 18 January 1967.

There is no doubt that the advice which influenced David Steel most came from the medical organizations and in particular from the Royal College of Obstetricians and Gynaecologists (RCOG) and the British Medical Association (BMA). At this time both organizations were opposed to a major liberalization of abortion law. As Madeleine Simms and Keith Hindell claim:

> Officially these organisations were not opposed to reform but merely opposed to particular sections of Steel's Bill. In the event the influence exerted by both organisations on Parliament and on the Government served to jeopardise the very life of the Bill and almost wrote into it a clause which might have made it worthless, namely the consultant clause.[13]

The RCOG had published a report on abortion in April 1966 and the BMA one in July 1966.[14] Both reports then appeared before the publication of the Steel Bill and recommended that abortion be restricted to circumstances where there was 'serious' risk to the life of the mother, or 'substantial' risk that the child would be born abnormal. The RCOG also argued that all abortions should be authorized, and carried out, by or under the supervision of a gynaecologist. This view was not originally supported by the BMA. When the Steel Bill was published the two organizations formed a committee to consider it which reported in November 1966.[15] This report condemned outright the 'social grounds' for abortion contained in the Bill although it did recommend that a sub-clause should be added to allow a doctor to take into account a patient's 'total environment'. In addition the report argued that one of the two doctors who approved an abortion should be a consultant, noting that as far as the RCOG were concerned a gynaecologist would be preferable.

Steel had several meetings with representatives of the BMA and the RCOG before in December he himself tabled an amendment to his Bill which seemed to accept the arguments of the two groups. The amendment allowed a doctor to take into account 'the patient's total environment actual or reasonably foreseeable' when taking a decision on abortion. At the same time Steel proposed to withdraw the two more directly 'social clauses' in the Bill which would have allowed abortion if the woman was likely to be totally inadequate as a mother, or if the pregnancy was a result of rape. In consequence many of the leading abortion law reformers believed that the heart of the Bill had been removed.

Despite the concession by Steel the Bill was strongly opposed during 12 sittings and 30 hours of debate in Standing Committee.[16] The full range of parliamentary tactics were used against it by its opponents; a large number of amendments were tabled, speeches were long, and numerous points of order were introduced. However only one other significant amendment was approved and it too was supported by Steel. It allowed doctors, nurses and other medical staff to abstain from abortion on the grounds of conscience, although the burden of proof rested with the person claiming this exemption. In contrast the opposition was unsuccessful in introducing an amendment to require that one of the two doctors authorizing an abortion be a consultant, despite the continued lobbying of the RCOG and the BMA both inside and outside Parliament. Nevertheless although they had little success in amending the Bill in the Committee Stage the opposition did delay it so that it appeared unlikely that it would pass through its remaining stages in the single day available. In fact it was only saved because Roy Jenkins, the Home Secretary, and Richard Crossman, leader of the House, who were supporters of the measure, persuaded the Cabinet on two occasions to give the Bill more time.

The Report Stage thus lasted for three sessions and a total of 28 hours, but after the Third Reading which lasted two hours the Bill was finally approved by 167 votes to 83 on 13 July.[17] It then passed through the House of Lords although not without a number of alarms, and received the Royal Assent on 27 October 1967. For administrative reasons, however, it did not come into operation until 27 April 1968. In its final form the Act allowed for a pregnancy to be terminated by a registered medical practitioner if two registered doctors were of the opinion, formed in good faith, that:

> (a) the continuance of the pregnancy would involve risk to the life of the pregnant woman, or of injury to the physical or mental health of the pregnant woman or any existing children of her family, greater than if the pregnancy were terminated; or
> (b) that there was a substantial risk that if the child were born, it would suffer from such physical or mental abnormalities as to be seriously handicapped.[18]

Why Was Steel Successful?

Why did the Steel Bill pass successfully? This is an important question here because without understanding why this Bill passed it is difficult fully to appreciate why subsequent amending legislation has proved unsuccessful.

A number of factors were obviously crucial to the successful passage of the 1967 Abortion Act. In particular the liberal atmosphere which existed in Parliament and in the country in the 1960s was important. Indeed the two Parliaments between 1964 and 1970 saw the passage of a variety of liberal reforms:[19] capital punishment was abolished by the Murder (Abolition of the Death Penalty) Act in 1965; homosexuality between consenting adults was legalized by the Sexual Offences Act in 1967; censorship in the theatre was abolished by the Theatres Act in 1968; and divorce was significantly liberalized by the Divorce Act of 1969. Once such an atmosphere was established it made MPs more likely to introduce reforming bills and perhaps also made the government more willing to give such private members' bills parliamentary time.

Of course this doesn't explain why Parliament was more liberal. Perhaps this liberalism owed something to the temporary euphoria of the 'white-hot technological revolution' and 'swinging London', or perhaps it reflected the changing moral values of the population. However it certainly did owe a great deal to the more liberal views of the new wave of MPs elected into Parliament in 1964 and 1966. As the Labour Party had 59 more MPs in 1964 and 105 more in 1966 than they had in 1959 many of the new MPs were Labour supporters whose views on social issues were, and have remained, generally more liberal than those of Conservative MPs (see Table 7.2(a), p. 200). Indeed of the 167 MPs who supported the Third Reading of the Steel Bill 72 per cent were Labour and only 23 per cent Conservative, while of the 83 who opposed it 73 per cent were Conservative and only 27 per cent Labour. However although this influx of Labour MPs largely explains the more liberal nature of the two Parliaments there is also evidence that younger MPs and those elected at the 1964 or 1966 election of both parties were more likely to support the Abortion Bill, and indeed, other liberal reforms, than their older and more experienced colleagues.[20]

In 1967 then Parliament was more disposed to support abortion reform because of its party composition and because of an influx of younger more liberal MPs. However this only explains why the Bill had a better chance than other bills — not why Steel's Bill in particular was successful. Six other factors appear important. First, an MP willing to promote an abortion bill achieved a high place in the ballot, an almost essential prerequisite for any private member's bill to progress.[21] Secondly, the thalidomide tragedy had a marked impact and predisposed some MPs to favour abortion where a child might be born with horrifying handicaps. Thirdly, the MP who introduced the Bill, David Steel, proved an able parliamentarian. He consulted widely and made major concessions to the medical profession. In retrospect his judgement seems to have been excellent. Even Simms and Hindell, who were advocates of a more liberal reform than that enacted, admitted, when referring to Steel's concessions to the BMA and the RCOG: 'In view of the tremendous effort which was later needed to get even the amended and watered-down version through Parliament it is very difficult to fault Steel's political judgement.'[22]

The fourth significant factor was the activity of the interest groups on the issue. We shall be dealing at length with the growth of the interest groups in this field in the next chapter, but it is important here to stress the role of the Abortion Law Reform Association (ALRA), whose members formed a small but very active group which played a crucial role both in persuading Steel to introduce the Bill and in helping him to pilot it through Parliament. Indeed after an analysis of all the conscience issues dealt with in Parliament in the 1960s Peter Richards claims: 'Of all the pressure groups noticed in this study ALRA has been the most influential.'[23] In addition ALRA was helped by the fact that the first anti-abortion interest group, the Society for the Protection of the Unborn Child (SPUC), was not formed until after the Second Reading of the Steel Bill and remained small and relatively ineffective during its passage. As Richards says: 'Compared with ALRA, the Society for the Protection of Unborn Children was very unsuccessful.'[24]

Moreover although members of the Roman Catholic Church campaigned against the Steel Bill, they were nothing like as organized or vociferous in opposition to the Bill as they were to prove in support of later amending legislation. Indeed Barker and Rush, who happened to be undertaking a survey of Parliament Members' sources of information at the time of the Steel Bill's Committee Stage, could conclude:

> On the basis of our limited information from the 1966-7 Session we would speculate that the Roman Catholics were on this issue at least, less monolythic in their reaction (than might be expected) and that local priests are moving towards Anglican priests in their individual freedom either to preach and organise against legislation which official Catholic teaching opposes, or to keep quiet.[25]

This conclusion, as we shall see, would be difficult to substantiate in the case of John Corrie's Bill.

The fifth factor which probably helped persuade some MPs to vote for the Steel Bill was public opinion. It was not until the middle of the 1960s that the opinion polls began to ask questions about abortion. When they did, the results came as a surprise to many. According to a NOP study in 1965, 72 per cent of the population favoured reform, including 60 per cent of Roman Catholics. In a subsequent NOP poll published in mid-February 1967, 65 per cent of the voters believed that abortion should be possible on 'social' grounds. Although such findings may have strengthened MPs in their liberal convictions, and persuaded some to vote who might not otherwise have done so, it is unlikely that they changed many minds.

The last factor and by far the most important one in ensuring the success of the Bill was the attitude of the government. In the Second Reading debate Roy Jenkins declared that the government's view was one of benevolent neutrality — but in the event it was more benevolent than neutral. As we have shown, the majority of the Labour Party supported reform and so did the majority of the Cabinet. Roy Jenkins and Richard Crossman were both strong advocates of liberal reform, and the Minister of Health, Kenneth Robinson, had himself previously introduced a bill to reform abortion law. So at every stage the government lent the Bill a hand as it did with other liberal reforms in the same period. When the Bill was delayed in going to the Standing Committee which considered private members' bills by the extended consideration of a previous bill, the government allowed the Abortion Bill to go to a Standing Committee normally reserved for government bills. Subsequently and more crucially it allowed 25 hours of government time to the later stages of the Bill. Without such concessions from the government the Bill would have been successfully talked out by its opponents.

The Steel Bill succeeded, but there were signs during its passage that the struggle was not over. The Third Reading vote of 83 against the Bill indicated a concern, particularly, although not exclusively, among Conservative MPs, that it was too liberal. In addition it reflected the improved organization of the anti-abortion campaigners both inside and outside Parliament during the Bill's later stages. While SPUC may have been unsuccessful in this instance it grew in both size and experience during its fight against the Steel Bill. At the same time the opposition in the Commons to the Bill gathered around a few MPs who were to be influential in attempts to amend the Act over the next decade, particularly MPs such as Sir Bernard Braine, Jill Knight and Norman St John Stevas.

After Steel

The Abortion Act became operational on 27 April 1968. Within 15 months the first attempt to amend it was made, and in all, seven amendment bills were introduced before the Corrie Bill. Once again it is important that we examine these bills, and the voting on them, because they provide an essential part of the background to the Corrie Bill. The major changes in the pattern of parliamentary voting on the abortion issue up to the Corrie Bill are clear from Table 1.1. Between 1967 and 1975 there was a movement towards support for amending legislation among MPs. However after 1975 until 1978 this pattern was reversed with the support for amending legislation significantly declining. We look at these two periods separately.

1967-75

In this period there was a movement towards support for amending legislation which was well established by 1969 but was accentuated afterwards. In fact there were five amending bills introduced during the period. The first which was sponsored by Norman St John-Stevas in 1969[26] contained only one provision. The bill if passed would have required one of the two doctors who recommended an abortion to be a consultant in the NHS, or a doctor of equivalent status. This amendment had been promoted by the medical associations and debated at length, before being defeated, at the Committee Stage of the Steel Bill. As Norman St John-Stevas's Bill was a ten-minute rule bill it had little chance of progressing even if it had obtained a First Reading. Such bills can only progress after being successfully introduced if they are allowed an unopposed Second Reading, or if the government grants them time. No abortion bill is likely to be unopposed, and

Table 1.1: Parliamentary Voting on Abortion, 1966-78

Year	Sponsor and type of bill	Voting (expressed as % of those voting) for	against	Majority	No. of MPs voting
1966	David Steel, Private Member's Bill (1967 Abortion Act), Second Reading	88 (N 223)	12 (N 29)	+194	252
1967	David Steel, Private Member's Bill (1967 Abortion Act), Third Reading	67 (N 167)	33 (N 83)	+84	250
1969	Norman St. John-Stevas, Ten-Minute Rule Bill, First Reading	49 (N 199)	51 (N 210)	−11	409
1975	James White, Private Member's Bill, Second Reading	70 (N 203)	30 (N 88)	+115	291
1977	William Benyon, Abortion (Amendment) Private Member's Bill, Second Reading	56 (N 170)	44 (N 132)	+38	302
1978	Sir Bernard Braine, Abortion (Amendment), Ten-Minute Rule Bill, First Reading	51 (N 181)	59 (N 175)	+6	356

Note: This table together with Table 6.1 are the only tables in this book which do not include Tellers. A vote for the two votes on Steel and against all the subsequent bills is a pro-abortion vote.

the Labour government tacitly supported the Abortion Act, so St John-Stevas's Bill was doomed from the start. Indeed St John-Stevas's aim in introducing the Bill was restricted to airing the issue in Parliament again and testing the opinion of the House. However, he was denied permission to introduce his Bill by 210 votes to 199.

The campaign against the Abortion Act continued six months after the defeat of the St John-Stevas Bill when the Conservative member for Rye, Bryant Godman Irvine, introduced a similar measure which was talked out.[27] Subsequently in the 1970-4 Parliament two more bills were introduced specifically to prohibit the charging of fees for referring or recommending persons to doctors or clinics for treatment. The first bill, introduced by John Hunt, Conservative member for Bromley, excluded charities from this prohibition.[28] However, Hunt's Bill failed to reach

Second Reading, while the second bill brought forward by Michael Grylls, Conservative Member for Surrey NW, which did include charities, fell with the dissolution of Parliament in February 1974. Michael Grylls obtained permission to reintroduce his Bill in the new parliament and it was given an unopposed Second Reading, but as soon as it reached Standing Committee it ran into difficulties. Deadlock was reached when four members walked out refusing to return to make up a quorum and the Bill never finished its Committee Stage.[29]

In the meantime, in 1971, the Secretary for Social Services, Sir Keith Joseph, under pressure from the anti-abortion lobby, appointed a Committee of 14 under the chairmanship of the Hon. Mrs Justice Lane. Its remit was to examine the operation of the 1967 Act, but its terms of reference only allowed it to look at administrative questions concerned with the operation of the Act; it could not examine evidence or arguments about the morality of abortion. These terms of reference were regarded by the anti-abortion pressure groups, and particularly by the newly formed group LIFE, as very restrictive. In addition neither of the two major anti-abortion groups SPUC and LIFE were happy about the composition of the Committee which they felt was pro-abortion. The Lane Committee sat for two-and-a-half years, took evidence from the Ministry of Health and all the interested parties and published its report in three volumes in April 1974.[30] Its members were unanimous in supporting the Act and its provisions concluding that where abuses existed they could be more effectively controlled by administration than by legislation. Indeed they recommended only one legislative change: an amendment to the 1929 Infant Life (Preservation) Act which would have reduced the time limit for legal abortion from 28 to 24 weeks.

However despite the Lane Committee's report support for an effort to amend the 1967 Abortion Act was growing and it was against this background that a radical private member's amendment bill was introduced by James White, Labour MP for Glasgow (Pollock).[31] Its sponsors argued that the main aim of the Bill was to curtail abuses in the operation of the Abortion Act. Nevertheless, there can be no doubt that, if the Bill had become law, it would have resulted in a substantial reduction in the availability of legal abortions in Britain.

The Bill had three main elements: (1) it attempted to prevent abuses in the private sector and to prevent referral bureaux being financially associated with abortion clinics; (2) it laid down statutory conditions for the approval of private clinics; and most important (3) it removed the clause in the original Act which provided the basis for the so-called 'statistical argument' for abortions. Under this clause an abortion was legal if on balance the risk of continuing pregnancy was greater than that of termination; anti-abortion supporters believed that this clause allowed some doctors to offer abortion on demand, because one could show statistically that abortion was less risky to all mothers than continued pregnancy. The White Bill would have replaced this clause with one specifying that abortion was only legal if there was a 'grave' risk to life or a 'serious' risk to health.

The voting on the Second Reading of the White Bill in 1975 shocked the supporters of the Abortion Act. The Bill was given a Second Reading by a majority of 203 to 88. This was a radical change since the Steel Bill and even represented a major revision since the voting on the St John-Stevas Bill. Despite this massive favourable vote the Bill did not, however, progress further because the sponsors accepted a government proposal that it should be referred to a parliamentary Select Committee which would consider it in the light of a review of abortion law. With hindsight this appears to have been a successful attempt by the government in general, and perhaps the Ministry of Health in particular, to defuse the abortion issue and remove any hope that the White Bill had of progressing.

How can the changes in voting which occurred in this period be explained? In fact there were two separate changes. The shift between 1967 and 1969 occurred largely, although not exclusively, among Conservative MPs, while that between 1969 and 1975 mainly concerned Labour MPs.

The change among Conservative MPs is not difficult to understand. In 1967 Conservative MPs had been much more reluctant to support the details of the Steel Bill than its principle. So from the start the prevailing atmosphere within the Conservative Party did not favour any liberal interpretation of the Abortion Act. Indeed only 31 Conservatives supported the Third Reading of the Steel Bill, and many had voted against individual clauses in the Bill at Report Stage. This attitude probably significantly influenced some Conservative MPs who had been prepared to abstain in 1967 and allow the legislation through, but who voted for the St John-Stevas Bill. So although only seven Conservatives who voted for the Third Reading of the Steel Bill voted for the St John-Stevas Bill, over half of the Conservative MPs who supported the St John-Stevas Bill had not previously voted on the issue. The main point here is that although there was certain evidence of taxi-touting at Heathrow airport and Victoria station and of overcharging in the private sector, MPs actually had little experience of, or evidence about, the operation of the Act, which had only been fully operative for just over a year. Thus it is evident that most Conservative MPs were in 1969 reasserting their normal, conservative, stance on abortion. This view is confirmed by the fact that the vast majority of Conservative MPs who vote on the issue have remained in favour of amending legislation ever since. In fact as far as Conservative MPs are concerned the most surprising thing is that so few of them opposed the original Steel Bill.

In the entire period between 1967 and 1980 the most significant changes in parliamentary voting on abortion have occurred among Labour MPs. As Table 7.2(a) (p. 200) shows they have been far from consistent on this issue. The first major change among Labour MPs occurred between 1969 and 1975. This change did not result from an influx of less liberal Labour MPs at the 1970 or 1974 elections. Indeed Labour MPs newly elected in 1974 were more liberal on the abortion issue than their colleagues who had been there in 1969. In fact it was the movement in the views of Labour MPs who had been in Parliament in 1969 which was crucial. So 14 Labour MPs who had voted against the St John-Stevas Bill and 23 Labour MPs who had not voted or abstained on that Bill voted for the White Bill. In addition, 47 Labour MPs who had voted against the St John-Stevas Bill abstained in 1975. How can we account for these changes?

There can be little doubt that the opinions of MPs on the issue in 1975 were considerably influenced by two major aspects of the operation of the 1967 Act. It is evident that MPs were surprised by the absolute number of abortions carried out in the early 1970s. If MPs had little evidence of the Act's operation in 1969 by 1975 they had ample material. As Table A.1 (p. 216) shows, there was a rapid increase in the number of abortions performed after 1970 together with a sharp increase in the number of abortions performed on women not resident in England and Wales. This latter fact in particular disturbed many MPs who felt that London was in danger of becoming the 'abortion capital of the world'.

At the same time, and perhaps more significantly, MPs were increasingly aware of the much publicized 'abuses' which were occurring in the operation of the 1967 Act. These 'abuses' were examined by the Lane Committee which identified the major cause for concern as the private sector. In addition the Lane report had criticized the medical standards of some clinics and the ethics of a small number of unnamed doctors, while still concluding that these 'abuses' could be removed by administrative action.[32] Nevertheless the 'abuses' of the 1967 Act continued to be stressed in a much less circumspect, more sensational and often distorted way in the media. The revealing point is that it appears that MPs' perceptions of the abuses were more influenced by the media than by the Lane Committee's report. It is interesting here to look in some detail at the treatment of the abortion issue in the press prior to the publication of, and debate on, the White Bill in February 1975. In this period the work of two young journalists, Michael Lichfield and Susan Kentish was especially important.

On 29 February 1974 the front page of the *News of the World* carried the headline, 'Phantom Babies Sensation'. The article reported the results of a 'thorough investigation' by Lichfield and Kentish into the activities of private clinics and agencies. The article alleged that Kentish, who was not pregnant, had been declared so by seven pregnancy testing agencies which referred her to private, or charitable, abortion clinics. She claimed that at four of the clinics doctors declared her pregnant, and in each case she was offered an abortion without there being any serious attempt to discover whether she had justifiable grounds under the 1967 Act. This article attracted considerable attention, but more was to follow. In December 1974 Lichfield and Kentish published a book called *Babies for Burning,* which was nothing short of horrific. It contained reports of a doctor selling aborted babies alive for experiments, of a London gynaecologist selling foetuses to be made into soap, and of cases of babies being aborted so late as to be taken living to the incinerator. In addition, some doctors performing abortions were said to have Nazi sympathies, with rooms full of books on fascism.[33]

Some of the book's more extreme allegations have been discredited and others remain unproved while its authors have been subject to successful libel actions.[34] The tone of the book is polemical and exaggeration is common. Nevertheless the *News of the World* article and the book had significant influence in the year following publication. The 'research' was widely used, and quoted from, in articles in the press, for example, by Malcolm Muggeridge in the *Sunday Times* and Ronald Butt in *The Times.*[35] At the same time the work was heavily utilized as a source by the anti-abortion lobby and by a number of MPs who favoured amending the 1967 Act. In particular, James White and Leo Abse, one the sponsor and the other the MP most associated with the Bill, were impressed by the book. James White, asked about his research on abortion, named the book as his chief source of knowledge,[36] while Leo Abse reviewed the book in the *Spectator* claiming that the authors came to the problem as 'virgin and pristine as only young journalists can be'. He concluded that 'The need to amend the law, as Lichfield and Kentish's book corroborates, is urgent.'[37]

The media during the run-up to the Second Reading vote on White was generally favourably disposed to the Bill. At the same time the role of the interest groups themselves must not be overlooked. SPUC had grown in numbers and organization while the formation of LIFE, a more extreme anti-abortion group than SPUC, had added an impetus to the reformers' zeal. Both organizations lobbied in Parliament and both organized meetings and write-in campaigns in the constituencies. They were strongly supported in the constituencies by the Roman Catholic Church whose ministers preached in favour of the White Bill and whose faithful provided a crucial source of funds to both groups.

In addition, the pro-abortion side had lost its impetus as we shall see later. ALRA lost support once it had achieved abortion law reform and many of its activists had moved on to other concerns. The younger more radical pro-abortion groups which were to play an important role on the Corrie Bill were only formed during or after the White Bill. Indeed the lobbying activity on the White Bill from outside Parliament was almost as one-sided as it had been on the Steel Bill, although now the anti-abortion lobbyists had replaced ALRA and were making the running. Inside Parliament the Labour supporters of liberal abortion law were regrouping themselves and were not as effective as they were later to prove to be.

On the White Bill there is no evidence of medical opinion playing a crucial role. By the time of the Lane Committee's report both the BMA and the RCOG had come to support the Abortion Act, and indeed the White Bill only received the support of the nurses among the medical organizations.[38] Hence given the strong vote for the White Bill it is difficult to see how professional opinion could have exercised much influence over MPs. At the same time public opinion remained fairly firmly opposed to amending the law (see Table A.2 (p. 217) so that this too can have had little effect on MPs' voting decisions.

It seems unlikely, then, that MPs were much influenced by medical opinion or public opinion, yet they were significantly influenced by their perception of the 'abuses' in the operation of the Act. In forming this opinion they appear to have been influenced by reports in the media and evidence from *Babies for Burning*, and by letters from constituents and representations from interest groups, rather than by the Lane Committee's report, medical or public opinion.

The role played by the Department of Health is also important and worthy of consideration. Indeed, the behaviour of the Department had a crucial influence on MPs' voting on the White Bill. The Department was not only very circumspect in its administration of the Act but also very secretive. Initially the Department seemed unsure of its powers under Section 1(3) of the 1967 Act. It believed that this only entitled it to scrutinize the medical or 'physical' standards of the clinics. This meant that the government was tardy in preventing abuses and in tightening controls. Indeed David Owen, then Minister of Health, admitted this in the White Debate when he said:

> I deeply regret that such abuses have been allowed to continue for such a long time ... I wish that, immediately following the passage of the Act, when the abuses were at their height, successive governments had used administrative measures to prevent abuses.[39]

Despite this by the time of the debate upon the White Bill, administrative action had stopped the majority of these 'abuses'. However, the Department was still reluctant to publicize its actions, and remained unsure of its power under Section 1(3) of the 1967 Act. When action was taken against certain nursing homes, the Department was loathe to reveal its reasons for this action: no ministerial statement was issued, nor did the Department give the Lane Committee any assurances that abuses would be controlled. The Department seems to have been afraid that, if it revealed the reasons for closing clinics, this might lead to court actions by the clinics to test the extent of the Minister's powers. This view of the Department action was confirmed by its evidence to the Select Committee which considered the White Bill.[40]

There is no doubt then that the Department responded to its experience of the operation of the Act.[41] However because it shunned publicity a large number of MPs were unaware of its efforts to stem the 'abuses' when the White Bill was debated in 1975. So, some MPs voted on the White Bill without appreciating what the Department was doing, largely because of its failure to inform Parliament of the true current position.

It is clear then that in voting on the White Bill many MPs were influenced by the extent of the 'abortion trade' and by their perception of the 'abuses' in the operation of the 1967 Act. This interpretation is reinforced by the response to our letter from MPs who had changed their vote between 1969 and 1975. We received replies from six Labour MPs, and the one Liberal MP who voted for the White Bill after voting against the St John-Stevas Bill. Of these all except one of the Labour MPs gave the 'abuses' of the Act as their only reason for changing votes.

Two other points should be emphasized. First, a number of MPs who were in favour of abortion seemed to vote for the Second Reading of the White Bill in the mistaken view that they were voting for the establishment of a Select Committee which would consider the Report of the Lane Committee as well as the White Bill. Indeed the other Labour MP who responded to our request for information on his changed vote explained his vote for the White Bill in this way. Similarly, Eddie Loyden, then Labour MP for Liverpool (Garston), contended:

> My experience, after speaking to people in the House, is that quite a number would not have voted for the bill if they had not believed that this was the only way of getting the findings of the Lane Report ... discussed by the Select Committee.[42]

This confusion was not surprising given that a few days before the Second Reading vote the sponsors of the Bill had reached an agreement with the government. James White agreed to withdraw his Bill if the government set up a Select Committee to examine and report on its proposals. This meant that the Bill would be withdrawn without a Second Reading vote. The government, to convince the sponsors that it was not using the Select Committee as a delaying tactic, gave an assurance that should consideration of the bill not be completed by the end of the session it would re-establish the Select Committee in the new session. However, James White lost control of events when his Bill was debated. His attempt to withdraw the Bill was resisted and a vote taken.

Secondly, we must remember here that we are dealing with a Second Reading vote. A vote on Second Reading does not commit an MP to supporting a bill in its final form. Indeed some MPs who voted for the Second Reading of the Steel Bill voted against it on Report, and at Third Reading. However in the case of the White Bill a rather different pattern emerges. By the 1974 elections abortion had become a major political issue in a number of constituencies, particularly although not exclusively, Labour constituencies with large Roman Catholic populations. There is evidence from our interviews with MPs that some Labour MPs 'bought off' opposition on this issue in their constituencies by committing themselves to vote for any amendment bill on Second Reading while intending to vote against it during the later legislative stages. Thus they voted for the White Bill. This is a pattern which as we shall see later was repeated in the case of the Corrie Bill but it was significant even in 1975.

In the period between 1967 and 1975 two patterns have become apparent. First, by 1969 and the vote on the St John-Stevas Bill many Conservative MPs had reasserted their conservative position and supported amending legislation. Obviously such MPs were reinforced in that conservative belief by the evidence of abuses which grew after 1969. However, few

Conservatives changed their view between 1969 and 1975 because in 1969 few Conservatives had taken a liberal stand on abortion. Secondly there was a large swing between 1969 and 1975 in the voting of Labour MPs. The change appears to have occurred mainly because MPs believed that there were numerous 'abuses' of the legislation, but at the same time some Labour MPs voted for the White Bill at Second Reading for political or tactical reasons.

1975-78

The White Bill was given a Second Reading and as such would normally have been referred to a Standing Committee. However, after this vote it was agreed without a vote to forward the Bill to a Select Committee where it would be examined in the light of a review of the operation of the 1967 Act. This strategy was supported by the sponsors of the Bill but it meant that its legislative stages were suspended and it lapsed at the end of the parliamentary session.

Almost as soon as the Select Committee was established, it became clear that its 15 members were deeply divided, with nine members strongly in favour of the main provisions of the White Bill, and six against. Initially, however, the Committee concentrated upon the area of 'abuses' which both sides felt could be effectively controlled by administrative action. This enabled them to reach agreement on nine recommendations before the end of the parliamentary session. These recommendations covered such areas as counselling, examination, certification and nomination, fees and financial agreement in the private sector, the restriction of termination of pregnancy after the twentieth week to NHS hospitals or specially approved places, and the introduction of a list of approved referral and pregnancy advisory bureaux.[43] These recommendations were all accepted and acted upon by the Secretary of State for Social Services, Barbara Castle.[44]

The government decided that the decision on whether the Select Committee should be re-established should be decided by the House and in February 1976, after a debate, a majority of 141 MPs voted in favour of this proposal. The Committee therefore began sitting again with the same membership. At this stage there was an unusual development. The minority of six who were against any significant changes to the 1967 Act resigned because they felt that the Committee, by its very composition, was sure to recommend the emasculation of the original Act. Only one of the six vacancies thus caused was filled, but the rest of the Committee continued to take evidence and produced two further reports before finally completing its deliberations in November 1976.

The major report of the reconvened Select Committee contained 15 recommendations.[45] Surprisingly in the light of its composition the Committee made no recommendation on the grounds upon which abortion could be carried out. It did however suggest that legislation should be introduced to: reduce the time limit for abortions to 20 weeks; make it easier for doctors and nurses to claim conscientious objection to carrying out abortions; and require the licensing of abortion clinics, referral agencies and pregnancy testing agencies.

In 1977, William Benyon, Conservative Member for Buckingham, introduced a private member's bill based on the first report of the re-formed, but truncated, Select Committee.[46] The Bill would have had less effect on the operation of the 1967 Act than James White's Bill. Nevertheless, it would have restricted the availability of abortions in three ways: first, by changing the wording of the provision on eligibility for abortion; secondly, by shortening the period during which abortions could take place; thirdly, by requiring that one of the two certifying doctors should have been registered for not less than 5 years, and that the two doctors should not be partners. In addition, the Bill would have affected the operation of the charitable pregnancy advisory services, notably the Pregnancy Advisory Service and the British Pregnancy Advisory Service, by ensuring that no one clinic could advise on, and carry out, abortions. The Benyon Bill was given a Second Reading by 170 votes to 132 (see Table 1.1).

The Benyon Bill was thus the first amendment bill to reach and complete its Committee Stage. As such it proved an educative experience for the supporters and opponents of reform inside and outside Parliament. The Bill reached the Standing Committee fairly late in the session, and the Committee itself was composed of opponents and supporters of the Bill in direct proportion to the Second Reading vote. Thus the Bill's supporters had a majority and ensured that the Committee met frequently, completing its consideration of the Bill after ten sittings, including three all-night sittings and 19 sessions, including one which lasted 11 hours 48 minutes.[47] Despite this the Bill came out of Committee largely unscathed but there was not time available for its Report Stage, and the government refused to give it time, so that it fell at the end of Parliament. Nevertheless the Benyon Bill was important particularly for the pro-abortion side because of what they learnt from the experience. Indeed MPs from both sides who were on the Committee told us that the Benyon supporters had outmanoeuvred their opponents at the Committee Stage. This was largely because the resources of the pro-abortion side were severely stretched by the frequent and extended sittings. In the first place there were only six opponents of Benyon's Bill on the Standing Committee and two of these, Renée Short and Maureen Colquhoun, were missing from four of the sittings because of a trip to America. This meant that the remaining members were under enormous physical pressure. In addition the aid provided by the pro-abortion interest groups to their supporters on the Standing Committee was not of equal strength to that provided on the Corrie Bill. The chief adviser was initially Peter Jackson who, as an MP in 1966-7, had been chief whip among the Labour supporters of the Steel Bill. However he proved less adept on this occasion partly because his knowledge of parliamentary draftsmanship was limited and partly because no one person could carry such a load. It was thus only when a number of individuals from the pro-abortion lobby played an active role in the later stages of the Committee that the pro-abortion side was as well served as its adversaries. Here again the defenders of the 1967 Act learnt a great deal from this experience.

The Benyon Bill lapsed at the end of the 1977-8 parliamentary session. However, in October 1977 an attempt was made by the Labour Government to defuse the abortion controversy. It thought that if one amending bill was passed by Parliament this would satisfy the anti-abortion lobby and prevent the issue returning to Parliament again and again. The then Minister of State for Health, Roland Moyle, initiated a series of discussions with pro- and anti-abortion MPs to see whether some compromise could be reached. Talks centred around a reduction in the upper time limit for abortions. Jo Richardson recalls being asked to attend one of these meetings which were held at the DHSS; other MPs invited included Leo Abse, Sir Bernard Braine,

William Benyon and Robert Rhodes-James. However, as soon as she and other supporters of the 1967 Act realized that the government intended introducing a compromise bill they withdrew from any further discussion, stating that no changes in the abortion law were necessary. These talks, therefore, broke down and nothing more was heard of the intended compromise bill.

In the next session Sir Bernard Braine introduced a ten-minute rule bill, the provisions of which followed closely those of the Benyon Bill.[48] As a ten-minute rule bill it had no chance of progressing but Sir Bernard was given leave to introduce the bill, with 181 voting in favour and 175 against. Once again then we can see that a significant change in parliamentary opinion had occurred between 1975 and 1978. In particular two trends are apparent if we examine individual MPs' voting patterns over the period. There was an increase in the number of Conservative MPs voting for amending legislation. More specifically, 53 Conservative MPs who abstained or did not vote on the issue in 1975 subsequently supported the Benyon Bill. At the same time, many fewer Labour MPs supported amending legislation in 1977 and 1978 than had done in 1975. In addition, 35 Labour MPs who had abstained or not voted in 1975 voted against the Benyon Bill. Overall, then, while the trend between 1975 and 1978 is away from support for amending legislation, there are important party differences.

It is not difficult to explain the changing views of most Labour MPs, or of those few Conservative MPs who moved away from support for amending legislation. In particular it is evident that many of those MPs who had been confused in 1975 as to whether they were voting for the White Bill, or the establishment of a Select Committee, reasserted their opposition to amending legislation in 1977 and 1978. Our replies from MPs who supported White and voted against Braine and/or Benyon confirms this argument. Three Labour and one Conservative MP of the 15 who responded said they had supported White to get the issue and the Lane Committe's report referred to a Select Committee. Each subsequently reasserted his opposition to amending legislation.

At the same time, by 1977, there was ample evidence that many of the 'abuses' in the operation of the 1967 Act were being removed. In the debate on the White Bill, the DHSS had made clear for the first time the steps it was taking to prevent abuses. The Department had also accepted, and acted upon, the initial unanimous recommendations of the Select Committee on the White Bill. All this meant that the private clinics were much more tightly controlled, that taxi-touting was dramatically reduced and that standards in the private sector were radically improved. This action was made very clear to MPs in the debate on the Benyon Bill by Roland Moyle, Minister of State at the DHSS.[49] The Department's action on 'abuses' obviously influenced some MPs. Indeed all the other eleven MPs who supported White and opposed Benyon and/or Braine, and replied to our request for information, gave the curtailment of the 'abuses' as the reason for their changed vote.

In addition, it was evident from Mr Moyle's speech that the Department believed that legislation to amend the 1967 Act was unnecessary. It is true that the Minister refused to give a departmental view, but his speech represented a defence of the way the Act was operating after administrative action by the government. What is more, David Ennals, then Secretary of State for Social Services, had sent a private, but well publicized, letter to David Steel before the Benyon debate in which he argued that legislation was unnecessary.[50] This view is likely to have affected the voting of some Labour MPs.

In Conclusion

After the 1978 vote, opinion in the House appeared evenly divided. The two sides had learnt a great deal from their experience on the Benyon Bill although it is probable that the pro-abortionists had learnt more, particularly about the problems of organization in Standing Committee. However both sides at this time awaited the outcome of the forthcoming election knowing that, given past voting patterns, if the Conservative Party won a comfortable overall majority at such an election, the chances of a successful amendment to the Abortion Act would increase substantially.

Notes

1. For an analysis of the history of abortion and English Law see Glanville Williams, *The Sanctity of Life and the Criminal Law,* London, Faber, 1958, pp. 139-224.
2. For a fuller analysis of the evolution of the law on abortion see B.M. Dickens, *Abortion and the Law,* London, MacGibbon and Kee, 1966.
3. See ibid. and A. Bourne, *A Doctor's Creed,* London, Gollancz, 1962.
4. HC Debs., 27 February 1953, vol. 511, col. 2506.
5. HC Debs., 10 February 1961, vol. 634, cols. 853-92.
6. HC Debs., 15 June 1965, vol. 714, cols. 254-58.
7. HC Debs., 26 February 1966, vol. 725, cols. 837-56.
8. HL Debs., 30 November 1965, vol. 270, cols. 1139-242; 1 February 1966, vol. 272 cols. 284-356; 3 February 1966, vol. 272, cols. 491-557; 7 February 1966, vol. 272, cols. 581-601 and 605-39; 22 February 1966, vol. 273, cols. 92-152; 28 February 1966, vol. 273, cols. 520-76; 7 March 1966, vol. 273, cols. 910-20 and 929-46.
9. HL Debs., 10 May 1966, vol. 274, cols. 577-605; 23 May, vol. 274, cols. 1206-50.

10' The original Bill is printed as appendix 1 to M. Simms and K. Hindell, *Abortion Law Reformed,* London, Peter Owen, 1971, pp. 245-8. This book offers a very thorough analysis of the evolution and passage of the Steel Bill.

11. The Bill's title was changed because of an amendment tabled by the House of Lords and accepted by the House of Commons, HC Debs., 25 October 1967, vol. 751, col. 1780. Two reasons were given by David Steel. First, two bills had been passed in the Lords (1965 and 1966) under the title 'Abortion Bill'. It was natural, he felt, that they should prefer their own title. Secondly, Lord Brooke had pointed out during debate that the term 'termination of pregnancy' could be used up to full term. As the Bill did not provide for abortion in the case of a viable foetus the title 'Abortion Bill' was therefore technically correct.
12. HC Debs., 22 July 1966, vol. 732, cols. 1067-166.
13. Simms and Hindell, *Abortion Law Reformed,* p. 167.
14. Royal College of Obstetricians and Gynaecologists, 'Report on Legalised Abortion', *British Medical Journal,* 2 April 1966; British Medical Association, 'Report of Committee on Therapeutic Abortion', ibid., 2 July 1966.
15. 'Medical Termination of Pregnancy Bill: Views of BMA and RCOG', ibid., 31 December 1966.

16. HC Debs., *Reports of Standing Committees, Session 1966-7,* vol. X, *Committee F on Medical Termination of Pregnancy Bill,* cols. 1-616.
17. HC Debs., 2 June 1967, vol. 747, col. 448-536; 30 June 1967, vol. 749, cols. 895-1102; 13 July 1967, vol. 750, cols. 1159-344. The Third Reading followed the last Report Stage debate, HC Debs., 13 July 1967, vol. 750, cols. 1346-86.
18. The full Act is printed as appendix 2 in Simms and Hindell, *Abortion Law Reformed,* pp. 249-53.
19. See P. Richards, *Parliament and Conscience,* London, Allen and Unwin, 1970.
20. Ibid., pp. 181-2.
21. For a thorough analysis of private members' bills see P. Bromhead, *Private Members Bills,* London, Routledge & Kegan Paul, 1956, and P. Richards, 'Private Members Legislation', in S. Walkland (ed.), *The House of Commons in the Twentieth Century,* Oxford, Clarendon Press, 1979, pp. 292-328.
22. Simms and Hindell, *Abortion Law Reformed,* p. 178.
23. Richards, *Parliament and Conscience,* p. 206.
24. Ibid., p. 104.
25. A. Barker and M. Rush, *The Member of Parliament and His Information,* London, Allen and Unwin, 1970, p. 55.
26. HC Debs., 15 July 1969, vol. 787, cols. 411-24.
27. HC Debs., 13 February 1970, vol. 795, cols. 1653-703.
28. The Medical Services (Referral) Bill was presented by John Hunt and given a formal First Reading on 1 December 1971, HC Debs., vol. 827, col. 460, but was never debated because no time was available. HC Debs., 18 February 1972, vol. 831, col. 861.
29. Michael Gryll's Abortion (Amendment) Bill was given a First Reading on 28 November 1973, HC Debs., vol. 865, col. 411. Its Second Reading was not due until after the February 1974 election. He was given leave to introduce the Bill in the next session on 8 May, HC Debs., vol. 873, cols. 403-6. It was given an unopposed Second Reading on 10 May 1974, HC Debs., vol. 873, col. 853.
30. *Report of the Committee on the Working of the Abortion Act* (The Lane Committee Report), 3 vols., cmnds 5579-1 and 5579-11. HMSO, 1974.
31. HC Debs., 7 February 1975, vol. 885, cols. 1757-868.
32. Lane Committee Report, vol. 1, para. 605 , '…we are unanimous in supporting the Act and its provisions. We have no doubt that the gains facilitated by the Act have much outweighted any disadvantages for which it has been criticised.'
33. M. Litchfield and S. Kentish, *Babies for Burning,* London, Serpentine Press, 1974. The particular references are pp.1, 146, 143 and 52.

34. The two most notable were brought by the British Pregnancy Advisory Service in early 1978 and by Dr Bloom in 1977.
35. M. Muggeridge, *Sunday Times,* 2 February 1975, and R. Butt, *Times,* 23 January 1975.
36. James White as quoted in an article in the *Scottish Daily Record,* 5 December 1975.
37. Leo Abse, review of 'Babies for Burning', *The Spectator,* 18 January 1975.
38. The attitude of the professional organizations was very clear in the evidence they gave to the Select Committee which considered the White Bill. The BMA gave evidence on 23 June 1975, *Special Reports and Minutes of Evidence of the Select Committee on the Abortion (Amendment) Bill 1974-75*, HMSO 692-11, pp.186-210. The RCOG gave evidence on 30 June 1975, ibid., pp.226-39. The RCN gave evidence on 27 October 1975, ibid., pp.333-49.
39. David Owen, HC Debs., 7 February 1975, vol. 885, col. 1800.
40. See the evidence of Mr Fogden, a Principal in the Department of Health, to the Select Committee. He explained: 'The Secretary of State's action may be open to challenge in the Courts and the Secretary of State may wish to protect her position publicly, so it has never been the policy to state publicly why they have been closed down.' First Report of the Select Committee, *Special Reports and Minutes of Evidence of the Select Committee on the Abortion (Amendment) Bill,* p.18 para. 13.
41. This is evident in the Department's response when Leo Abse, a member of the Select Committee, asked why the Department appeared at that time (1975) to be interpreting their powers under Section 1(3) much more widely than previously. Mr Hume, Under-Secretary to the DHSS, replied: 'What has happened historically is that over the years we have gradually added to the undertakings required of the proprietors of the homes. Mr Butcher will be able to elaborate on this, but this means that our legal advice has evolved during this period. Action is taken in the light of experience, and whether a particular decision has been challenged or not. Until there is a case tested in the Courts, there must be an element of doubt about what our powers are.' Ibid., p.18, para. 13.
42. Personal communication.
43. *Recommendations of the Select Committee on the Abortion (Amendment) Bill, Third Special Report,* HMSO HC 552, 30 July 1975.
44. HC Debs., 21 October 1975, vol. 898, col. 244-7.
45. *First Report from the Select Committee on Abortion, Session 1975-76,* vol. 1: *Report,* HMSO HC 573-1, 12 July 1976, pp. 21-3.

46. HC Debs., 25 February 1977, vol. 926, col. 1783-896.
47. HC Debs., *Reports of Standing Committee C on the Abortion (Amendment) Bill, Session 1977-8,* fourth sitting on 5 July 1977, HMSO, 1977.
48. HC Debs., 21 February 1978, vol. 944, cols. 1213-24.
49. R. Moyle, HC Debs., 25 February 1977, vol. 926, vols. 1805-15.
50. D. Steel, HC Debs., 25 February 1977, vol. 926. col. 1825.

2
The Abortion Lobby

It is impossible to explain what happened during the Corrie Bill without first examining the development of the abortion lobbies. When the Steel Bill was first introduced the Abortion Law Reform Association (ALRA) and the professional medical associations, particularly the Royal College of Obstetricians (RCOG) and the British Medical Association (BMA), were the only organizations lobbying on the issue. In contrast, by the time of the Corrie Bill there were nine organizations campaigning in defence of the Steel Act (including ALRA) as well as the medical organizations, and seven anti-abortion groups.

The growth of the lobby has been dramatic. What we now have is a genuine plurality: a large number of interest groups taking a wide variety of stances, all attempting to influence legislation in this field. However, out of all the groups involved only the professional organizations — the BMA and RCOG — are 'insider' groups with good contacts with the major department concerned, the DHSS.

The main battleground for all the groups involved is Parliament, although at the same time groups attempt to influence both the administration of the current legislation and public opinion. Most of the lobbying is conducted in the open, rather than behind the closed doors of Whitehall, which provides an opportunity to observe what must be described as a near-classic case of parliamentary lobbying — possibly unrivalled in the postwar era. In fact, all the MPs we talked to reported that their postbag on abortion bills was at least two or three times as large as that on any other issue.[1] The mass lobbies held by the

Society for the Protection of Unborn Children (SPUC) on 30 January 1979, and by the Campaign Against the Corrie Bill (CAC) on 5 February 1979 created scenes which were almost unprecedented, with hundreds of people milling around the Central Lobby and feelings running very high. One story will serve to illustrate the intensity of emotion and activity involved.

On the day of the SPUC lobby one newly elected Scottish MP was meeting a group of about 15 anti-abortion supporters from his constituency. He was a strong supporter of the 1967 Act and told his constituents that he had made this clear at the election and had no intention of supporting the Corrie Bill. He told the delegation that he would have been more impressed with their declaration that they 'spoke for the majority in his constituency' if he had received a lot of correspondence from his constituency supporting the Corrie Bill. In the next month the MP received 1,000 letters from his constituency and another 1,000 from the surrounding area, calling upon him to support the Corrie Bill.[2]

There can be no doubt, therefore, that the issue provokes high levels of commitment among activists, a level of commitment and activity rarely reached even on economic issues. What is more the abortion lobby has become increasingly sophisticated. Of all the non-economic interest groups this lobby must be the most politically aware and knowledgeable. This is largely because the various groups have had a great deal of experience and practice in a short time. At the same time, as we shall see in detail later, the previous parliamentary debates served in many ways as a learning process which informed and shaped the lobbying on the Corrie Bill. Indeed, by the 1979-80 parliamentary session this lobby was, in British terms, very sophisticated. Its activists had learnt from their mistakes and had changed strategy and tactics.

This chapter examines how the lobby grew and identifies the changes which occurred in the interest groups' views, personnel and tactics. This helps to establish the background against which to analyse the lobbying on the Corrie Bill. For the most part the chapter examines the extra-parliamentary lobby prior to the Corrie Bill. This is dealt with in six sections. The first two sections look at the growth, structure and strategies of the pro-abortion lobby and the anti-abortion lobby respectively; the third looks at the changing attitudes of the parties; the fourth deals with the growing involvement of the TUC; the fifth looks at the role of the

Church; and the sixth section examines the changing views and lobbying of the professional organizations, the BMA, RCOG and Royal College of Nursing (RCN). The remainder of the chapter identifies the development and activities of the parliamentary lobby, before the introduction of the Corrie Bill.

The Pro-abortion Lobby

Abortion Law Reform Association (1936)

The passage of the Steel Bill was the culmination of 32 years of persistent and at times intensive campaigning by a small but highly organized pressure group, the Abortion Law Reform Association. ALRA was founded in 1936 and its history until the passage of the 1967 Abortion Act has been well documented by Madeleine Simms and Keith Hindell.[3] It has never been a large organization and even at the height of its campaign in support of the Steel Bill had only approximately 1,000 members. Nevertheless, as was emphasized in the last chapter, it was very effective in persuading David Steel to sponsor an abortion bill and in helping him pilot it through Parliament. It relied for this effectiveness on the dedicated efforts of a handful of people who had a detailed knowledge of the issue, rather than on a mass membership or sophisticated organization.

Once the Abortion Act became law ALRA was faced with a problem common to all successful 'issue' interest groups. With its declared aim achieved it became difficult to hold the interest and support of its members and ALRA's membership and income declined significantly after 1967. In addition ALRA lost a number of key active members and several crucial sources of finance in the five years after the passage of the Abortion Act. All this weakened its effectiveness as a lobby.

Some of the ALRA activists moved on to different issues but others found it impossible to continue working unpaid for long hours. Indeed these difficulties were spelt out by Alastair Service, then chairman of ALRA, in an internal memo:

> ALRA has been losing some of its hard working executive committee members, mainly because they can no longer

> neglect their livelihoods nor their personal affairs... There may be other members who can devote the time to ALRA's affairs that existing officials have done in the past seven years, in which case ALRA could continue to function at the present level. Unfortunately they are not so far evident and if they do not become so by the next AGM ALRA faces a crisis.[4]

In fact these full-time activists have never really been replaced by ALRA. The crisis worsened in 1972 when finance from two United States foundations which had given ALRA regular grants dried up. The Hopkins Funds were liquidated while the Lalor Foundation was affected by changes in the American tax laws which made it almost impossible for such charities to support foreign organizations unless the aims of these organizations were fully approved. In addition one individual supporter who had regularly given sizeable grants to ALRA died. ALRA's resources were drastically reduced at a time when opposition to the Abortion Act was growing quickly.

ALRA's response to its loss of activists, members and finance was fairly dramatic. The executive committee believed that the decline in membership could only be reversed and more funds found if they launched a positive rather than a defensive campaign. They ruled out the possibility of advocating a liberalization of the abortion law as there seemed little support for such a move. Instead they decided to direct their attention towards birth control and merging ALRA with a new pressure group to be called the Birth Control Campaign (BCC). Its principal aims would be: to campaign for free contraception on the NHS; to defend the 1967 Abortion Act; to press for better abortion facilities on the NHS; and to call for wider attention to be paid to the problems of overpopulation.

This merger was viewed with alarm by parliamentary opponents of abortion, such as Leo Abse and Sir Bernard Braine. They felt that BCC would merely be ALRA campaigning under another name, but that the contraception campaign would give respectability to the abortion campaign. Therefore, they approached the then Secretary of State for Social Services, Sir Keith Joseph, to express their alarm. In the face of the publicity that followed the ALRA executive decided that it would be damaging to launch BCC as a merger with ALRA and so it was established in April 1971 as a separate group.

The establishment of BCC allowed the pro-abortion lobby to fight on a new front and gain interest, funds and membership again. However, it did leave ALRA rather bare as much of its resources, and some of its personnel, were channelled into the new organization. This meant that for the next four or five years the efforts of many pro-abortion activists were directed away from abortion at a time when the anti-abortion interest groups SPUC and LIFE were gathering momentum.

In fact, although ALRA continued to exist after the formation of BCC, its position in the pro-abortion lobby changed. Never a mass organization, and with no real interest in being one, by the late 1970s it was much smaller in size than the National Abortion Campaign (NAC). However, ALRA still had as members a number of individuals with wide knowledge of the abortion issue and considerable experience and skill in lobbying. Individuals like Dilys Cossey, Vera Houghton, Diane Munday and Madeleine Simms continued to play a major role, particularly through their position on Co-ord, even though ALRA itself became less active and less noticeable. In fact the key role played by certain ALRA activists is in keeping with the whole history of the organization: the original Steel Bill had been helped through by the prodigious efforts of a relatively small number of ALRA activists and certain of them continued to play a similar role in defending the 1967 Act.

However, by 1975 the political terrain had changed dramatically. The anti-abortion lobby was now well organized in the constituencies and active within Parliament. The pro-abortion side needed a stronger and wider grass-roots organization than ALRA. Therefore, although ALRA continued in much the same way as it had always done — if a little less effectively — a whole variety of other pro-abortion groups proliferated around it, responding to changes in the political environment.

Doctors' Pressure Groups

From 1970 onwards a large number of doctors became increasingly disturbed at attempts to amend the Abortion Act. Within the next nine years three separate doctors' pressure groups were established.

The first of these groups, the Doctors and Overpopulation Group (DOG), was formed in January 1972 by Dr George Morris, a London GP. DOG's aim is to alert the medical profession, the public, the government and Parliament to the problem of overpopulation. In particular they campaign for the retention of the abortion law, more readily available NHS facilities for abortion, and facilities for voluntary sterilization.[5] Within a year of its formation the group had approximately 2,000 members who were either doctors or medical students. This level of membership has remained more or less the same over the last eight years. Notable among its early supporters were Dr Gerard Vaughan (the present Minister of Health) and Dr David Owen (Minister of Health from 1974-6).

The second group, Doctors for a Woman's Choice on Abortion (DWCA), was established late in 1976 by two doctors, Judy Bury and Nadine Harrison. This is a more radical group which wishes to hand the decision on abortion over to the woman. They believed that simply to defend the Act in the face of constant attacks would lead to a gradual erosion of abortion provisions. In the early days of the group's activities the co-ordination was undertaken by Judy Bury and it soon became highly organized and effective. Members include GPs, family planning doctors, gynaecologists and psychiatrists. By 1980 this group had around 600 members and the workload of the co-ordinator had increased so much that specific tasks had to be delegated. There is now a library and information officer as well as three press officers covering different parts of the country.

The third group, Doctors in Defence of the 1967 Abortion Act (DDAA), was established as a result of activity in Parliament. When the reconvened Select Committee on the James White Bill issued its recommendations in 1976 it was clear that if the recommendations were enacted they would seriously restrict the availability of legal abortions. This report provoked a letter to *The Lancet*[6] from more than 500 doctors, from all sections of the medical profession, who deplored the prospect of a return to restrictive legislation. The letter was initiated by Dr George Morris, founder and secretary of DOG. The expressions of support prompted Dr Morris to form another doctors' pressure group with the sole aim of defending the 1967 Abortion Act — the beginning of DDAA. This new group enabling doctors to speak with one voice against restrictions to the Abortion Act soon had a membership of around 2,000 of whom approximately half are also members of DOG. The chairwoman of the group is Dame Josephine Barnes, a consultant gynaecologist who was President of the BMA in 1979, and the secretary is Dr Morris.

The importance of these three doctors' pressure groups cannot be overemphasized. Because of their professional experience their views tend to have a considerable impact on MPs and the press. The anti-abortion campaigners have no similar organization, a fact which was very noticeable during the Corrie Bill.

The National Abortion Campaign (1975)

Until 1975 ALRA was the only group campaigning specifically and solely on abortion, although DOG joined them in their defence of the 1967 Act. In addition there was one other group campaigning for free, safe and reliable contraception on the NHS and a woman's right to choose on abortion. The group was called Women's Abortion and Contraception Campaign (WACC) and was most active where there was a strong women's liberation group, for instance in Leeds, Nottingham, Exeter, Bristol and Liverpool. The groups activities fluctuated, but they prepared the ground for the National Abortion Campaign (NAC) which developed with the introduction of James White's Bill in 1975. White's Bill was the first major attack on the 1967 Act and it made many people realize, some for the first time, the extent of the threat to the abortion law. The renewed expansion of the pro-abortion lobby began in 1974, but it was not until restrictive legislation was actually introduced in 1975 that these new activists organized themselves.

In 1974 Diane Munday, ALRA's general secretary, retired and went to the British Pregnancy Advisory Service (BPAS). At the same time the other members of ALRA's executive committee took the unusual step of retiring, handing the committee over to a new, younger generation, because they felt the campaign needed new life — just as in 1963 they themselves had taken over the committee because they did not think it was radical enough. The new committee's campaign was launched after the introduction of James White's Bill with the slogan 'A woman's right to choose' and a meeting was organized in Central

Hall on the day of the Second Reading of the Bill. This was the first mass meeting to be held on the pro-abortion side and the organizers were surprised at the number who attended (500), and at the level of commitment shown. At this meeting it was decided that all the pro-abortion groups must campaign together to fight restrictive legislation. Therefore one organization was needed to co-ordinate these groups. This decision was acted on when in March a second meeting was held and the National Abortion Campaign (NAC) was founded. Initially it acted as an umbrella organization through which all other pro-abortion groups could campaign in the country. However, NAC soon became a totally independent group with a radical voice in the pro-abortion lobby.

Perhaps surprisingly, the new ALRA did not assume the role now taken on by NAC. However, as we have said, ALRA has never been a mass based organization, and has never wanted to be. Moreover, the new generation of radical feminist activists who joined NAC would not have fitted happily within ALRA. ALRA is hierarchical and decisions are taken by a small group of activists on the executive committee. NAC is completely different. It grew out of the women's liberation movement and is overtly democratic. Its supporters called for a broadly based mass organization with loose structures through which decisions would be arrived at after full discussions with all members. NAC has been most concerned to politicize public opinion generally and women in particular on the issue. In contrast ALRA has concentrated much more on parliamentary lobbying.

It would be wrong therefore to see NAC and ALRA in competition with each other. Instead they have tended to complement each other. Particularly, in its early days, NAC owed a great deal to ALRA, which carried out most of the administrative work and gave advice and help on how to campaign against restrictive legislation.

By July 1975 a national demonstration had been organized and 20,000 people marched against James White's Bill in the biggest demonstration on a woman's issue since the suffragettes. Support for the march was even more remarkable given that the campaign had only been launched four months previously. It was an indication of the strength of feeling that existed, and of the opposition to restrictive abortion legislation.

The structure of NAC was decided at its first conference in

October 1975 and it has not changed significantly since then. It is ultra-democratic, reflecting its origins in the feminist movement. Although men can be members of NAC it is women who control and organize the campaign. The local groups which are the focus of the organization are completely autonomous, deciding their own policy and method of campaigning. There are no elected officers or delegated structures. National policy is decided at the annual conference and at six-weekly planning meetings, all of which are open to all members. The NAC national office gives back-up to the local groups in the country and co-ordinates activities, and a steering committee deals with day to day work. However, any member can participate in steering committee meetings and the committee and the national office are accountable to the six-weekly planning meetings.

When it was originally formed NAC's aim was to defend the 1967 Abortion Act. However, at its first conference in October 1975 it adopted the policy of 'Free abortion on demand — a woman's right to choose.' Over the years NAC has developed a clear programme. At present they campaign alongside other organizations to defend the 1967 Act, but their aim is to liberalize the Act. Ultimately they are campaigning for abortion to be treated like any other medical procedure so that it cannot be used to enforce a measure of sexual control on women. NAC's advocacy of abortion up to term has caused tension in the pro-abortion movement as the majority of other pro-abortion groups favour the retention of the current time limit of 28 weeks. Indeed NAC itself is aware that its radical position alienates some potential supporters. It was partly for this reason that NAC sponsored the formation of the Campaign Against the Corrie Bill (CAC) as a separate organization in 1979, so that individuals who supported the current legislation, but who felt less than committed to an organization which advocated abortion up to term, could be drawn into the campaign.

NAC's strategy centres around demonstrations and local picketing of MP's surgeries, health authorities or hospitals. It also organizes day-schools and conferences on abortion and fertility control, and sponsors short educational films on abortion procedures. In other words, NAC is in essence a proselytizing group, rather than a parliamentary lobbying group. As such its achievement has been to make MPs aware that there is substantial grass-roots support for the Abortion Act. Until NAC was formed SPUC and LIFE had had almost a clear run in the constituencies while ALRA had concentrated more on parliamentary lobbying. The formation of NAC redressed the balance. NAC grew in membership every time an amending bill was introduced so that by 1979 approximately 350 groups were affiliated. Its action against the three amending bills in 1975, 1977 and 1978 politicized the group. In effect NAC's actions in the streets complemented the parliamentary elements of ALRA and other groups in a way which was to prove very effective in the pro-abortion campaign on the Corrie Bill.

One other aspect of NAC's strategy is particularly important. Although NAC is an avowedly non-partisan organization, most of its members are radicals and some are active in the trade union movement and in the Labour Party. In addition NAC maintained from the very beginning that women would not win control of their own bodies without the committed support of the trade union movement. Therefore, right from the outset NAC tried to recruit trade union members and encourage links with individual unions. At the same time NAC sought, through its members, to get resolutions supporting the 1967 Act and calling for abortion on request, introduced at union conferences and at the Labour Party Conference. Initially this strategy had little effect but it was to prove important, as we shall see later.

Christians For Free Choice (1976)

During the parliamentary passage of the White Bill Elfreda Fuller began writing to her local papers and the religious press, to express her anxiety that so many fellow Christians were supporting the Bill. She was encouraged by ALRA, of which she was a member, to establish a group in order to demonstrate that not all Christians were against abortion. In response she formed Christians for Free Choice (CFFC) in 1976.

The group has a membership of around 600 which includes clergy and lay people and is drawn from every Christian denomination. Patrons include Rev. the Lord Soper, Rt Rev. J.A.T. Robinson, Rev. Dr Chad Varah and The Rev. T. Robinson. Members play an important role writing letters to the press and MPs in defence of the Abortion Act. In taking this action CFFC plays a significant role within the pro-abortion lobby because its existence demonstrates that a fairly large proportion of Christians oppose any restriction on legal abortions as provided under the 1967 Act.

Labour Abortion Rights Campaign (1976)

LIFE, one of the two major anti-abortion groups, was actively recruiting members in the Labour Party after 1976. The Labour Party's changing stance on abortion is examined later in this chapter, but in 1975 a motion calling for abortion on request was passed overwhelmingly at the Labour Party Conference. Despite this, however, some Labour Party members believed that a great deal of work needed to be done to remind MPs of the Conference decision and that a Labour Party pro-abortion group should be formed. LARC was formed at the end of 1976 and its first meeting took place on 12 December. Approximately 50 people attended, coming from 22 constituency parties. The group has never been large: at the time of writing it claims a membership of around 200.

The main aim of the group is to convince Labour MPs that abortion is not a matter of conscience to be left to predominantly male MPs, but is a basic political right for the women they represent. As such the group is radical and feminist and shares many of NAC's views. LARC's three principal aims are: to defend and extend the 1967 Abortion Act to allow abortion on request; to campaign for better birth control facilities; and to abolish the free vote on abortion and replace it with a three-line whip. In order to carry through these policies it organizes an active campaign in the constituencies, raises the matter wherever reselection of MPs takes place, and continually puts pressure on Labour MPs who insist on voting against Party Conference decisions on the matter. In addition LARC often organizes fringe meetings on abortion at Party Conferences.

The group has strong links with the National Council of Working Women's Organizations, the Labour Women's Advisory Committee, the Young Socialists, the National Organization of Labour Students and with various pro-abortion interest groups, especially NAC. It also has special links with ASTMS, AUEW/TASS and NUPE. As an example of this relationship the women's section of AUEW/TASS sends out LARC mailings on a national scale, usually when there is a campaign being waged against a restrictive bill, whilst other unions will often circulate and publish LARC material in union journals.

Tories for Free Choice (1977)

The pro-abortion lobby has always been well organized among Labour MPs and Labour supporters but poorly organized on the Conservative side. This deficiency was partly remedied by the formation of Tories for Free Choice (TFFC) in 1977. Sharon Spiers, a member of ALRA, was encouraged to form the group and begin lobbying among Conservative MPs during the lead up to the Benyon Bill in 1977.

TFFC has been, from the outset, a small group consisting of a few activists whose main aim is to lobby Conservative MPs rather than to influence Conservative Party opinion. Initially the leading role was taken by Sharon Spiers and her key contact was Sir George Sinclair MP. It is not an easy task given the opposition of most Conservative MPs to liberal abortion policy. However, as a result of the group's activities a small number of Conservative MPs began to oppose amending legislation and speak against it. This support was important to the pro-abortion lobby because it went at least some way towards dispelling the impression that the pro-abortion lobby was composed solely of Labour MPs. This meant that the efforts of TFFC, and their success in lobbying Conservative MPs has been important to the pro-abortion side.

Co-ordinating Committee in Defence of the 1967 Abortion Act (1976)

In March 1976 a new umbrella organization, incorporating all the groups campaigning on the issue, was established. This group, the Co-ordinating Committee in Defence of the 1967 Abortion Act (Co-ord) began in 1976 with 16 member-organizations — by 1980 it had 56 member-organizations and had developed into an effective defensive lobby.

The formation of the group was brought about by the events surrounding the re-establishment of the Select Committee on

James White's Bill in March 1976. The six pro-abortion MPs on the Committee felt that no further agreement between the two sides in committee could be reached and that any further recommendations were totally unnecessary and would serve only to restrict the provision of abortion. Therefore, they announced their withdrawal from the Committee. Their action was supported by NAC's refusal to give evidence because it felt that to do so would only lend credibility to the Committee. NAC went on, at a press conference, to criticize the biased composition of the Committee, which carried on sitting without the six MPs, and the 'illusion of impartiality' given to it.[7] These remarks and actions by NAC were referred to the Committee of Privileges as an alleged contempt of Parliament. Four days later NAC was officially backed by a further 15 organizations.

On 4 March, BCC called a meeting to which it invited 18 representatives of other organizations, and a number of individuals, who were concerned about the constant attacks on the 1967 Act. At this meeting NAC proposed that all pro-abortion groups should unite and agree not to give evidence to the Select Committee in support of the six MPs who had resigned. Furthermore, it suggested the establishment of a public forum to 'receive and publicly consider evidence' which would have the interests of women principally in mind.[8] However, this latter proposal was not accepted by the meeting. Instead it was decided that all those organizations attending should join together in one forum so that consultation could take place and, wherever possible, collective decisions be reached on matters of common interest and concern. To do this they formed the Co-ordinating Committee on Abortion Legislation (later renamed Co-ordinating Committee in Defence of the 1967 Abortion Act). The 16 organizations which formed Co-ord stated that they would not give evidence to the Select Committee until reference to the Committee of Privileges was disposed of, and the Select Committee was reconstituted 'to command the respect of the defenders of the principles of the 1967 Abortion Act'.[9]

This was the beginning of a strong and highly effective defensive lobby. The groups aims are not only to defend the 1967 Act, but also to ensure a more equitable provision of abortion facilities throughout the country. Co-ord receives no funds. It works as a co-operative with each member-organization contributing as much effort as it can. It is housed by the Birth Control Trust which is a registered charity whose aims are to advance medical and sociological research into all methods of fertility control and to attempt to educate the public in the field of procreation and contraception. It also seeks to protect and preserve the health of parents, young people and children and prevent the poverty and hardship caused by unwanted pregnancy. As the Trust is a charity Co-ord can only take defensive action as the charity laws do not allow charities to campaign for changes in legislation.

The group normally meets every two or three months — more frequently if there is an amending bill before Parliament. A regular newsletter keeps members informed of all studies and activities going on in the abortion field. Co-ord has in fact proved of crucial importance to the pro-abortion lobby. It has managed to keep such diverse organizations as TFFC, LARC, ALRA, NAC and CFFC united with the single aim of defending the 1967 Act. Although there have been disputes over strategy and tactics, differences have in the end always been resolved in order to further the one common aim.

By 1979 the group covered a wide spectrum, incorporating doctors; representatives from the three main political parties; trade unions, such as the Confederation of Health Service Employees and the National Association of Public Employees; the major providers of abortion and family planning in the charitable sector; organizations representing social workers, such as the British Association of Social Workers and the National Association of Probation Officers; and indeed all the groups campaigning on the issue. The existence and activities of Co-ord has ensured a co-ordination of effort, knowledge and expertise.

Co-ord Lawyers (1978)

In a memo sent to Co-ord members after the defeat of the Benyon Bill it was suggested that in any future campaign a team of lawyers and Co-ord advisers should draft amendments to a proposed bill before the Committee Stage, and that MPs should be consulted on amendments and strategy.[10] Accordingly in June 1978 a group of lawyers, brought together by Bill Birtles, who had worked on the Benyon Bill, met with Co-ord representatives and one or two MPs. They resolved that by the time the next restrictive bill was introduced they would be well prepared on the parliamentary front. It was decided that approximately 15 lawyers should be invited to join the group. They would have to be prepared to offer their advice and help voluntarily and to meet whenever necessary to draft amendments throughout a bill's progress through Parliament. This group proved vital to the pro-abortion lobby, as later chapters will show.

British Pregnancy Advisory Service and Pregnancy Advisory Service (1968)

BPAS and the Pregnancy Advisory Service (PAS) are the two major abortion charities in the country. They have both played an important role in providing facilities for abortion at low cost, and in defending the 1967 Act. It would, therefore, be remiss to conclude this part of the chapter without explaining the role they have played in the defence campaign.

When the 1967 Act came into force in 1968 the demand for abortion exceeded all expectations. In the first five full years of the Act's implementation the number of pregnancies terminated on residents of England and Wales rose from 49,800 in 1969 to a peak of 110,600 in 1973 — the numbers then began to stabilize. The NHS was completely unprepared for this demand and facilities were hopelessly inadequate. If anything, the NHS provision of abortion facilities has deteriorated over the years. In 1969 the NHS performed 62 per cent of all legal abortions in England and Wales, but in 1979 this figure had fallen to 46 per cent. Moreover, facilities vary considerably throughout the country. For instance, in Newcastle-upon-Tyne 86 per cent of all abortions were performed in the NHS in 1979, but in Dudley this figure fell to 6 per cent.

In an attempt to improve facilities, iron out the discrepancies, and offer a low-cost but safe and efficient service, BPAS (originally called the Birmingham PAS) and PAS (originally called the London PAS) established advisory bureaux in 1968. BPAS now has approximately 30 advisory bureaux, and PAS has one. Although the charities offer low-cost abortions many women cannot afford any fee. Therefore, the charities operate a loans and grants system so that no woman who is legally entitled to an abortion is turned away because of lack of money. To ensure the highest standard of care for their patients both charities now own and administer their own nursing homes. These are strictly controlled and licensed by the DHSS like all commercial nursing homes.

As registered charities, PAS and BPAS are governed by the strict limitations of the charity laws which proscribe any active promotion of legislation. Their role concerning the 1967 Act is a purely defensive one, but even here they must exercise considerable caution. Therefore, they have confined their activities to giving evidence to various committees and providing details of their work to MPs at appropriate times.

Conclusion

The pro-abortion lobby had grown considerably since the introduction of the Steel Bill when ALRA was the only group campaigning on abortion. ALRA itself diminished in importance as other groups, such as DOG, DWCA and CFFC, developed in specialist areas; others, such as NAC, were helped into existence by ALRA, and still others such as BCC and Co-ord emerged through the ideas and with the help of the ALRA executive, old and new. Therefore, although ALRA declined in importance, some of its executive committee members played and continue to play a vital role in the development of the pro-abortion lobby.

The development of NAC was of enormous importance. At last the pro-abortion lobby could begin to counteract the pressure that was building up in the constituencies led by SPUC and LIFE. In addition NAC provided the main channel for feminists actively to campaign and this politicized a great many people who might otherwise have remained outside active politics.

Although the groups on this side of the lobby have different aims and strategies they are all united in defending the 1967 Act and this strong commitment is brought together by Co-ord. This does not prevent member-organizations of Co-ord acting independently outside the group, but ensures that activity is not duplicated and that the specialist knowledge and functions of each group are used to their full.

In addition, this side of the lobby learnt quickly from their mistakes and developed strong parliamentary links, chiefly through the establishment of the Co-ord lawyers group, which during the Corrie Bill met weekly with MPs. All of this meant that by 1979 the pro-abortion lobby was well prepared both in the country and in Parliament to deal with restrictive legislation.

The Anti-abortion Lobby

Society for the Protection of the Unborn Child (1967)

The first anti-abortion group was launched in a blaze of publicity at a press conference in the House of Commons on 11 January 1967. Its initial aim was to prevent the passage of David Steel's Bill. However, once the Bill became law as the 1967 Act it made reform of the Act its immediate aim, and its repeal a long-term ideal. Since the group's founding, there have been a number of debates about strategy and tactics. These have usually involved a discussion of what can realistically be achieved by any one piece of amending legislation. However, since the final report of the Select Committee on abortion in 1976 their intermediate goal on the way to repeal of the abortion law has been to achieve the passage of a radical amendment bill, based on that Select Committee's report.

The two principal founders of SPUC were Phyllis Bowman and Elspeth Rhys Williams. At the same time the group had the support of three prominent gynaecologists, Prof. Hugh McLaren, then at Birmingham University, Prof. Ian Donald of Glasgow University and Prof. J.S. Scott of Leeds. At this stage, and in the years to follow, the group's chief parliamentary supporters were Jill Knight and Norman St John-Stevas.

SPUC membership grew substantially during the passage of the Steel Bill, but lost nearly half of its members when the Bill succeeded. Its fortunes began to revive when a bill introduced by Norman St John-Stevas won considerable support in the House. By 1972 membership had grown to 10,000. This figure had doubled by 1973, possibly because of reports in the press during 1971-3 of 'abuses' of the 1967 Act. SPUC currently claims a membership of 26,000, although this probably underestimates its support. The organization's membership list is in fact its mailing list so only one member is counted from each household. In addition SPUC has some organizations as members, including some Anglican and Baptist Churches and the Knights of St Columba.

Initially the group was run by voluntary help but in 1975 it appointed as salaried director Phyllis Bowman, and a general secretary. The latter post was held by Jennifer Murray until 1978 when she was replaced by the current general secretary, John Smeaton. SPUC at present has five full-time paid officials and one part-time.

The structure of SPUC is democratic. The local branches, of which there are at present 250, exercise considerable autonomy over their activities and lobbying efforts. However, policy is made by an elected council of 51 members which meets at least twice a year. This policy is enacted by a 15-20 strong executive committee which includes the SPUC national officers and other elected members. At first Roman Catholics were excluded from the executive committee for practical and political reasons. None of the original handful of activists was Catholic and it was generally agreed that if Catholics were excluded from the executive committee it would forestall criticism that it was a Catholic 'front' organization. However, in 1975 the decision was taken to remove this bar — a natural development, given the large number of Roman Catholic members.

It is still common among pro-abortion activists to view both SPUC and LIFE as Roman Catholic 'front' organizations. The organizations are in their turn anxious to play down their connections with all religious groups, as SPUC's initial decision to exclude Roman Catholics from its executive committee indicates. Certainly SPUC has no formal connection with any religious organization and receives no funds from the Anglican or Roman Catholic churches. In fact it draws its membership from all denominations and most political persuasions and pointedly avoids using church buildings for its meetings. Nevertheless there is little doubt that a large proportion of its membership have strong religious views or that many of them are Roman Catholics. At the same time it is clear that the teaching of the Roman Catholic Church on abortion has helped the anti-abortion groups. Roman Catholic congregations do provide a rich seam of membership, activists and funds for both SPUC and LIFE.

There have been two crucial elements in SPUC's strategy.

First, it has attempted to mobilize opposition to abortion within the constituencies and, through its local groups, to put pressure on MPs to vote for amending legislation. At the same time the central organization has built up close contacts with a number of MPs with the aim of persuading those who draw favourable positions in the private members' ballot to introduce an abortion amendment bill. Both strategies have been successful.

In the constituencies SPUC has been much better organized than the pro-abortion groups. The real strength of SPUC and LIFE is in the constituencies — the weak spot of the pro-abortion lobby. Part of the reason for this success must be attributed to the support that the churches give to the anti-abortion campaign. They provide a ready-made structure from which to launch and fight a campaign. It is usual during campaigns on amending legislation to see notices and leaflets in many churches supporting the amendment. Messages of support are frequently part of regular sermons and parish newsletters.[11] Indeed, as Anthony Barker and Michael Rush have said:

> It has been suggested that Roman Catholics are the only 'true' pressure group in British politics as no other body is continuously poised to raise a campaign on a variety of issues by ordering their local professional leaders, the priests and bishops, to obtain the desired mass response from their followers.[12]

In Parliament SPUC has been successful in persuading a number of MPs to introduce amending legislation and has given advice and support to others who have sponsored bills. In particular SPUC was instrumental in the introduction of the St John-Stevas Bill in 1969 and the Benyon Bill in 1977; it also gave support to James White's Bill in 1975 and Sir Bernard Braine's Bill in 1978. SPUC's achievements in this respect owe much to the efforts and experience of its director, Phyllis Bowman, who like a number of others in the field, has become a skilled political lobbyist. However, SPUC's performance in the parliamentary lobby has been only moderately effective. The organization's main effort is directed towards encouraging its members to influence MPs at the constituency level, and in this respect has been extremely successful. Even so, the relations between SPUC and the MPs who support amending legislation within Parliament have not been particularly close, a failure which stems partly from SPUC's emphasis on constituency activity, which leaves limited resources available, but probably owing more to a marked reluctance on the part of many anti-abortion MPs to become too intimately identified with SPUC or LIFE.

LIFE (1970)

The second of the two major anti-abortion interest groups, LIFE, was founded in August 1970. Like SPUC its immediate aim is to oppose the 1967 Abortion Act, but its long-term goal is to repeal the Act. Since October 1974 LIFE has had a draft bill prepared called the Equal Protection of Unborn Children (Criminal Law) Bill which they hope an MP will sponsor. This Bill would only permit abortion where there was no chance of the foetus surviving, for example in the case of an ectopic pregnancy, or where there is cancer of the womb. In contrast SPUC, while it wishes to see the Abortion Act repealed, would condone abortion under slightly less restricted circumstances, such as where the life of the mother is endangered. LIFE is, therefore, marginally more fundamentalist in its attitude than SPUC.

LIFE was in fact formed by breakaway SPUC members who were unhappy with aspects of the aims and strategy of SPUC. The individuals who formed LIFE and especially its first national chairman, Jack Scarisbrick, Professor of History at Warwick University, felt that SPUC's strategy was too cautious and negative. In particular Prof. Scarisbrick and his co-founders believed that it was not enough merely to campaign against abortion: positive action must be taken to help women with unwanted pregnancies by providing advice and housing. In addition LIFE places more stress on education about abortion, providing and distributing anti-abortion literature for use in schools, churches and youth clubs. SPUC, while it is concerned with these problems and particularly with education, concentrates mainly on achieving repeal by parliamentary pressure. The difference between the two organizations is, therefore, one of strategy and emphasis rather than of ultimate aims.

LIFE's principal concern is to show, through its education and 'caring' work, that abortion is unnecessary as well as morally wrong. In fact LIFE was established with the full knowledge and approval of SPUC officers and in many ways their work is complementary: SPUC concentrates on the political dimension and LIFE on the educative and 'caring' work. Nevertheless relations between the two organizations have remained cordial rather than close.

LIFE quickly began to lay the foundations for a highly organized campaign in the country. Its membership has grown steadily and by 1980 it claimed a membership of nearly 20,000. Individual members belong to locally-based LIFE groups which fix their own membership fees and decide on their own activities. There are at present about 220 such groups covering roughly 50 per cent of the English, Scottish and Welsh constituencies. In fact there are groups in most sizeable towns and some towns have a number of groups — for example there are twenty-three in London, five in Birmingham and three in Coventry. While the local groups have considerable autonomy they are linked together in a regional structure. There are 17 regions each of which has a regional committee which is elected. Each committee consists of a chairman, a political officer, an education officer, a treasurer and a secretary. These regional committees act as a link between the centre and the groups and have a particular responsibility for organizing training courses for volunteers who wish to help with LIFE's 'caring' or educational work. The organization's policy is decided at the national conference which has met annually since 1972. At the conference a central committee is elected which has full powers to decide and administer policy between conferences. This central committee is composed of one representative elected by each regional committee, and all the national officers who are themselves elected at the conference. LIFE has a chairman, a vice-chairman, an administrator, a national caring officer, a national political officer and a national treasurer all of whom are unpaid.

LIFE's stress on the 'caring' side of its work is reflected by the fact that most of the LIFE groups run telephone counselling services and provide free pregnancy testing advice and counselling. These services are usually advertized in the local press or on hoardings. Counsellors are trained by LIFE and emphasize that abortion will not solve a woman's problems and may cause severe physical and mental problems. LIFE counsellors never recommend or advise abortion. At the same time LIFE counsellors do not give advice on contraception or refer women to agencies that give such advice.

In mid-1977 LIFE's aim to help women avoid abortion by offering them advice and accommodation before and immediately after the birth of the child was developed when they established a charity called the LIFE Housing Trust, which in 1978 became the LIFE Care and Housing Trust. The Trustees are all members of the national committee of LIFE. The first house opened in November 1977 and since then a further 40 houses have opened, and over 60 are in various stages of negotiation.

The houses are managed by LIFE caring officers. The Trust emphasizes that residents of their houses are not tenants and do not pay rent. The weekly payments they do pay are taken as contributions towards the cost of living in the house. This side of LIFE's work was greatly enhanced with the passing of the 1977 Homeless Persons Act which transferred responsibility for dealing with homelessness from the Department of Social Services to local housing authorities. One section of the Act states that pregnant women and parents of dependent children are to be given priority and that local authorities are to co-operate and give all possible help to local voluntary organizations that cater for the homeless. In 1980 the national housing officer of LIFE received a grant from the Department of the Environment of £5,500 to supervise the LIFE Care Centres. The Department explained that this grant was to assist in meeting the salary and associated costs of a housing officer for the period 15 October 1979 to 30 June 1980. The grant was renewed in July 1980 for another year.

The strategy of LIFE is therefore significantly different from that of SPUC. LIFE concentrates its work almost exclusively at the local level. The majority of the work is done by the local groups which are crucially concerned with the provision of alternatives to abortion for pregnant women through counselling and the provision of accommodation. At the same time these local groups are also involved in trying to influence public opinion on abortion and in attempting to persuade local MPs to support amending legislation. The role of the central and regional organization is mainly to facilitate the local activities by providing information, advice and expertise. The LIFE national officers provide information to MPs who ask for it and occasionally they mail information to all MPs, but LIFE has played a less significant role inside Parliament than SPUC. Like SPUC it has campaigned very effectively in the constituencies by organizing large write-in campaigns to MPs and co-ordinating and taking part in local and national demonstrations against abortion. However, SPUC has devoted greater attention to political work and has had more consistent and close contacts with MPs.

One other element in LIFE's strategy is important. Since 1974 LIFE has established a series of national groups to organize particular sectors of its membership. For instance LIFE Nurses and the LIFE Labour Group were formed in 1974, and these were followed by LIFE Anglicans in 1976, LIFE Teachers and LIFE Conservative Group in 1977.[13]

In many ways these groups perform the same role in the anti-abortion lobby that various groups, such as LARC and CFFC do within the pro-abortion lobby. Their aim is to co-ordinate the efforts of LIFE members in particular sectors, to spread information about LIFE's aims and activities, to attempt to influence opinion and to gather material about abortion for use by the central organization. In this way LIFE Nurses, which has a membership of about 2,000, aims to organize nurses who are opposed to the current abortion law. In particular the group provides advice and help to any nurse who wishes to opt out of abortion operations under the conscience clause of the 1967 Act. In addition it attempts to collect evidence about 'abuses' in the operation of the Act, especially in relation to late abortions.

By contrast LIFE Anglicans is more concerned to influence opinion. It has a membership of around 500 which includes six Bishops and concentrates on attempting to influence the Church of England's attitude to abortion. It consistently lobbies both outside and inside the Church of England Synod.

The Association of Lawyers for the Defence of the Unborn (1978)

In May 1978 the Association of Lawyers for the Defence of the Unborn was formed. Its founder and first chairman was Michael Bell. This group is deliberately independent but obviously shares a related interest with SPUC and LIFE. The aims of the group are to inform and influence the legal profession and to provide legal advice for reformers. It claims a membership of approximately 560 of whom about 100 are students or articled clerks. Its existence and aims have been widely publicized through advertisements in legal journals and ALDU publishes leaflets on the law relating to abortion and a regular newsheet. The organization also holds an annual conference.

The members of the group are in favour of the repeal of the Abortion Act and work towards that end. The group is potentially of considerable importance to the anti-abortion lobby as a source of legal advice. There are obvious problems in drafting and redrafting parliamentary bills and private members need legal advice. ALDU would appear to be in a position to provide such advice and assistance although, as we shall see later, there is little evidence that it played this role in relation to the Corrie Bill.

The National Pro-life Committee (1974)

It is evident from the previous discussion that there are fewer independent groups on the anti-abortion side, although of course LIFE and SPUC have very large memberships. Co-ordination is therefore less of a problem. Nevertheless in 1974 the anti-abortion lobby established a National Pro-life Committee to co-ordinate their efforts. The Committee has no aims or formal membership but provides a convenient meeting point for individuals and organizations who otherwise would merely have telephoned one another. It is chaired by George Crozier, a Scottish lawyer who played a considerable part in the drafting of both James White's Amendment Bill in 1975 and John Corrie's Bill. There is no published formal membership of the Committee although all the organizations so far dealt with on the anti-abortion side, including the offshoots of LIFE, are members. Meetings are held bi-monthly but attendance is irregular (for instance LIFE has not attended for the past year).

It is clear that the National Pro-life Committee does not in any sense fulfil the role performed by Co-ord on the pro-abortion side. The Committee is merely a forum in which information is exchanged about activities. It is not a means of evolving a common strategy or co-ordination of local and national efforts. The view of both LIFE and SPUC is that as both organizations are autonomous each should pursue its own aims and strategy. The local SPUC and LIFE groups do co-ordinate their efforts, so that if, for example, LIFE is organizing a strong campaign in one constituency SPUC will not duplicate that effort but will rather concentrate its work elsewhere. Nevertheless it is very noticeable that the efforts of SPUC and LIFE at the national level are nothing like as effectively co-ordinated as are those on the opposing side. In one way this is surprising, given the greater resources of the anti-abortion groups and the greater diversity of view of the pro-abortion groups. However, once again it results mainly from the emphasis within the anti-abortion lobby on activity at the local level.

Conclusion

The main strength of the anti-abortion lobby lies in the constituencies. The memberships of SPUC and LIFE are very large and up until the Corrie Bill the anti-abortion lobby were always more active and more numerous in the constituencies. However, as we have seen, this side of the lobby lacks the co-ordination of the pro-abortion lobby. This was particularly apparent during the passage of the Corrie Bill when splits occurred over what, and how much, could be achieved. These splits were apparent both inside and outside Parliament, and were a major factor in the Bill's ultimate downfall. However, it must be said that it is always more difficult to achieve co-ordination when trying to promote a bill than when defending an Act.

The anti-abortion lobby also lacks the close parliamentary links of the pro-abortion lobby, partly because with such strong support in the constituencies it has tended to ignore Parliament. However, it is also due to a strong wish of anti-abortion MPs to keep their distance from the pressure groups.

By the time the Corrie Bill was introduced, therefore, the anti-abortion pressure groups were strong in the constituencies but weak in Parliament. This was to become very obvious during the Bill's passage.

The Parties

The Labour Party

The Labour Party's policy on abortion was to prove an increasingly important factor influencing the effectiveness of the pro-abortion lobby in the later half of the 1970s. Indeed the conversion of the Labour Party to a definite liberal abortion stance had significant consequences for the strategy adopted by the pro-abortion lobby both inside and outside Parliament.

Within the Labour Party the first move on abortion came in 1934 from the Co-operative Women's Guilds, which called for abortion to be treated like any other operation and opposed the imprisonment of women who performed illegal abortions. However like the TUC the Labour Party left the consideration of so-called 'women's issues', such as abortion, to the women's organizations within the Labour movement: the National Council of Working Women's Organizations and the Labour Women's Advisory Committee, both run from Transport House.[14] The Labour Party itself took no position on abortion either when the Steel Bill was being discussed or when subsequent attempts were made to amend the Act in the following years. However feeling was building up in the party, particularly, although not exclusively among women, that the party should take a stand on the issue. The first breakthrough as far as the pro-abortion lobby was concerned came in 1975.

At the Party Conference in 1975 a radical resolution was passed overwhelmingly on a show of hands. The resolution read:

> This conference calls for extended facilities for pregnancy testing, contraception, and abortion so that they are available to all women on request, free of charge, and opposes moves to restrict the availability of abortion on social grounds.

The size of the majority surprised the proposers and the party leadership but did not entirely satisfy the pro-abortion lobby. The motion had been buried among a large number of other resolutions and had not been debated, and the lobbyists believed it had received insufficient attention. However they were not totally agreed on strategy. All wanted the defence of the 1967 Act to be adopted as party policy but many also wanted the Parliamentary Labour Party to endorse the policy and enforce a three-line whip on MPs to vote against amending legislation.

We have already seen that LARC was formed in 1976 to harness the efforts of the radical elements within the pro-abortion lobby in the Labour Party. The main element in LARC strategy has been to call for the enforcement of a three-line whip by the PLP in support of the conference decision in favour of a liberal abortion law. However this strategy has not gained widespread support within the Labour Party and certainly has little support among the PLP. In fact the main impetus towards acceptance by the Labour Party of a liberal abortion policy has probably come from within Transport House itself, and particularly from the efforts of Joyce Gould, the chief women's officer of the Labour Party.

The intention of Joyce Gould and others within the Labour movement was to get as many motions as possible calling for liberal abortion policy put forward to the Labour Party Conference so that the issue would be fully debated and a card vote taken. This would ensure that the Conference decision on the issue became recognized party policy and that it could be considered for inclusion in the next manifesto. Joyce Gould mailed all members of the National Joint Committee of Working Women's Organizations and the National Women's Advisory Committee advocating that they persuade their constituency parties to put forward resolutions on abortion. At the same time LARC and NAC were urging their members to exert similar pressure in the constituencies.

This effort bore fruit in 1977 when seven resolutions on abortion were forwarded to conference; in fact abortion was the third most popular issue for resolutions in that year. As always at Labour Party Conferences these seven resolutions were composited. In fact as a result of pressure from Transport House they were composited into two separate resolutions. The first resolution supported the 1967 Act and abortion on request. The second resolution, promoted by LARC, called for the use of a three-line whip on the issue by the PLP. The first motion was overwhelmingly successful while the second was defeated.

Since 1977, therefore, official Labour Party policy has been to defend the 1967 Abortion Act and to call for abortion on request.

This had been a very large bonus to the pro-abortion lobby for three reasons. First, the Labour Party women's organizations have continued to mail supporters and MPs on the issue reminding them of party policy. The members of these women's organizations are often experienced Labour Party activists who have easy access to their MPs and whose views are likely to be more respected by those MPs than those of NAC or LARC radicals. Secondly, as we shall see later, Joyce Gould attended all the Report Stage debates on the Corrie Bill 'keeping an eye' on Labour MPs. She is well known to Labour MPs who were aware that if they voted for the Bill she would be around to see them in the next few days. This 'party supervision' probably had an influence on those Labour MPs who were not strongly committed on the issue. Obviously such supervision would not have been possible unless the defence of the 1967 Act was official party policy. Thirdly, and perhaps most significantly, the pro-abortion members of the PLP were able to use the weekly PLP meetings as a means of communication with their colleagues. The meetings were an important forum, particularly during the weeks of the Report Stage of the Corrie Bill, in which MPs could be told of the issues which would be raised and the votes which would occur in the following Friday's debate. At the same time the very fact that the matter was raised in the official PLP meetings reminded MPs of Party policy and helped legitimize the pro-abortion lobby's position. In fact this gave the pro-abortion lobby a marked advantage over their opponents who had no equivalent forum.

The Liberal Party and the Conservative Party

The Liberal Party like the Labour Party also has an official policy on abortion. In the middle of the 1970s, particularly after the shock provided to the pro-abortion lobby by the huge Second Reading vote for the White Bill, considerable pressure built up, especially among Young Liberals, for the party to take a pro-abortion stand. In 1975 the Council of the Party noted the finding of the Lane Report and stated: 'Council ... resolves to oppose the Abortion (Amendment) Bill on the grounds that it severely restricts the right to legal abortion.' In November 1979 the Council reaffirmed its support of the 1967 Act when a resolution was passed deploring the introduction of the Corrie

Bill. However, this policy is not binding in any sense on members of the Parliamentary Liberal Party which is probably more split on the issue than either the Labour or the Conservative parties. In fact the Parliamentary Liberal Party has never discussed the issue, partly because it is regarded as a matter for the conscience of individual MPs, and partly because of the divisions among members on the issue. As such the fact that defence of the 1967 Act is Liberal Party policy appears to have had little effect on behaviour or votes of MPs.

The Conservative Party has no official policy on abortion which it also regards as an issue for individual conscience. As we have seen, both the pro- and anti-abortion lobbies are active within the Conservative Party but both are aware that the party is very unlikely ever to adopt a policy on the issue, therefore they concentrate on trying to influence individual Conservative MPs. The absence of an official anti-abortion stance in the Conservative Party despite the views of most of its MPs means that the Parliamentary Conservative Party cannot provide an official focus for the parliamentary anti-abortion lobby in the way that the PLP does for the pro-abortion lobby.

The Trade Union Congress

The TUC had never had a policy on abortion which, like the Labour Party, it had regarded as an issue to be considered by their women's organizations. Indeed the TUC refused to submit evidence to the Lane Committee in 1971 suggesting instead that the committee might 'like to invite individual unions to submit evidence, particularly [those which] have a large women's section or have members employed in the Health Service'.[15] The TUC itself was reluctant to take a stand because it believed that its individual member unions held a variety of different opinions on the issue and that, as such, the TUC would have difficulty in agreeing a policy and would therefore have more to lose than to gain by taking a stand on the issue.

The first Trade Union Congress document, entitled *Women at Work,* was published in 1963 and republished in 1968, and contained no mention of abortion. Neither did the updated version, published to mark International Women's Year on 8

March 1975. However, the London Trades Council published its own document in 1975, entitled *The Working Women's Charter* in which item 8 called for 'Family Planning Clinics, supplying free contraception to be extended to cover every locality, free abortion to be readily available.' There was support for this alternative document from Berry Beaumont (ASTMS/Medical Practitioners' Section) and P. Knight (Croydon Trades Council) at the Women's TUC Conference that year.

At the same Women's TUC Congress however the support for a liberal abortion policy went much further. Two amendments on contraception and abortion were introduced into a resolution on the Health Service which had been moved by the Health Visitors' Association. One of these called for contraception and abortion facilities to be freely available for all women through the NHS. The other called for additional funds to provide for more research into safe and effective methods of birth control and expressed the view that women should be able to obtain an abortion on the NHS where contraception had failed. It also called for the elimination of private clinics and unauthorized facilities. Both amendments were carried with almost unanimous support.

Even so the TUC was reluctant to adopt this as TUC policy. Its view was clearly expressed by Ethal Chipchase, Secretary to the Womens' Advisory Committee, in a letter to a member:

> We do appreciate that this is an issue on which there would not be unanimity of opinion among all trade unionists or even among all women trade unionists. It is because of this that there is no reference to contraception or abortion in our revised Charter of trade union aims for women workers...[16]

Similarly the TUC General Council Report in 1975 explained in Section 103 that abortion had been omitted from its *Aims for Women at Work* because it was not one of those issues 'on which the movement as a whole is agreed at present'. The Council did however present evidence to the Select Committee on abortion in 1975, saying that it felt the White Bill would reduce safe, legal abortion, but supporting moves to control private clinics.

However the pro-abortion lobby was far from defeated. At the 1975 annual congress a motion was introduced which called for free abortion to be readily available. It was opposed by the general council which, however, admitted that abortion had become an important issue within the movement. The motion was defeated on a card vote by 6,224,000 votes to 3,697,000. A composite motion was then moved which opposed James White's restrictive amendment Bill and called for abortion on request within the NHS. This composite motion was carried on a show of hands almost unanimously. The vote surprised the general council but because it had only been passed by a show of hands it did not necessarily have to become official TUC policy. The pressure in the movement was however very strong and the general council, despite its reluctance to become too involved in the issue, was forced to recognize the strength of feeling. Nevertheless it was only in 1977 that the official TUC *Aims for Women at Work* was rewritten to include a section calling for free abortion to be readily available.

In 1977 therefore the TUC lent its backing to the pro-abortion lobby. It had adopted this policy despite rather than because of the efforts of the general council. Pressure had built up among the rank and file, partly as a result of the efforts of organizations like NAC and to a lesser extent LARC, but perhaps mainly because individual men and women in the Labour movement had become increasingly aware of the challenge to the 1967 Abortion Act being mounted by the anti-abortion lobby. The conversion of the TUC was of crucial importance to the pro-abortion lobby because of its size and position within the Labour movement. If the TUC could be mobilized to help campaign against any future amending legislation then this would help counteract the superior local organization of the anti-abortion groups. So when the Corrie Bill was on the horizon the pro-abortion groups, and NAC in particular, devoted a great deal of effort to mobilizing the TUC. The success of that effort was a very important factor in the campaign against the Corrie Bill.

The Church

This section deals largely with the Roman Catholic Church, the church most active on the issue. The role of the Church of England, the established church, is also considered.

Roman Catholic Church

The Roman Catholic Church has, since 1869, taught that abortion is a crime from the moment of conception. This belief did not change during the period 1966-80 but the public emphasis on the condemnation of abortion did intensify during the Corrie campaign. This was partly due to the election of a new Pope, John Paul II, in 1978, who chose to make condemnation of abortion one of the key themes of his Papacy. Pope John Paul II is a younger, more energetic and more populist Pope than his immediate predecessors. He has already travelled widely and in every country he has visited has condemned the practice of abortion. For instance, in one of his major speeches during his visit to America in 1979 he stated: 'All human life — from the moment of conception and through all subsequent stages — is sacred.'[17]

In this country during the Corrie Bill, the Roman Catholic hierarchy for the first time joined together to condemn the practice of abortion. This unity reached a peak when, just before the Report State, the two Roman Catholic hierarchies of Scotland and England and Wales issued a joint statement on the human rights of the unborn. This statement, which gained wide coverage in the daily and provincial papers, stated: 'We speak in defence of life against the evil of abortion.' It went on to call for a renewed national campaign against abortion and in defence of the nation's 'weakest, totally silent minority group' — the unborn. In conclusion the statement said:

> By practising and condoning abortion, our society has lost its way... To our fellow-Catholics we can add this: when we acknowledge and respect the sanctity of human life we acknowledge both the unique value of every human individual made in the image and likeness of God, and the dominion of God over that life and over its creation and its ending.[18]

It is difficult to assess the effect of these declarations. Certainly none of the MPs we spoke to cited them as factors which influenced the way they voted on the Bill, and they were not mentioned by any MPs during the debates at Second Reading or at the Report Stage, whereas statements by the BMA and RCOG were often mentioned. It is more likely they acted as a moral booster to those groups and individuals campaigning for the Bill.

Church of England

The attitude to abortion of the Church of England Board of Social Responsibilitiy has hardened over the last 15 years. In 1965, two years before David Steel introduced his Bill, the Board issued a pamphlet entitled *Abortion An Ethical Discussion.*[19] This pamphlet recognized that there were certain circumstances under which abortions could be justified. These were where

> it could be reasonably established that there was a threat to the mother's life or well-being, and hence inescapably her health, if she were obliged to carry the child to term and give it birth. And our view is that, in reaching this conclusion, her life and well-being must be seen as integrally connected with the life and well-being of her family.[20]

The decision as to whether such a threat existed would be left up to the medical practitioner concerned, in consultation with a consultative group representing different professional and personal interests.

Conditions which could lead to the deterioration of the mother's 'well-being' included where the mother's life was threatened by the continuation of the pregnancy; where there was a risk that the foetus would be born handicapped; and where rape or incest had occurred. However, the report added that risk of deformity, rape or incest were not sufficient grounds for termination of pregnancy in themselves. They had to be looked at in conjunction with the effect the birth would have on 'the health of the mother, her family situation, and her capacity and that of the family to accept the extra strain which might be thrown upon it'.[21]

By 1975 these views were being questioned by the Board itself. In a report called *Abortion Law Reform*[22] published in 1974/5 the Synod stated: 'It must be asked ... whether there is no less drastic remedy than abortion for possible threats to existing children.'[23] With the number of abortions running at approximately 150,000 a year the Board believed that the 1967 Act was 'having a deleterious effect on the sexual behaviour of young unmarried people'.[24] They regretted that the 1967 Act went much further than they had recommended in 1966 and supported James White's Bill: 'more [as a] gesture to indicate Christian's general anxiety about the whole development of abortion in our country than the discovery of a real answer to the deeper questions which are being asked'.[25]

In January 1980 the Board issued a statement which brought them nearer the Roman Catholic teaching on abortion than ever before. Headed 'Abortion A Great Moral Evil' it stated that although an abortion should be permitted where the woman's life was put at risk by the continuance of the pregnancy 'the right of the innocent to life admits surely of few exceptions indeed'. If a choice had to be made between the life of the mother and the life of the foetus (a situation rare in today's advanced society, the report noted) 'precedence should be given to the mother's interests; but such a choice would only arise if no less drastic remedy for the ill existed'.[26]

However, in making this statement the Board emphasized that they could not issue authoritative statements committing all members of the Church of England, adding that deep differences of opinion concerning abortion existed in the Church of England.

The Professional Organizations

The British Medical Association

Obviously on an issue like abortion the views of the professional organizations are particularly important and potentially influential. The attitude of the BMA to abortion in general and the 1967 Abortion Act in particular has changed dramatically over time. As we said in Chapter 1, the BMA at the time of the David Steel Bill came out strongly against abortion on social grounds arguing that social abortions were against the ethics of the medical profession. Indeed at the time of the passage of the Bill there was even talk of expelling doctors who performed such abortions from the BMA. At this stage the few supporters of a liberal abortion law at the annual representative meetings of the BMA, and the conferences of representatives of local medical committees were often vitriolically attacked.

This mood remained unchanged for a number of years. At the annual representative meetings of 1968 and 1970 proposals that the BMA should reconsider its opposition to the social clauses in the Act were overwhelmingly defeated, while the matter was not even discussed in 1969 despite the appearance of the St John-Stevas Bill.

The first real indication of a change in attitude came with the evidence that the BMA gave to the Lane Committee. Actually the BMA Council had anticipated the government by establishing a panel to examine the working of the Abortion Act in October 1970. This working party reported in February 1971 but was immediately re-established to prepare the BMA's evidence to the Lane Committee. The working party was however extended to include representatives of the general practitioners, the consultants and the junior doctors.

The chairman of the working party both before and after it was reconvened was Ian Donald a gynaecologist from Glasgow and a strong anti-abortionist. At the first meeting of the reconvened and extended working party he attempted to resign from the chair in order to be able to intervene more directly in the debate. However the working party refused to accept his resignation as chairman and the result of its deliberations offered little comfort to Dr Donald. The working party's recommendations were slightly modified by the Board of Science of the BMA, approved by Council and submitted to the Lane Committee. The BMA evidence came out fairly firmly in support of the 1967 Act arguing that most of the problems of 'abuse' could be removed through administrative action by the Department of Health. It opposed any suggestion that the Bill should be amended in order to restrict the availability of abortion.

The evidence to the Lane Committee thus marks a substantial change in the BMA's view. It had accepted the existence of, and need for, abortions carried out on social grounds. This change in view was confirmed when the BMA came out unequivocally against the radical Abortion (Amendment) Bill introduced by James White in 1975. The BMA prepared as evidence a strongly worded attack upon the purposes and provision of James White's proposal. Two extracts give a flavour of the tone:

> In general, the Association supported the recommendations of the Lane Committee on the working of the Abortion Act 1967, and it has grave doubts whether the proposed Bill would achieve the purpose of its sponsors to find a reasonable consensus of opinion which would make sensible provision for reviving some of the abuses of the Act.[27]

This was elaborated on later in the statement:

> So far as risk to life of the patient is concerned, the need for existence of a 'grave' risk would clearly put the law in this particular connection back to what it was before R. v. Bourne in 1938.[28]

Until this time, although the BMA Council's policy had changed, and the annual representative meeting had, by approving the Council's report, approved of those changes, neither that annual representative meeting nor the conference of representatives of local medical committees had specifically voted in support of the 1967 Act. However the picture changed totally in 1975. Initially at the conference of representatives in June 1975 a motion which read 'this Conference is firmly opposed to the legal changes proposed by the Abortion (Amendment) Bill at present before Parliament', was overwhelmingly carried with only four dissenters. Similarly a month later at the annual representative meeting of the BMA eleven motions on abortion were put forward. After a lively debate the meeting passed a resolution which said 'this Meeting takes note of the approval by Council of the evidence submitted to the Abortion (Amendment) Bill and is of the opinion that the current abuses could be controlled by a simple change in the Regulations.'

By 1975 therefore the BMA was committed to oppose any attempt to amend radically the 1967 Abortion Act, and this policy was confirmed at subsequent representative meetings. In 1977 there were nine motions on abortion, one of which directly opposed the Benyon Bill and was overwhelmingly carried. Similarly in 1978 a motion 'deploring persistent attacks on the Abortion Act' received almost unanimous support.

The position of the BMA was obviously a great help to the pro-abortion lobby. It was not merely that the BMA's policy was so strongly in support of the 1967 Act but also that the Association was willing and able to ensure that its views were well known. For example, the BMA proved quite active on the issue during the Corrie Bill when, as we shall see later, John Havard, the secretary of the BMA, wrote to all MPs stating clearly the BMA's views on the issue and its opposition to the bill. At the same time a number of BMA representatives were very willing to speak on platforms in support of the Abortion Act. Notable among these was Dr John Marks, deputy chairman of the BMA's representative body and a strong and able campaigner from 1967 onwards against attempts to amend the law. The BMA's oft stated policy, together with the support of the Abortion Act by the Royal College of Obstetricians and Gynaecologists, conferred a legitimacy on the pro-abortion lobby which the anti-abortion lobby found difficult, if not impossible, to match.

Royal College of Obstetricians and Gynaecologists

As we have seen the RCOG also put pressure on Steel to restrict his Bill. In fact Simms and Hindell[29] argue that it was the RCOG's opinion which guided the BMA at this time. It also supported both the amending bills of 1969 and 1970.

Its major concern about the 1967 Act was expressed in evidence to the Lane Committee. In this paper the RCOG stated its belief that the 1967 Act could be interpreted so widely as to allow 'abortion on demand', and that it was time 'For the public and legislators to decide if they want abortion on demand or request... If they do they should say so openly and modify the Act. If they do not, then it should be made clear that only medical and medico-social indications are acceptable.'[30] In advocating this approach it was made clear that the RCOG was not in favour of abortion on request.

However, when questioned about this statement by the Select Committee in 1976, Professor Sir Stanley Clayton, then president of the RCOG, denied that this was any longer the view of the RCOG. He explained that both his predecessor, Sir Norman Jeffcoate, and he had given evidence to the Lane Committee, but that it was his evidence that was now the view of the RCOG. In this evidence he stated that the RCOG no longer believed that any change was necessary in the grounds for abortion as the great majority of consultants interpret the grounds as they were intended and do not authorize abortion on demand. This view had been endorsed by the Council of the RCOG, by an overwhelming majority of twenty-eight to two.[31]

Since 1974 the RCOG has also consistently opposed any restrictions to the 1967 Act, although it has preferred to maintain a lower profile than the BMA and would not resist a reduction of the upper time limit from 28 to 24 weeks.

The Royal College of Nursing

When David Steel introduced his Bill the RCN decided that as the decision whether or not an abortion should be performed was a medical one, it was not a subject upon which it could formulate a policy. It did however make a statement on the need for safeguarding the right of all nurses who, on grounds of conscience, did not wish to participate in abortion work.[32]

However, concern over the way the Act was being interpreted led the RCN Representative Body (the national delegate body of the organization) to pass a resolution in 1969 which urged the Secretary of State to review the working of the 1967 Act 'particularly in relation to the resultant pressure on hospital beds and the effect upon nursing staff'.[33]

The RCN's central concern has always been that the Act is interpreted differently throughout the country and that this creates unequal provision of facilities. This, it claims, often leads to the workload of nurses being increased in abortion work which means they miss out on training in other areas of their profession. To ameliorate these problems and to ensure that nurses have the opportunity to opt out of abortion work if they wish to the RCN has often suggested the setting up of separate abortion units.[34]

While the RCN was always keen to ensure abortions were carried out under conditions which were safe and adequate for the woman, and did not wish to see abortion made too difficult for women to obtain, it did believe that 'abortion on demand' was a mis-use of health service resources, including the time and skills of staff involved in the procedure.[35] In order to prevent the practice of 'abortion on demand' it gave support to James White's Bill and William Benyon's Bill. However, the RCN's view has changed since 1977. Although still not condoning 'abortion on demand' it did not support the proposed change in the grounds for abortion in John Corrie's Bill.

Conclusion

The change of opinion towards the 1967 Abortion Act by the BMA and RCOG took place principally as a result of their experience of the Act. As doctors began to realize the benefits the Act brought to women and to themselves their opposition began to decline. It soon became very rare for them to have to treat women who had either attempted to induce an abortion themselves or had sought the help of a back-street abortionist. This was an enormous relief to doctors who found the work of clearing up after these illegal abortions particularly distressing and it was the major reason for their determination to resist any measure which sought to restrict legal abortions and might cause women to seek them, once again, illegally.

By the time James White's Bill was introduced in 1975 any fears that the BMA or RCOG did have about abuses of the Act had been dispelled by the administrative action taken by the DHSS to control the private sector. Therefore, from 1975 onwards they became active campaigners to defend the 1967 Act — although the BMA has always been the more outspoken of the two organizations.

The RCN on the other hand remains unhappy with the law. Although during the Corrie Bill it did not wish to see a change to the grounds for abortion it did continue to support a widening of the conscience clause. This will no doubt remain a contentious issue until either the law is changed or outpatient abortion units are established throughout the country so that abortion patients are taken out of general hospital wards.

The Growth of the Parliamentary Lobby

The Pro-abortion Lobby

Alongside the growth of the extra-parliamentary lobby a strong lobby developed in Parliament to defend the abortion law. The growth of this lobby began amongst some of the Labour women elected in 1974 and also involved, up until 1979, two Conservative MPs, Sir George Sinclair and Robin Hodgson. Both of these MPs were lost in the 1979 election, when Sir George Sinclair retired and Robin Hodgson lost his seat. Other Conservative MPs began to emerge during the Corrie Bill, such as Bowen Wells, Anthony Nelson and Sheila Faith, who were willing to lobby their colleagues but as yet the prominent role played by Sir George Sinclair has not been completely filled.

The most interesting development in the parliamentary lobby was amongst Labour women. Elizabeth Valance in her book *Women in Parliament*[36] describes how the abortion debates prompted a group of Labour women to meet together to discuss tactics and strategy. This unity was completely *ad hoc* and completely new. On no other issues have women in the House grouped together in such a manner. She goes on to explain how these women felt compelled to act together because of the appalling lack of interest shown by their male colleagues towards the issue. Although the men were prepared to turn up and vote against restrictive legislation, they were not prepared to organize opposition so that a bill did not go through by default.

This strong group sense can be seen most openly during abortion debates when the Labour women sit together on the backbenches. During James White's Bill in 1976 Valance notes how 12 of them sat together. When this happened during the Corrie Bill one reporter referred to them as 'a terrifying cabal of ginger perms vitriolitically united'.[37]

By the time the Corrie Bill was introduced into Parliament this small group of women MPs had organized themselves into a very efficient and knowledgeable lobby. Jo Richardson and Oonagh McDonald had both sat on the Benyon Committee and had learnt a great deal from the Bill. Since that time they have led and organized the pro-abortion lobby in the House of Commons.

Their experience was put to the test during the Report Stage of the Corrie Bill. Other restrictive bills had either fallen at Second Reading or in Committee. It is always difficult lobbying at Second Reading, especially on abortion bills when the contents of the bill are not known until the last few days. At this stage uncommitted

MPs always say they must wait to hear what is in the bill. During the Committee Stages it is helpful to keep other MPs informed on the bill's progress but it is on Report that it is vital to pull out as many supporters as possible. Corrie's Bill was the first of many restrictive bills to reach the Report Stage and it was possible, for the first time, to judge the effectiveness of each side's lobbying. As we demonstrate later the pro-abortion lobby's knowledge and skills began to pay off at this stage. It was far more co-ordinated and effective than the anti-abortion side. This ensured it of victories on one or two crucial votes and played a significant part in the Bill's downfall.

This side of the lobby has particularly strong links with the extra-parliamentary lobby as became particularly noticeable during the Corrie Bill when regular meetings were held between the two wings of the lobby. These meetings were used to discuss strategy and tactics and provided an opportunity for the advisers of the extra-parliamentary lobby to give detailed briefs to the MPs. This close contact was maintained throughout the bill's progress and was instrumental in the Bill's eventual defeat.

Elizabeth Valance describes how the united action by a group of women MPs at times provoked laughter and suggestive comments from male MPs. But it had a far more profound effect. By taking this stand the many women showed their male colleagues how strongly they, and other women outside Parliament, felt on this issue. Moreover, they demonstrated that it was important precisely because they as women defined it as such. The strength of this feeling at times surprised the men who began to realize they could no longer carry on ignoring women's issues. Most important of all it gave the women confidence to fight on their own terms, and not those defined by men.[38]

The Anti-abortion Lobby

When David Steel's Bill was going through Parliament it was bitterly fought by a small group of MPs, most notably Norman St John-Stevas and Jill Knight. Since that time this side of the lobby has grown but it differs in four significant ways from the pro-abortion lobby in Parliament. First, with the exception of Jill Knight, its members are male. Secondly, it is all-party: including Labour MPs Leo Abse, Stan Cohen, James Dunn and James White and Conservative MPs include Michael Ancram, William Benyon, Sir Bernard Braine and Jill Knight. In addition Liberal MP Cyril Smith is a strong supporter of restrictive legislation. These are the MPs who are in the forefront of the anti-abortion lobby. There are, of course, many others who support amending legislation but who take a less prominent role in the campaign.

The third difference lies in the lack of unity on this side. This was most striking during the Corrie Bill when splits occurred over strategy and tactics on major clauses of the Bill. These differences of opinion led to a lack of co-ordination between the MPs so that, for instance, when Corrie became ill during the Committee Stage nobody on his side knew how he intended to redraft one of the major clauses of the Bill. In addition it led to a difference of opinion during the vital Report Stages on the importance of MPs voting for or against amendments. As later chapters will show these splits were fatal and one of the major reasons for the Bill's ultimate downfall.

The fourth difference is the lack of co-ordination between the intra- and extra-parliamentary lobby among the anti-abortionists. Throughout all the amending bills the sponsors of the bills have preferred to keep themselves at one remove from the campaigning groups, such as SPUC and LIFE, and this remained the case during the Corrie Bill. Although the sponsors of Corrie's Bill had meetings with one or two members of the extra-parliamentary lobby during the Committee Stages, these meetings were short and irregular. They were nothing like the regular weekly meetings which took place between the intra- and extra-parliamentary lobby on the pro-abortion side. Nor did the Bill's sponsors seek briefing material from their supporters outside Parliament, as the pro-abortion MPs opposing the Bill did.

The anti-abortion lobby has now realized the usefulness of regular contact between MPs and supporters outside Parliament. After the Corrie Bill it set up a committee to which the leading campaigners both inside and outside Parliament were invited in order to discuss future action. However it is questionable whether the opponents of the 1967 Act can be as united and co-ordinated as the pro-abortion lobby. It is in the position of trying to promote legislation, and under such circumstances it is always more difficult to reach agreement.

Conclusion

This chapter has demonstrated the extraordinary growth of the abortion lobby since the passing of the 1967 Abortion Act. Both sides have become highly skilled and knowledgeable lobbyists so that today the abortion lobby is perhaps the most sophisticated amongst all the non-economic pressure groups.

The strength of the anti-abortionists, as we have shown, lies principally in the constituencies where they have a large number of members and good local organizations. The backing given to the campaign by the Roman Catholic Church is an important element in this success in the constituencies as it means that the anti-abortion groups have a ready-made platform from which to launch a campaign whenever it is needed. Up until 1979 these local efforts were not matched by the pro-abortion lobby. However this reliance on constituency pressure has led SPUC and LIFE to pay insufficient attention to Parliament where their links could be stronger.

In contrast by 1979 the pro-abortionists had become stronger on all fronts. Their position in the constituencies had improved considerably with the inception of NAC and, during the Corrie Bill, activity at this level, for the first time, matched that of SPUC and LIFE. They were helped enormously in this by the active support of the TUC and Labour Party which meant that at last the pro-abortion lobby had the support of an organization which could match the strength of the Roman Catholic Church. In addition this side of the lobby had the active support of the BMA and the passive support of the RCOG, as well as every other professional medical organization.

They were also well organized within Parliament after the setting up of the Co-ord lawyers and advisers group. The pro-abortion lobby was, therefore, in a better position than ever before to fight a restrictive bill.

Notes

1. See below p. 99.
2. Personal interview, 8 July 1980.
3. M. Simms and K. Hindell, *Abortion Law Reformed,* London, Peter Owen, 1971.
4. Internal memorandum from Alastair Service to ALRA executive, April 1970.
5. The group's intentions were summarized in a letter, signed by 55 doctors, published in *The Lancet* and *British Medical Journal,* 8 January 1977.
6. *The Lancet,* 7 August 1976.
7. NAC press statement, undated (2 or 3 March 1976).
8. NAC press statement, undated (2 or 3 March 1976).
9. Co-ord press statement, undated (early March 1976).
10. Internal memorandum to Co-ord member-organizations, 28 July 1977.
11. Evidence of Church involvement: *Ardrossan and Salcoats Herald,* 13 July 1979; *Kirkby Reporter,* 13 July 1979; *Finchley Press,* 25 January 1980; *Durham Advertiser,* 25 January 1980; *Western Morning News,* 7 February 1980.
12. A. Barker and M. Rush, *The Member of Parliament and His Information,* London, Allen and Unwin, 1970, pp.54-5.
13. The LIFE Labour Group and LIFE Conservative Group were disbanded at the beginning of 1980 and a national political secretary appointed in their place.
14. Interview with Joyce Gould, 16 September 1980.
15. Letter from Ethal Chipchase, Secretary of the Womens' Advisory Committee, to Secretary to Committee on the Working of the Abortion Act, 13 August 1971.
16. From Ethal Chipchase to TUC member, 25 March 1975.
17. *Observer,* 14 October 1979.
18. *Abortion and the Right to Live,* Catholic Information Services, 24 January 1980.
19. *Abortion An Ethical Discussion,* Church Information Office, 1965.
20. Ibid., p.61.
21. Ibid., p.43.
22. *Abortion Law Reform,* Church Information Office, 1974/5.
23. Ibid., p.7.
24. Ibid.
25. Ibid.
26. Press statement, January 1980.

27. BMA memorandum submitted on 23 June 1975, *Special Reports and Minutes of Evidence to the Select Committee on the Abortion (Amendment) Bill,* HMSO 692-11, pp.178-81.
28. Ibid.
29. Simms and Hindell, *Abortion Law Reformed.*
30. RCOG evidence, Lane Committee Report, vol. 1, paras. 68 and 70.
31. Evidence submitted on 30 June 1975, *Special Reports and Minutes of Evidence to the Select Committee on the Abortion (Amendment) Bill,* para. 1208.
32. The RCN and the National Council of Nurses of the United Kingdom, 'The Working of the Abortion Act', January 1972, para. 2.
33. Ibid., para. 4 (a).
34. Ibid., para. 26 and evidence submitted on 27 October 1975, *Special Reports and Minutes of Evidence to the Select Committee on the Abortion (Amendment) Bill,* para. 1847.
35. RCN memorandum submitted on 27 October 1975, ibid., item 7.
36. Elizabeth Valence, *Women in Parliament,* London, Athlone Press, 1979.
37. *Sunday Times,* 10 February 1980.
38. Valance, *Women in Parliament,* p.89.

3
Second Reading — a Battle but not the War

It was clear to both supporters and opponents of the 1967 Abortion Act that the result of the 1979 general election would have a large bearing on the chances of a bill to amend the Act being successful in the next Parliament. We have already indicated that although abortion is an unwhipped issue there are clear party positions in the voting; with certain striking exceptions Conservatives tend to vote for amending legislation and Labour MPs against it. This conclusion is confirmed in Table 7.1 (pp. 196-7). Obviously then, if the Conservative Party won a clear majority at the 1979 election an amending bill would have a much greater likelihood of success.

The 1979 Election Campaign

The interest groups were therefore very concerned about the outcome of the 1979 general election and both sides made some efforts to influence the views of candidates and the votes of electors. However there is no doubt that the anti-abortion side was much more active in this area or that this activity reflects a major element in its strategy. The anti-abortion groups SPUC and particularly LIFE have continually emphasized the need to influence and educate the public and to encourage their members to press candidates and MPs in the constituencies. Obviously the pro-abortion groups, and particularly NAC, do this also, while the anti-abortion groups, notably SPUC, lobby in Parliament. Nevertheless there is a marked difference of emphasis in the strategy and tactics of the two sides which will become even clearer later. The anti-abortion groups have continued to be most active and most effective in the constituencies, although more recently they have had less of a clear run because of the activities of NAC and, on Corrie, CAC. In contrast the pro-abortion groups have tended to concentrate upon parliamentary lobbying, first through ALRA and later through Co-ord.

The activity of the two sides in the lead up to the 1979 election provides an excellent example of their different strategies. The pro-abortion side was largely inactive and not well co-ordinated at the constituency level, while the anti-abortion groups were very active and were co-ordinated from the centre by their respective leaderships.

In the two elections in 1974 SPUC had encouraged its local groups to ask the candidates for their views on the abortion issue and then publicize those views around the constituency. It followed a similar strategy in 1979. In the edition of the SPUC newspaper *Human Concern* which preceded the general election, a list was published of the past voting patterns of all the MPs who were standing again and members were urged to discover the views of other candidates and publicize them.[1] At the same time SPUC produced a large number of *Value Your Vote* leaflets about abortions to be given out in the street or pushed through letter boxes. No leaflet was produced, however, with specific instruction to its members (who cover some 500 constituencies) about what to do in the election.

In contrast LIFE's advice to its membership was much more detailed. In September 1978, in expectation, like most other observers, of an election in October, LIFE issued a list of guidelines to all its groups,[2] asking them to find out the views of all candidates and to campaign for pro-LIFE candidates. Groups were advised to assess the local political situation and to support other LIFE groups if their group was in a safe seat. They were also given advice about how to meet their candidates and what to show them. The LIFE central organization produced a large number of copies of a single-page leaflet called 'Your vote — His Life', and of a more detailed one entitled 'Which way will you vote?' Local groups, which cover about 250 constituencies, were also asked to prepare leaflets on the views of their local candidates. Anyone distributing leaflets about the election near election time must avoid infringing the Representation of the People Acts of 1949 and 1969. It is an offence under those Acts for an organization or individual to try to promote or secure the election of any candidate by any means (including producing and distributing literature) except with the consent of the candidate's agent and as part of his election budget. As such LIFE advised its members very carefully about what to do and how to set out their leaflets in order to keep within the law.[3]

By comparison the pro-abortion groups were relatively inactive during the election period. Co-ord produced a manifesto on abortion which went to all candidates in constituencies with majorities of less than five thousand votes. These manifestos were accompanied by an index card which asked for each candidate's views on abortion. In addition ALRA wrote to all candidates in marginal constituencies before the election and followed this up by writing to all newly elected MPs immediately after the election asking for information on their likely voting intentions on the issue. However this exercise was probably more useful as a means of gathering the views of new MPs than as an attempt to influence candidates. Indeed the noticeable thing is not only that the supporters of the 1967 Act were less visible at election time but also that they made little attempt to influence the votes of electors, in direct contrast to the strong efforts of the anti-abortion groups. This pattern is not difficult to understand. The main pro-abortion group active in the constituencies before the Corrie Bill was NAC. The majority of NAC's supporters are 'radical' in a broad sense and few of them would vote, or work, for a Conservative candidate. Indeed NAC could not, nor would it want to, mount a campaign in support of all pro-abortion candidates regardless of party without alienating most of its membership. So NAC's activities in the 1979 campaign were local and directed at helping pro-abortion Labour candidates in marginal seats.

There is then an obvious difference between the tactics and strategies of the two sides at election time. The anti-abortion groups were very active in the 1979 election campaign but did they have very much success? Both LIFE and SPUC claim notable victories. In particular LIFE claims to have significantly helped anti-abortion Conservative candidates win against pro-abortion Labour MPs in Dartford and Gravesend[4] while SPUC claims influence in Redbridge, Ilford North and Ormskirk.[5] The particular results in these constituencies are examined in Table 3.1.

Table 3.1: Effects of the Anti-abortion Groups' Efforts in the 1979 Election

Constituency	Labour candidate and vote	Conservative candidate and vote	Swing to Conservatives in constituency, 1974-9 %	Swing to Conservatives in area of which constituency is part %
Dartford	S. Irving 19,803	R. Dunn 21,195	+7.7	+6.0
Gravesend	J. Ovendon 28,246	T. Brinton 37,592	+8.2	+6.0
Redbridge Ilford North	T. Jowell 19,186	V. Bendall 20,381	+7.8	+6.4
Ormskirk	R. Kilroy Silk 37,222	B. Keefe 36,364	+5.7	+4.4

In each of these constituencies the swing to Conservatives was higher than general in that region. However in none of the constituencies did that higher swing result in the loss of a seat by a Labour member who would have held it if the swing had only been in line with the regional average. Nevertheless the pressure in constituencies like these was intense, with the Roman Catholic Church playing a major role in attempting to influence voters. One of our interviews was with one of these three new Conservative MPs who said:

> In [my constituency] there is a strong Roman Catholic element. Before the 1979 election all the candidates in the constituency were asked their views on euthanasia, abortion and pornography by a Catholic organisation. The answers were then posted on the notice boards of the local Catholic churches. In addition the Catholic priests were preaching on the abortion issue advising parishioners not to vote for my main [Labour and pro-abortion] opponent.[6]

In fact we have heard of numerous cases of Roman Catholic priests attempting to influence the voting of their flocks by sermons or through articles in their parish magazines. Many of these cases we can directly substantiate. However it is much harder to assess the effect of such efforts. Working-class Roman Catholics have economic reasons for voting Labour and most anti-abortion candidates are Conservative; faced 'with such conflict many Catholics will choose to vote in line with their perceived economic interests'.[7] Nevertheless Table 3.1 does suggest that the efforts of SPUC and LIFE may have a marginal, perhaps ½ per cent to 1 per cent, effect in some constituencies.

The Result of the Election: a Changing Balance of Forces

After the election the composition of Parliament was substantially changed. Whereas in the October 1974 election the Labour Party won 319 seats to the Conservatives' 277, in the May 1979 election the Conservatives returned 339 MPs and the Labour Party only 269. This election result obviously had major consequences for parliamentary opinion on the abortion issue given the tendency of Conservative MPs to vote for amending legislation. What is more the pro-abortion side seemed to lose even more supporters than one might expect given the swing to the Conservatives. Indeed of the MPs who retired or were defeated at the 1979 election, almost twice as many (46) had voted against the Braine Bill as had voted for it (24).

The loss to the pro-abortion lobby at the 1979 election was qualitative as well as quantitative. Some of their key supporters on the Labour benches like Lena Jeger, Joyce Butler and Barbara Castle retired, while Audrey Wise, Maureen Colquhoun and Helene Hayman all lost their seats. In fact the reduction in the number of women MPs from 27 to 19 was a severe blow given the activism of Labour women MPs on this issue.[8] However for all this the main loss felt by the pro-abortion side was on the Conservative benches. Robin Hodgson who after being elected at a by-election in 1976 had proved to be a strong speaker on the subject was defeated, while, most important, Sir George Sinclair retired. He had been the pro-abortion side's main champion on the Conservative benches since the Steel Bill, serving as a member of the Standing Committees on the Steel and Benyon Bills and of the original Select Committee on the White Bill. He had been particularly important as the organizer and 'whip' of the small group of Conservative MPs who opposed amending legislation. The rest of the pro-abortion activists were all Labour MPs who had few contacts on the Conservative benches so that the loss of Sir George Sinclair was felt particularly on the Second Reading of the Corrie Bill. Later other Conservatives like Bowen Wells, MP for Hertford, took a more active role lobbying on the issue, and the efforts of Sharon Spiers of Tories for Free Choice were important in collecting information on Conservative MPs and voting intentions. However although Sir George Sinclair's advice and efforts were always missed the loss was most apparent in the early stages of the Bill's progress.

The Private Members' Ballot

The private members' ballot takes place under Standing Order No. 6 on the second Thursday of every session. All members who wish can enter their names although by convention Ministers do not. The Speaker is responsible for arranging the ballot and the number of names drawn depends upon the amount of time available for private members' business in that session. Standing Order No. 6, which dates from 1927, specifies that ten Fridays will be set aside for such business but in fact a sessional order has been laid before Parliament by the government to supersede that order in every year since 1939. In the 1979-80 session the government laid a sessional order before Parliament on 21 November 1979. This order was approved and set aside 12 Fridays for private members' business with half of those being allocated to Second Reading debates and the other half to Report Stage and Third Reading debates. In this session on 24 May over 400 MPs entered the ballot and 24 names were drawn.

It must be emphasized that it is members' names which go into the ballot not bills so that an MP need not have any specific bill in mind when he or she enters the ballot. Indeed many MPs do not really think about a bill until after the ballot and as such interest groups often play an active role in persuading an MP with a high position in the ballot to adopt a particular bill. In this way, as we said earlier, ALRA originally approached David Steel who after some deliberation introduced his Bill in 1966.

In fact pressure groups are mainly interested in the first six to ten MPs in the ballot as the bills of MPs with lower places have little chance of progressing far. The procedure for deciding which bills are debated on which days is fairly straightforward. The MP with first place in the ballot can choose which Friday he wants for the Second Reading debate on his bill, the second MP then chooses one of the other five Fridays allocated for the Second Readings of private members' bills, the third MP subsequently chooses one of the remaining four Fridays and so on. The MP who has drawn seventh place in the ballot is then left to choose second place on one of the six Fridays and the process goes on until each of the successful members in the ballot (24 of them in the 1979-80 session) has chosen a position. Each Friday session lasts for four and a half hours and if the bill is opposed on Second Reading, as abortion bills invariably are, the first bill on any Friday is likely to occupy all that day's debate and be voted upon at a few minutes to four. Thus only the first six bills are guaranteed a Second Reading vote although other bills may get one. Indeed many private members' bills are non-controversial and have easy passages so that on rare occasions as many as three or four private members' bills will be discussed on one Friday.[9] All this ensures that if an MP draws a place between seven and twelve in the ballot he is very careful to choose to follow a bill which is likely to prove non-contentious. No MP with a good draw would choose to follow an abortion bill.

The pressure groups on both sides of the abortion issue are normally present in the House to find out the results of the ballot. However their lobbying at this point is not as intense as one might expect. The anti-abortion groups SPUC and LIFE seem to be somewhat reluctant to pressurize MPs. This appears to result partly from a belief that MPs resent such pressure. At the same time of course MPs are by now very politicized on this issue and some are strongly committed to amending the 1967 Act. This means that there is a good chance that one of these MPs will draw a place in the top ten of each ballot. In contrast the pro-abortion groups have no interest at present in promoting legislation so they are present to hear the result of the ballot largely to acquire information and keep MPs aware of their continued opposition to amending legislation.

When John Corrie won first place in the ballot it was not immediately clear that he would introduce an abortion bill and neither of the abortion factions were certain of his intentions. He was not one of the MPs whom SPUC or LIFE would have chosen to win the ballot and when he drew first place neither initially expected him to take an abortion bill. Indeed LIFE's first hope was that Robert Taylor, Conservative MP for Croydon North West, who drew third place in the ballot, would introduce a bill.

In fact in the Second Reading debate on his Bill Corrie claimed that abortion reform had always been in his mind:

> I walked into the House on the Wednesday night when the ballot had been drawn, I was told by a press man that I had won it and he asked me what I would do. At that moment I said that I would try to amend the Abortion Act because I had always felt strongly about it. No other person had spoken to me up to that moment. It was my decision made because I wanted to do it.[10]

However during the month between the declaration of the result of the ballot and the publication of the short titles of the bills which members intended to promote, Corrie was not always as certain of his intentions. On 26 May the *Guardian* reported that, 'Mr Corrie said yesterday that he now thought it considerably less likely that he would choose abortion as the subject for his Bill.' Later on 1 January the *Catholic Herald* reported that he was particularly worried about the level of opposition within Parliament to amending legislation. Indeed Corrie himself said in a letter to the *Daily Express* published on 4 June, 'I have not yet decided what bill I wish to present to Parliament', and later told the *Glasgow Sunday Mail,* 'I shall take my final decision on June 26, but I can say that the abortion issue is a front runner.'[11]

These reports are probably not as contradictory as they might first appear. John Corrie was more interested in abortion reform than most other MPs although not as committed to it as some MPs like William Benyon, Sir Bernard Braine, Jill Knight or Michael Ancram. In addition he had a personal reason for his concern:

> Let's not pretend I haven't been influenced by the fact that it has taken us 15 years to try to have three children. A lot of that time — while nurses were sweating to see that our child wasn't lost — they have been hurrying off to perform abortions on patients in beds flanking my wife's.[12]

So John Corrie had a personal as well as a moral reason for his support for reform. However at the same time John Corrie is a politician and as such he consulted widely with his friends inside and outside Parliament and with interested parties before he decided to take a bill through Parliament which he knew would be strongly opposed. Corrie asserted, as we saw earlier, that he was not influenced by SPUC or LIFE in his choice of his Bill and certainly neither SPUC nor LIFE have claimed a major role in its drafting. Nevertheless Corrie has also admitted receiving a large number of letters from supporters of abortion law reform, largely members of SPUC and LIFE, while he was deciding which bill to promote. Such pressure did not force him to take an abortion bill but it must have strengthened his belief that he would receive a great deal of support to offset against the inevitable opposition he would encounter. In the end then his choice probably depended as much on his political judgement as his moral and religious convictions. As such it is not surprising that he took time to make a definite commitment to take an amending bill.

It is clear that even before John Corrie had finally decided on the subject of his bill the two abortion lobbies were mobilized for action. At the end of May Co-Ord had written to Corrie urging him not to take an abortion bill while on 8 June they wrote to all MPs asking them not to support amending legislation. In addition they called upon all their members to write to their MPs, to John Corrie, and to the Minister of Health, Dr Gerard Vaughan. SPUC and LIFE's tactics were different. They were more concerned to get their members to write to Corrie and to their MPs urging them to support him, rather than writing directly to MPs themselves. This is a definite strategy as they believe that MPs are most influenced by their constituents' letters. Nevertheless the groups only began to move into top gear after 27 June when Corrie's Abortion (Amendment) Bill received a formal First Reading. At this stage a private member still only has to declare the short title, not the content of his bill, so that over the next two and a half weeks until the full text of the Bill was available on 10 June only three days before the Second Reading, no one was entirely sure of its contents although rumours abounded. During this period Corrie saw a number of organizations to discuss with them the detailed content of his Bill. He talked to SPUC, the BMA and the RCOG, and Doctors in Defence of the 1967 Act. Each group appears to have received a different understanding of the likely content of the Bill: SPUC was happy because it felt Corrie intended to alter the grounds for abortion to remove the 'statistical argument', and to prevent financial links between abortion referral agencies and clinics. In contrast Doctors in Defence of the 1967 Act came away from their meeting with Corrie on 25 June convinced that he planned a bill which would not significantly change the grounds or affect the operation of the charities BPAS and PAS.[13]

Once again Corrie does not seem to have been greatly influenced in drafting his Bill by the direct pressure from the anti-abortion interest groups. In fact he appears to have been most influenced by his parliamentary colleagues. All private members' bills are almost inevitably sponsored by a number of MPs from different political parties. An MP agrees to sponsor a bill after discussions with its promoter and in return for his support may request changes in, or additions to, the bill. The sponsors of John Corrie's Bill were Sir Bernard Braine, Jill Knight, Elaine Kellett-Bowman, William Benyon, Michael Ancram and Janet Fookes (all Conservative MPs), Leo Abse, James Hamilton, James White and Ian Campbell (all Labour MPs); and Gordon Wilson, the Scottish Nationalist. There can be no doubt that some of these, notably Michael Ancram, Jill Knight and Elaine Kellett-Bowman take a more fundamentalist or absolutist view on abortion than the one favoured by Corrie. In his discussions with us John Corrie made it clear that the Bill was larger in scope than he had originally intended because this was the price he paid for the support of sponsors with a more fundamentalist view.[14] In particular it is evident from our interviews that the sponsors were split on clause 4 of the Bill which dealt with the separation of referral agencies and clinics, a split which became evident in Committee.[15] William Benyon and, to a slightly lesser extent, John Corrie had little belief in this clause yet to others like

Bernard Braine and Jill Knight it was a, if not the, key clause in the Bill.

The role of George Crozier was also important in influencing the shape of the Bill. George Crozier, a Scottish lawyer from Dunbarton, had played a crucial part in drafting James White's Bill in 1975, and he took a similar role in the Corrie Bill. Mr Crozier is chairman of The National Pro-life Committee which is the umbrella organization for all the anti-abortion groups. He is a devout Roman Catholic and a fundamentalist on the abortion issue. As such it is perhaps not surprising that the Bill which John Corrie produced was the most radical attempt to reform the 1967 Act which has so far been proposed.

John Corrie's Bill became readily available in the House of Commons on 10 July only two days before Second Reading. This is unusual in the case of most private members' bills which are normally published at least seven days before the date of the Second Reading in order to ensure time for consultations and discussions between MPs and interested outside parties. It is less uncommon in the case of abortion bills. The James White Bill in 1975 was not available until seven days before Second Reading.[16] In fact John Corrie claimed that his secretary delivered the Bill to the Bill Office in the House of Commons, which is responsible for printing the bills, seven or eight days before 13 July. This view was in direct contrast to the report in the *Catholic Herald* which suggested that release of the Bill was delayed partly because of disagreement among its backers as to what would get passed by the House of Commons and partly to prevent the abortion campaign launching an attack on it.[17] Corrie dismissed this report in the Second Reading debate[18] but it is revealing that a draft of the Corrie Bill which was significantly different from the final form was still circulating around the House for comments on 9 July.[19]

The Bill: a Radical Measure

When the Bill was published it was soon clear that it attempted to radically amend the 1967 Act, and the 1929 Infant Life (Preservation) Act.[20] In fact it had four main elements:

The Time Limit

The Bill introduced a time limit of 20 weeks into the legislation, whereas before it had been assumed that under the 1929 Act abortion could be legal up to 28 weeks. There was to be one exception to this time limit. An abortion could be carried out legally up to 28 weeks if two doctors decided in good faith that the child would be born severely handicapped.

The Grounds for Abortion

In many ways the major aim of the Bill was to tighten the regulations upon the granting of abortion and in particular to prevent doctors using the so-called 'statistical argument' to justify abortion. In this way the Bill deleted the provision in the original Act which allowed a doctor to terminate a pregnancy if two doctors in good faith decided that the risk to the life or health of the mother or other children of a continuing pregnancy was *greater than* if the pregnancy were terminated. Instead two sub-clauses were substituted. An abortion would be legal only if the continuance of pregnancy involved '(i) *grave* risk to the life of the pregnant woman or (ii) *substantial* risk of *serious* injury to the physical or mental health of the pregnant woman or any existing children of her family'. The terminology here is crucial. The aim of the new sub-clauses was to make abortion legal in many fewer circumstances, to remove the 'statistical argument' and significantly to reduce the social grounds for abortion.

The Conscience Clause

The Bill also amended the conscience clause which was in the original act. It allowed any person to object on 'religious, ethical or other grounds' to taking part in an abortion operation. The most important change however was that the Corrie Bill removed the proviso in the original Act which specified that the burden of proof of conscientious objection lay with the person claiming it. In effect this meant that any doctor or nurse could refuse to take part in abortion operations on moral grounds.

Licensing and the Charities

The Bill would have significantly tightened up the licensing procedure for clinics and advice or referral bureaux. More important, it required the separation of referral agencies from clinics carrying out abortions. This would have affected the work of the charitable agencies BPAS and PAS.

The Drafting of the Bill

The drafting of the Corrie Bill played an important part in its fate. The drafting of parliamentary bills is a skilled job. Government bills are prepared by professional parliamentary draftsmen and still they usually have weaknesses or unclear passages which have to be tightened up in Committee. Private members have no such luxury; they must initially draft their bill with help from lawyers or colleagues, although it is common for departments to give advice and help in redrafting once the bill has obtained a Second Reading. Private members' bills are thus invariably accused, often by their supporters as well as their opponents, of being 'badly drafted'. The more complex the legislation the more likely that there will be serious drafting problems. The John Corrie Abortion (Amendment) Bill proved no exception and indeed many accused it of being particularly badly constructed.

Corrie himself opened his speech on the Second Reading with an apology about the drafting:

> I found it a complicated matter to try to amend the Abortion Act 1967, which in turn must be read in conjunction with the Infant Life (Preservation) Act 1929, which in turn does not cover Scotland. I was working with Scottish lawyers and we encountered difficulties. I apologise to the House. I regret that the Bill is now in its present form, due to circumstances beyond my control. Any drafting errors can be corrected at a later date.[21]

Later in the same debate Dr Gerald Vaughan, Minister of Health confirmed that 'the Bill as it stands is unsatisfactorily drafted in many respects. We would not want to see it go onto the Statute book in its present form.'[22] One of the main problems in drafting resulted from the use of terms like 'grave', 'serious' and 'substantial' in the grounds clause which many lawyers thought would be extremely difficult to interpret. In addition part of the section in the Bill dealing with licensing was unclear and very complicated. Such drafting problems were to prove important because the Bill's supporters did not find it as easy to remove them in Committee as Corrie had hoped and they presented the pro-abortion side with great scope for amendments and discussion.

Approaching Second Reading

There can be no doubt then that the Corrie Bill was a radical measure. Prof. Scarisbrick, chairman of LIFE, claimed that it would have reduced the number of abortions performed in England and Wales by two-thirds.[23] This was at best an informed guess but there can be little doubt that the effect would have been dramatic. In the circumstances it is not surprising that reactions to the Bill were immediate, diverse and heated. In fact because the Bill was published so late the pro-abortion groups in particular had to anticipate its contents when they launched their campaign against it. By the end of June Co-ord had produced a brief on the Bill[24] which was initially distributed to all Co-ord member-organizations and subsequently distributed to MPs at a lobby organized by ALRA in the House of Commons on 4 July. This lobby was followed up by a letter sent from Co-ord to all MPs who were not known strong supporters of amending legislation. The letter contained what proved to be a very accurate guess as to the likely contents of the Bill and urged MPs to oppose it.

The anti-abortion side was in a different position. It immediately asked local groups to write to Corrie as soon as he appeared likely to take a Bill and subsequently asked the groups to urge their MPs to support the Corrie Bill. They were initially less concerned with the content of the Bill as SPUC and LIFE see such amending legislation as only a first step to repeal of the 1967 Act.[25] However there is no doubt that both organizations were happier when they saw that the Bill proposed a major reform of the grounds clause[26] and included a clause requiring the separation of referral agencies and clinics. The response to SPUC's and LIFE's calls for pro-Corrie letters was immediate. All the MPs we spoke to, with the exception of one or two very well known pro-abortion campaigners, reported receiving a large number of letters in support of the Corrie Bill before Second Reading. The balance between pro- and anti-Corrie letters evened out later during the passage of the Bill but initially the letters came overwhelmingly from SPUC and LIFE supporters. A few examples should suffice to underline this point. Frank Field, Labour MP for Birkenhead, reported receiving 80 letters from constituents before the Second Reading debate, only one of them opposing the Bill. Similarly, Barry Porter, Conservative MP for Bebington and Ellesmere Port, received 100 letters all urging him to support the Corrie Bill,[27] and Dr Mabon, a strong supporter of the 1967 Act, reported receiving 'several hundred' letters almost unanimously asking him to vote for Corrie.[28]

The short period between the publication of the Bill and Second Reading meant that the professional organizations had no opportunity to comment formally on the Bill before the Second Reading vote. However the BMA had made its position fairly clear when at its annual conference on 25 June a motion defending the 1967 Act had been ratified. In addition when Dame Josephine Barnes became President of the BMA at this conference she spoke in support of the 1967 Abortion Act in her inaugural address and subsequently issued a statement to the press on 29 July condemning the Corrie Bill.[29] Nevertheless the real response of the professional organizations was not felt until later in the passage of the Bill, and then it had a considerable effect.

The few days before the Second Reading debate also confirmed the fact that most national newspapers were likely to oppose the Corrie Bill as they had done the Benyon Bill. On 12 and 13 July the *Daily Star,* the *Daily Mirror,* the *Daily Express,* the *Evening News* and the *Guardian*[30] all carried articles which criticized certain aspects of the Bill. In addition the *Guardian* editorial on the day of the Second Reading supported the 1967 Act and was quoted by David Ennals in the debate.[31] Despite this however the media's main influence on the vote was exercised through the publication of three late-abortion stories at Wanstead, Whiston and Barnsley.

Under the 1929 Infant Life (Preservation) Act, abortions can be carried out up to 28 weeks, although in fact less than 1 per cent of notified abortions are carried out after 20 weeks. Nevertheless, the 'late abortion' issue is one that has consistently worried some MPs. However, it is difficult to look at these cases without receiving the impression that the anti-abortion groups, and LIFE in particular, manipulated them very skilfully to their advantage in a crucial political period. In the Wanstead case the foetus was alleged to have been of 20 weeks gestation, to have 'cried out' at delivery and to have been left unattended and struggling for life until it died. The abortion was carried out on a 16-year-old girl in July 1978 but the details were only released by LIFE to the press at the end of March 1979 in the run up to the general election. The case was first covered 'exclusively' by the *Sunday People*[32] but was subsequently reported in all the national newspapers. The stress in the reports was on this case as an 'abuse' of the Abortion Act. In fact the report was subsequently investigated by the Redbridge and Waltham Forest Area Health Authority which found that the foetus was incapable of sustaining independent life and that resuscitation equipment had been available but had not been used because the foetus was too young to inflate its lungs.

In the Whiston case the foetus was 18 to 20-weeks-old and the abortion took place on 4 January 1979. The case was released by LIFE to the press, and widely reported on 20 April. The foetus was said to have been left unattended for two hours and to have been baptized by a trainee Roman Catholic priest. The Medical Protection Union immediately investigated the case and found that the foetus was examined half an hour after the abortion and showed no signs of life. Subsequently an enquiry carried out by the St Helen's and Knowsley Area Health Authority confirmed this finding. Indeed, Dr Gerard Vaughan, in a written answer to David Alton MP, said:

> The medical examination showed that the foetus was not capable of an independent existence and I am advised that there can be no possibility that a different conclusion would have been reached at the time of the abortion.[33]

In the Barnsley case the foetus was 26-weeks-old and the mother had come into contact with German measles in about the fifteenth week of pregnancy but had not realized this until later. The foetus was allegedly left unattended for three and a half to five hours before it was put on a life support system. It had died some 36 hours later. The subsequent inquest returned an 'open' verdict. This case was released immediately to the press and widely reported in late April 1979. In this instance, many of the articles directly related the case to a call for a reduction of the upper limit for abortions from 28 to 24 or 20 weeks, a suggestion which was to become a major element in the Corrie Bill.

The point here is that these late abortion cases were used by SPUC and, particularly, LIFE in their campaign in the 1979 general election. Subsequently these cases were often quoted in the run-up to the vote on the Corrie Bill and the debate on the Bill centred mainly around one clause which would have reduced the upper limit for abortions from 28 to 20 weeks.

Perhaps the most significant activity in the lead up to the Second Reading debate occurred among MPs themselves. By the time of the Corrie Bill there were some very experienced campaigners on both sides of this issue in Parliament. Among Corrie's supporters Sir Bernard Braine, William Benyon, Leo Abse and Jill Knight in particular had a great deal of knowledge of the issue and experience of lobbying among Members on the issue. On the other side Willie Hamilton, Oonagh MacDonald, and Jo Richardson had similar experience. As soon as it became clear that Corrie would promote an abortion bill both sides began lobbying. Initially of course priority was given to discovering the views on the issue of the new MPs although some information on this was provided by the interest groups. At the same time all the activists were busy approaching colleagues attempting to persuade them to vote for their side. However the informal whipping system which was to develop at Report Stage on both sides, and which we shall deal with later,[34] did not really exist before Second Reading because of the limited time available. Nevertheless even at this stage the level of lobbying by MPs was more intense, and the quality of their information about voting intentions was a great deal better than is normal on private members' bills. The fact that the level of activity was to grow vastly at Report Stage is another indication of the degree of 'politicization' of this issue.

The Second Reading

The Second Reading Debate took place on Friday 13 June. There had been a last minute scare among the Corrie supporters that the debate would be lost when some Labour MPs had mooted a filibuster of the previous day's Education Bill.[35] If the bill had been filibustered so that debate lasted into Friday morning then the day's private members' business would have been lost and the Abortion Bill would have gone to the bottom of the private members' list with little chance of further consideration. Any such tactic was forestalled however when the government decided to adjourn the remaining stages of the Education Bill to Monday 16 July. So John Corrie rose to his feet at 11.34am and the debate lasted four and a half hours until a vote was taken at 4.00pm.

The debate is worthy of some consideration as it may have had some influence on a few MPs. It was very well attended with the Chamber usually two-thirds full for the whole debate. There were seven speakers supporting the Bill, five opposing it and the Minister of Health, Gerard Vaughan, whose speech criticized much of the Bill but who later said he would vote for Second Reading.[36] The debate was always heated, sometimes emotional and often personal. In this way David Ennals and Willie Hamilton, both strong opponents of the Bill, threw doubt upon Corrie's knowledge of the subject and understanding of his own Bill[37] while Leo Abse, a strong supporter of the Bill, accused Ennals of a pro-abortion bias when he was a Minister.[38] Only one MP, Dale Campbell-Savours, a supporter of the Bill, managed to complete his speech without numerous interruptions[39] and that was only because it was his maiden speech, and maiden speeches are by convention not interrupted. In fact 34 MPs intervened in the debate many of them more than once. Of these, seventeen were opposed to the Bill, nine supported it and eight either asked for, or gave, factual information.

A number of other significant impressions emerge from the debate. First, it was made clear by both the pro-abortion speakers and by Dr Vaughan that the investigations of the Wanstead and Whiston 'late abortion' cases revealed that the law was not broken and that the foetuses were not viable.[40] Secondly, and in contrast, some of the supporters of the Corrie Bill still cited these and other unspecified late abortion cases as evidence of abuses of the 1967 Act.[41] Thirdly, the main clause dealt with in the speeches was clause 1 concerned with the reduction of the time limit. Indeed there can be little doubt given the debate that many MPs voted on the basis of this clause. In an interruption to Corrie's speech John Bruce-Gardyne, Conservative MP for Knutsford claimed: 'The time limit is of crucial importance to some of us in deciding which way we shall vote at the end of this debate.'[42]

In the division taken at the end of the Second Reading the Bill was given a Second Reading by a majority of 242 votes to 98. This was the largest majority any amendment bill had enjoyed at Second Reading. The result did not surprise either side but the size of the majority did. Corrie and his supporters were obviously delighted while the Bill's opponents were concerned. The vote meant not only that the task of convincing MPs to oppose the Bill at the Report Stage would be extremely difficult but also that there would be no chance of amending the Bill in Standing Committee. Standing Committees on private members' bills are composed of supporters and opponents in direct proportion to the Second Reading vote. The overwhelming vote for the Corrie Bill meant that the Standing Committee was made up of ten supporters of the Corrie Bill and only five opponents. Obviously those five people would have to work extremely hard and be well serviced, and the extra-parliamentary and parliamentary lobbies would have to be highly organized if the Corrie Bill was to be defeated.

The Vote Explained

By 1978 and the vote upon the Braine Bill it appeared that there was a clear trend away from support for amending legislation in MPs' voting. Indeed the Braine Bill had only received a majority of six. However any such impression was dispelled by the overwhelming vote in favour of the Corrie Bill in July 1979.

How can such a change be explained?

Obviously much of the change can be explained by the Conservative victory in the 1979 election which brought 60 more Conservative MPs into Parliament than had been there in 1978. What is more, the Conservative MPs who were elected for the first time in 1979 were overwhelmingly supporters of abortion reform. Indeed 59 of the 60 new Conservative MPs who voted supported the Corrie Bill at Second Reading and they were more likely to support the Bill than those Conservatives who had been in the House prior to 1979 (see Table 3.2). However this only offers a partial explanation of the change.

Table 3.2: Voting Patterns on the Second Reading of the Corrie Bill, by Date of First Election and Party

(a) Conservatives

Date of first election	No. of MPs voting for	%	No. of MPs voting against	%
1974 or before	117	90	13	10
1979	59	99	1	1

(b) Labour

Date of first election	No. of MPs voting for	%	No. of MPs voting against	%
1974 or before	44	41	64	59
1979	10	36	18	64

In fact, while the number of Conservative MPs supporting amending legislation grew from 115 to 162 between 1978 and 1979, the decline in Labour MPs voting against amending legislation from 137 to 82 is at least as significant. Obviously this decline is partly the result of Labour's loss of 58 seats at the 1979 general election. However, just as many Labour MPs voted in favour of amending legislation in 1979 as had in 1978, so there are significant changes in both parties which need to be explained.

In the Conservative Party the main change, other than that involving new MPs, concerned 45 MPs who had abstained or not voted in 1978 but voted for the Corrie Bill in 1979. At the same time, 18 Conservatives who had voted against in 1978 abstained in 1979. The picture is complicated because 37 Conservatives who voted for the Braine Bill abstained in 1979. In the Labour Party the main change involved 48 MPs who voted against the Braine Bill but abstained in 1979, while 18 Labour MPs who had not voted in 1978 voted for the Corrie Bill. Overall then, although one Conservative MP changed sides, voting against Braine but for Corrie, the most significant changes result from Conservatives who abstained in 1978 voting for the Corrie Bill, and Labour MPs who voted against the Braine Bill abstaining in 1979. We have to explain both the overall pattern, and these two distinct, if related, trends.

Once again there is little evidence that MPs' views were changed either by medical or public opinion. As we have already indicated there was no evidence of any change in medical opinion on the abortion issue prior to the Second Reading vote. The main medical organizations continued to oppose amendment of the Abortion Act although they had no time to make new formal statements prior to the debate. The picture is very similar if we consider public opinion. In a poll published just before the vote Gallup found that while 38 per cent of its sample thought that abortion should be more difficult to obtain, 45 per cent were in favour of an abortion law as liberal or more liberal than the existing one.[43] In fact Table A.2 (p. 217) shows that while there has been a decline in the percentage wanting the Act to stay as it is, there has been no increase in the percentage preferring a more restrictive law between 1973 and 1979. Overall, a significant majority are opposed to amending legislation. It is clear that the changes in MPs' views hardly result from changes in medical opinion or public opinion.

In fact at this stage the anti-abortion interest groups probably had more influence on MPs' voting than either medical or public opinion. In particular SPUC and LIFE were involved in releasing to the press information about the three cases of 'late' abortions at Wanstead, Whiston and Barnsley. In addition a large number of members of these groups wrote to their MPs about the cases. The result was that the Second Reading debate, as we have indicated, was dominated by a concern with the time-limit clause in the Bill, and although the Minister denied the validity of the Wanstead and Whiston stories many MPs appeared to believe that there was no smoke without fire. The crucial point here though is that many MPs voted for the Second Reading because they favoured a reduction of the time limit believing either that this was the main element in the Bill or that the other clauses could, and would, be removed later, possibly in Committee. This view appears to be confirmed by the fact that while an amendment to reduce the time limit to 24 weeks received overwhelming support at Report Stage, most of the Bill's original clauses were voted down.

Our quantitative evidence reveals one other interesting relationship. The marginality of a constituency is clearly related to voting. As Table 3.3 shows, party is much more closely related to voting on the Second Reading of the Corrie Bill for those MPs in marginal constituencies. The *Lambda* in the case of MPs in safe seats is only 0.051 while if we consider MPs in marginal seats the *Lambda* is 0.692. In particular Labour MPs in marginal constituencies were more likely to oppose the Corrie Bill than were their colleagues in safe seats.

Table 3.3: Relationship between Party and Voting on the Second Reading of the Corrie Bill, Controlling for Marginality (Labour and Conservative MPs who voted)

(a) Only MPs in Safe Seats

	Labour %	Conservative %
Voted for Second Reading	48	92
Voted against Second Reading	52	8
Total	100	100

Note: *Lambda B* 0.051 significant at 0.001 level.

(b) Only MPs in Marginal Seats

	Labour %	Conservative %
Voted for Second Reading	20	95
Voted against Second Reading	80	5
Total	100	100

Note: *Lambda B* 0.692 significant at 0.001 level.

The most plausible explanation of this pattern is that MPs in marginal seats are likely to be more responsive to constituency pressure, particularly, although not exclusively, pressure from their constituency parties. Given the relationship between party allegiance and views on the abortion issue it is likely that Labour MPs in marginal constituencies are pressured by their general management committees and local party activists to support a liberal pro-abortion position, while Conservative MPs in similar precarious circumstances are pressed to support amending legislation.

There are particular reasons for the behaviour of Labour and of Conservative MPs which are evident from our qualitative material. Despite the overall pattern revealed in our quantitative evidence, our interviews did suggest that a number of Labour MPs in constituencies with sizeable Roman Catholic populations, or with a significant Catholic element on their GMCs, were influenced by this fact in casting their vote at Second Reading. Some of these MPs in fact promised the anti-abortion interest groups in their constituencies that they would vote for, or at least not oppose, amending legislation on Second Reading. They did this obviously for electoral reasons, although some of them informed their constituents that while they would not prevent a bill being considered by a Committee they would subsequently oppose it. It is difficult to know how many Labour MPs voted this way. However Jo Richardson, who was the co-ordinator of the pro-abortion side of the Standing Committee, and obviously closely involved in the Labour whipping, told us that at least 12 Labour MPs who voted for the Bill, or abstained, on the Second Reading made it clear to the Labour pro-abortion whips they they would subsequently oppose the Bill because their election promise was now fulfilled.[44]

In fact this pattern is an interesting variant on a line of reasoning which influenced the votes of a number of Labour and Conservative MPs. There is a tendency at Second Reading on private members' bills for MPs who are not particularly committed on the subject to vote for the Second Reading to 'give the bill a chance', or to 'air the matter thoroughly'. The reasoning behind this of course is that a Second Reading vote does not commit an MP to continue to vote for the bill when it comes back to the House. We talked to a number of MPs who gave this as an explanation of their vote. This means of course that a Second Reading vote is not always a good predictor of subsequent voting at Report Stage.

On the Conservative side two other factors possibly had a marginal effect on MPs' voting. In response to a point made by Willie Hamilton, Gerard Vaughan made it clear in the debate that he would vote for the Bill on Second Reading.[45] This may have influenced some Conservative MPs who saw him as a knowledgeable and dispassionate observer involved with the subject yet not associated with any of the interest groups. For those Conservative MPs, particularly new MPs, who were looking for a lead Dr Vaughan may have provided it. Certainly we interviewed two new Conservative MPs who mentioned it as a factor, although not the most important one, in their decision. In addition it is possible that some Conservative members were influenced by the fact that the Prime Minister, Mrs Thatcher, had made it clear that she intended to vote for the Bill at Second Reading.[46]

The overall pattern is fairly clear. The large vote for the Corrie Bill at Second Reading owes something to the Conservative victory at the 1979 election, something to the traditional parliamentary practice of giving a private members' bill a chance at Second Reading, and perhaps most to the belief among many MPs that something should be done about the upper time limit for abortions, a belief stimulated by the spate of late abortion stories in the press prior to the vote.

After Second Reading

On the evening of Second Reading NAC held a public meeting in Westminster Hall. It was addressed by Jo Richardson and the mood could at best be described as mixed. The people present were depressed by the result but determined to carry on the fight against the Bill. However the Second Reading vote had ensured that it would be an uphill fight for the pro-abortion side because of the composition of the Standing Committee.

The Composition of the Standing Committee

An all-party Selection Committee chooses which members will sit on a Standing Committee from a list of interested MPs drawn up by the Whips. As members are chosen because of the interest they have shown on the subject, it was fairly inevitable that Jo Richardson and Oonagh McDonald, both of whom had sat on the Standing Committee of William Benyon's Bill, should be selected to oppose Corrie's Bill in Committee. They were anxious to have, and succeeded in getting, Ian Mikardo to join them. Mikardo is well known for his knowledge of parliamentary procedure, and after the experience of the Benyon Committee, the pro-abortion lobby realized the need for someone as skilled as Mikardo. They were joined on the Committee by Willie Hamilton and Stan Thorne. This meant that all five pro-abortion members of the Standing Committee were Labour MPs. There was some attempt to recruit a Conservative member but, at this stage, none showed sufficient interest or willingness to lobby against the Bill.

In contrast the ten supporters of the Corrie Bill were drawn from both major parties. There were seven Conservatives, Michael Ancram, Vivian Bendell, William Benyon, Sir Bernard Braine, Jill Knight, Anthony Pollock, and, of course, John Corrie. The other three anti-abortionists were Stan Cohen, James Dunn and James White. The government was represented by Dr Gerard Vaughan and his parliamentary private secretary, Timothy Rathbone. The role of these two representatives was strictly to supply information, and they did not vote once throughout the Committee sittings.

The chairman of a Select Committee is chosen by the Speaker from a panel of senior backbenchers of both parties. The Chairman should act as an impartial arbiter in Committee in the same way as the Speaker does for debates on the floor of the House. In this case the chairman selected was Bonner Pink, Conservative MP for Portsmouth South, while James Lamond, Labour MP for Oldham East acted as his deputy. The Committee met for the first time on 25 July only two days before the summer recess. It was inevitable therefore that the only matter to be settled that day was the time table for the Committee sittings. The Committee agreed to meet again on 24 October and thenceforth every Wednesday at ten o'clock.

The scene was thus set. The Corrie supporters inside and outside Parliament had decisively won an important battle but the war continued. The pro-abortion side had learnt a great deal from their previous experience of the Committee Stage of the Benyon Bill and they had the advantage of fighting a defensive action. The various groups on their side could unite behind the simple aim of defending the 1967 Act. In contrast the anti-abortion groups, perhaps lulled into a false sense of security by their victory on Second Reading, had not agreed on either their priorities or their strategy.

Notes

1. *Human Concern,* no. 3.
2. 'Revised Guidelines for LIFE Groups Preparing for the General Election' issued by LIFE, September 1978.
3. Ibid., pp.3 and 4.
4. See *Human Concern,* no. 4.
5. Personal interview with John Smeaton, general secretary of SPUC, 21 August 1980.
6. Personal interview, 5 August 1980.
7. Personal interview, 5 August 1980.
8. This point is dealt with at some length above pp. 79-80 and below pp. 192-4.
9. E.g., six private members' bills introduced on 24 January 1975 (HC Debs., vol. 884, cols. 2123-211) eventually received Royal Assent in that session.
10. HC Debs., 13 July 1979, vol. 970, col. 908. Actually as we have said the ballot was drawn on Thursday 24 May.
11. The First Reading of his Bill was on 27 June 1979, HC Debs., vol. 969, col. 455.
12. *Scottish Daily Record,* 10 July 1979.
13. Interview with George Morris, chairman of Doctors in Defence of the 1967 Act, 12 August 1980.
14. Personal interview with John Corrie, 11 November 1980.
15. See below pp. 122-3.
16. James White's Bill was available one week before the Second Reading. A press conference was held on 29 January 1975 at which the contents were released.
17. *Catholic Herald,* 6 July 1979.
18. HC Debs., 13 July 1979, vol. 970, col. 920.

19. We have a copy of this draft bill with Corrie's comments handwritten upon it.
20. The original Bill is printed as Appendix 2 in this book.
21. HC Debs., 13 July 1979, vol. 970, col. 891.
22. Ibid., cols. 951-2.
23. In the *Guardian,* 11 July 1979, it was reported that, 'Professor Jack Scarisbrick, chairman of LIFE, said that he expected the number of abortions to be reduced by two-thirds if Mr Corrie's Bill went through.'
24. Co-ord memorandum to all member-organizations, 27 June 1979.
25. See above pp. 56-64.
26. LIFE in particular had been unhappy with the Benyon Bill because it had not included the phrase '*substantial* risk of *serious* injury'; they regard both adjectives as crucial.
27. As reported in the *Liverpool Echo,* 13 July 1979.
28. As reported in the *Greenock Telegraph,* 14 July 1979.
29. *Liverpool Daily Post,* 28 June 1979.
30. *Daily Star,* 12 July, 1979, carried an article on late abortions which was strongly against the Bill. The *Daily Mirror,* 12 July 1979, carried an article saying the choice should be with women. *Daily Express,* 13 July 1979, dealt with the circumstances under which women might need an abortion after 20 weeks. *Evening News,* 13 July 1979, dealt with the threat to the charities, notably PAS. *Guardian,* 12 July 1979, carried a report on doctors' opposition to the Bill.
31. HC Debs., 13 July 1979, vol. 970, col. 905.
32. *Sunday People,* 25 March 1979.
33. Written Answer, HC Debs., 20 July 1979, vol. 970, col. 825.
34. See below, pp. 139-40.
35. In fact Corrie mentioned this in his speech, HC Debs., vol. 970, col. 891.
36. Speakers in support of the Bill spoke for a total of 2 hours 16 minutes and speakers against for only 1 hour 24 minutes. Vaughan's speech lasted 45 minutes.
37. See HC Debs., 13 July 1979, vol. 970, cols. 903 and 955. Corrie did make two basic factual errors about the prior history of the Bill in his speech. He was wrong about the date of the St John-Stevas Bill (he said 1970 when it was 1969) and about the promoter of James White's Bill (he said it was Ian Campbell).
38. HC Debs., 13 July 1979, vol. 970, cols. 908 and 977.
39. Ibid., cols. 936-9.
40. Ibid., cols. 909, 923 and 948.
41. Ibid., cols. 938-9.

42. Ibid., col. 900.
43. Gallup poll published in *Woman's Own,* 9 February 1980.
44. Personal interview, 15 July 1980.
45. HC Debs., 13 July 1979, vol. 970, col. 955, Vaughan said, 'Personally I shall vote in favour of the Bill.'
46. This fact was mentioned in the debate by Willie Hamilton, ibid., col. 955.

4

Standing Committee — a Crucial Battle in which the Balance of Power Shifts

The composition of a Standing Committee on a private members' bill is determined by the Second Reading vote. In this case the overwhelming support for the Bill on Second Reading meant that there were ten supporters of the Bill and only five opponents of it on the Committee. Therefore, it was obvious from the outset that the Bill's opponents would have no hope of achieving major changes to the Bill in Standing Committee. In addition as it was the first private member's bill to go in to Committee in the 1979-80 session they had no hope of preventing its progress merely by filibustering in the Committee.

All this might lead one to dismiss the Committee Stage as unimportant; to see it merely as an interval between the Second Reading vote and the Report Stage where the crucial decision would be taken. However, such a view is shortsighted. This period had an important effect on the fate of the Bill in two ways. First, the supporters of the Corrie Bill failed to use the Committee Stage to improve the chances of its ultimate success. Secondly, this period saw a rapid growth of effective pro-abortion lobbying in the constituencies linked with the development of a particularly strong parliamentary lobbying organization.

When the Bill went to Standing Committee, both lobbies and the Department of Health accepted that it was badly drafted. At the same time many observers thought that it was too long and had too many clauses to have any realistic hope of ultimate success. In addition it was clear that many MPs, particularly although not exclusively Labour MPs, had supported the Bill at Second Reading largely because they favoured a reduction in the time limit for abortions, and that these MPs expected John Corrie and his supporters to accept a compromise which would result in the removal of some of the more radical elements in the Bill. Potentially then the Bill's sponsors might have used the Committee Stage to improve its drafting and reduce its scope. If they had done this there can be little doubt that the Bill would have passed in some form.

In fact while almost all the Bill's clauses were considerably redrafted or removed in Committee the scope of the Bill was not reduced, its radical provisions stayed largely intact and many drafting problems remained when it reached Report. This meant that the MPs who had hoped for a compromise in Committee were disappointed and they tended to blame the supporters of the Bill for failing to be realistic or 'particularly aware'. At the same time in one important sense the redrafting also made the position worse for the Bill's supporters. When the Bill went back to the House from Committee it was very different from the Bill to which the House had given a Second Reading. This almost inevitably ensured that the Speaker would call a large number of amendments on the Report Stage and allow detailed debate to give the House itself sufficient chance to consider the changed Bill. As time was of the essence at Report Stage this was virtually a death-blow to the Bill. It is obviously crucial then to examine the Committee Stage in order to establish how and why the Bill was redrafted and why its scope was not reduced.

The period between the Second Reading and the Report Stage also deserves particular attention because at this stage the two lobbies were very active inside and outside Parliament. There had been little time before Second Reading for much activity. However after the vote the extra-parliamentary lobbies began in earnest organizing meetings, demonstrations and lobbies. Their aim of course was to attempt to influence uncommitted MPs who were thus subjected to considerable pressure. In addition it was at this stage that the MPs on both sides organized their whipping system and began to approach and attempt to influence the undecided MPs. One of the major purposes of this chapter then is to chart the growth and organization of the lobby both inside and outside Parliament.

Because it has various aims this chapter is divided into three sections: the first and largest looks at the activity of the two sides within the Standing Committee and particularly at the strategies adopted by the two sides; the second examines the development of the parliamentary lobbies; and the third section looks at the activities of the extra-parliamentary lobbies during this period.

The Two Sides in Standing Committee

In this section we shall first analyse the strategy and tactics of the two sides in Committee, then the changes which occurred in the Bill and finally the role of the Minister in the Committee.

The Strategy of the Pro-abortion Lobby in Committee

The strategy of the pro-abortion lobbyists grew directly out of their experience of the Standing Committee on William Benyon's Bill. That had been the first time they had needed to block a bill in committee and they were badly prepared. However two very important lessons were learnt from the experience. It was clear that in future the pro-abortion side on any Committee should include one or more MPs with detailed procedural knowledge, and that in future improved co-ordination between the parliamentary and extra-parliamentary lobby was essential.

None of the pro-abortion MPs on the Benyon Committee had had sufficient knowledge of parliamentary procedure. This had meant that their side had been short of advice on the drafting and tabling of amendments. For this reason when the Corrie Bill obtained a Second Reading Oonagh McDonald and Jo Richardson approached Ian Mikardo to serve on the Standing Committee. Mikardo is one of the House of Commons elder statesmen who is steeped in knowledge of parliamentary tactics and procedure, and his advice proved crucial during the Bill's progress. In addition the pro-abortion lobby was also helped by the fact that Willie Hamilton, another knowledgeable parliamentarian, joined the Committee. Furthermore, the five pro-abortion members on the Committee all undertook different tasks so that their efforts were integrated. Oonagh McDonald was chief whip, Jo Richardson was the chief strategist, Willie Hamilton was in charge of tabling amendments, Ian Mikardo advised on procedure and Stan Thorne carried out a variety of tasks.

During the Benyon Committee the preparation of briefs and the drafting of amendments by the extra-parliamentary pro-abortion lobby had also been inadequate. In the early stages of that Committee only one person, Peter Jackson, an ex-MP attached to Jo Richardson as a research assistant, was co-ordinating activities inside and outside Parliament. It soon became apparent that the amount of work involved was far beyond the capabilities of one person. Therefore a group of people was formed to service the MPs in committee, but they had to work in the committee corridors finding space wherever they could. The MPs had no time to consider the material prepared which they often had to absorb as they rose to speak. Under these circumstances no forward planning was possible and when Benyon dropped clauses, as he often did to speed up the proceedings, the situation was almost unmanageable. As a result of this experience the pro-abortion lobby resolved to improve the servicing of MPs on future Committees by providing skilled advice from both lawyers and doctors.

The first step to implement this decision was taken in July 1978 when a Co-ord lawyers' group was established. The group, led by Bill Birtles, a barrister, was made up initially of 14 lawyers who agreed to meet with Co-ord advisers after the Second Reading of any future abortion bill to draft amendments. This would ensure that, before the Committee Stage, amendments and briefs would be prepared and discussed with the MPs on the Committee. This happened after the Second Reading of Corrie's Bill. During the summer recess this group of lawyers prepared a series of amendments to the Bill and new clauses which could be introduced. Subsequently when the Committee Stage started in earnest there were regular Monday evening meetings between the five MPs and a group of Co-ord advisers including both lawyers and doctors. In these meetings tactics were discussed and the MPs were continually briefed. In addition at least three members of the briefing team, as well as others associated with Co-ord, attended each meeting of the Standing Committee in order to advise MPs when required. This close contact between the extra-parliamentary lobby and the parliamentary lobby ensured that the MPs had a large number of amendments to choose from and were well briefed for the Committee debates.

The pro-abortion side was thus much better prepared for the

struggle in Committee on the Corrie Bill than they had been on the Benyon Bill. In consequence their tactics were better worked out. At the same time different tactics were necessary for dealing with the Corrie Bill than had been adopted on the Benyon Bill. In the case of the Benyon Bill time was very short when it reached Committee. As such the major objective of the pro-abortion side had been to extend the Committee Stage as long as possible by tabling large numbers of amendments, and by filibustering. Although they were not well prepared they had succeeded through the intensive effort of the MPs on the Committee in delaying its progress and ensuring that it had no time for debate on Report Stage. In the case of the Corrie Bill however they were faced with a very different situation. The Bill was first into Committee and was therefore guaranteed a Report Stage debate, so there was no hope of merely filibustering the Bill in Committee to prevent it reaching Report Stage. This meant that the tactics in Committee had to be devised with the Report Stage in mind.

In fact there were three main elements in the pro-abortion lobby's tactics in Committee. First, and most crucially, they decided to keep back a number of amendments, not tabling them for discussion in Committee but rather saving them to be introduced at the Report Stage. The reason for this strategy was simple. As the Bill would obviously reach Report Stage the main aim of the pro-abortion side throughout was to filibuster it on Report so as to ensure that the House did not have sufficient time to take a final decision on the Bill. In order to do that they needed to be able to guarantee that there were a large number of amendments to discuss on Report. Of course it is the Speaker who chooses which amendments are called at the Report Stage but he tends not to choose amendments which have been tabled and defeated in Committee. This is because the Committee is chosen to reflect the views of the House at Second Reading and as such in one sense the House itself has already rejected the amendments. The pro-abortion lobby was well aware of this so they deliberately kept back certain important amendments and new clauses which the Speaker was almost certain to call when they were subsequently tabled at Report Stage. The most notable of these amendments which were held back was one which would have altered the time limit in the Bill from 20 to 24 weeks. However there were many others, and indeed this tactic was partly responsible for the large number of amendments chosen by the Speaker for debate at Report Stage.

The second element in the pro-abortion side's tactics was much less successful and was in fact changed as the Committee Stage progressed. Initially although there was no hope of filibustering the Bill the MPs decided to extend the Committee debates in order to make Parliament and the public aware of its full contents. The pro-abortion side believed, with considerable justification, that many people thought that the Bill was largely, or even exclusively, concerned with lowering the time limit for abortions. So they felt that an extended Committee Stage, with thorough press coverage, would correct this impression. This tactic however was significantly changed as the Committee Stage progressed and once again the reason for this change was related to an assessment of the likely developments at Report Stage.

All private members' bills in a given session usually go to the same Committee. This means that any bill has to wait for the previous bill to come out of Committee before it can start its Committee Stage. There are normally six days available for the later stages (that is Report Stage and Third Reading) of private members' bills in any session. The first bill to come out of Committee has the first available day for its Report and Third Reading. It only has a second day if no other bill has come out of Committee by the time that day is reached. Otherwise it goes to the bottom of the list and is only reconsidered when all other private members' bills which have been approved in Committee have each had one day, or have completed all their legislative stages in the House of Commons. This is why few private members' bills get more than one day for the consideration of their later stages. It soon became clear to the pro-abortion side on the Corrie Committee that there was a danger that if the Committee Stage dragged on there would be a strong chance that no other bill would be out of Committee soon enough to prevent the Abortion (Amendment) Bill having at least two, and possibly more, days on Report. For this reason the pro-abortion MPs changed their tactics midstream and tried to speed up progress on the Bill in order to ensure that other bills would get into, and out of, committee in time to prevent extended debate on the Corrie Bill at Report Stage.

The pro-abortion side's tactics here could, with hindsight, have been improved, although they were faced with a difficult choice. If they offered little resistance in Committee in order to ensure that the Bill came out of Committee quickly, they would reduce its chances of having sufficient time for its later stages. However at the same time such a decision would have risked both giving the impression to Parliament that they condoned the contents of the Bill, and alienating their extra-parliamentary supporters who would have seen such a strategy as evidence of weakness. Nevertheless it is perhaps surprising that the pro-abortion lobby did not come to grips with this problem more quickly, as the delays in the Committee meant that no other private member's bill was ready for consideration on Report until the third available day.

The third element in the pro-abortion side's strategy was more successful. They were particularly anxious that their supporters inside and outside Parliament should be kept in touch with what was happening in Committee. The MPs on the Committee used PLP meetings as well as personal lobbying to keep Labour MPs aware of the Committee's deliberations. In such meetings and in the course of lobbying they gave particular emphasis to the fact that the Bill was not being de-radicalized in Committee. At the same time the regular Monday meetings ensured that Co-ord was aware of most, if not all, of what was going on. This in turn meant that Co-ord could inform its member organizations of the machinations in Committee. So the pro-abortion organizations and their members were much better informed about what was going on than they had been on the Benyon Bill and this helped ensure a sense of common purpose between the parliamentary and extra-parliamentary arms of the lobby.

The pro-abortion side was thus noticeably better organized than it had been previously. The MPs were well briefed and the tactics they adopted were most often both appropriate and successful. Their only error, and it might have proved a costly error, was their failure to prevent the Bill having so much time for debate on Report.

The Strategy of the Anti-abortion Lobby in Committee

There is no doubt that the efforts of the anti-abortion lobby were less co-ordinated than those of the pro-abortion side. There was less cohesion both between the parliamentary and extra-parliamentary branches of the lobby, and among the anti-abortion MPs on the Committee. In fact the anti-abortionists spent little time on discussion of strategy and were quite deeply divided on how to progress.

Throughout the Bill's passage there was less contact between the MPs and the anti-abortion interest groups than one might have expected. In so far as it did occur the contact was mainly with SPUC rather than LIFE and normally took the form of a request from one or more of the MPs for information. In this way John Corrie asked SPUC for evidence on late abortion cases, and on the activities of the charities. It is true that during the Committee Stage there were briefing meetings of the anti-abortion side but these were less frequent and shorter than those held by the pro-abortion lobby. In fact the meetings were mainly used to exchange information, rather than for any discussion of strategy, or for the extra-parliamentary lobby to brief MPs. Furthermore, there was no co-ordinated group of lawyers advising the anti-abortion MPs in the way that the Co-ord lawyers serviced the pro-abortion side. In fact none of the MPs on the Standing Committee had much, if any, contact with ALDU, the newly formed anti-abortion lawyers group. John Corrie himself was advised by George Crozier, who had been largely responsible for drafting the Bill, while William Benyon took his advice both from the Department of Health's lawyers and from his own parliamentary draftsmen. This meant that the legal advice given was uncoordinated and often conflicting.

There appear to be two major reasons for the lack of contact between the extra-parliamentary and the parliamentary branches of the anti-abortion lobby. First, John Corrie, like most of his predecessors as promoters of anti-abortion legislation, wanted to distance himself from SPUC and LIFE. This was due partly to the natural reluctance of MPs to be seen as the 'creature' of any lobby. It was accentuated in this case however by the fact that the anti-abortion interest groups were seen by Corrie, and some of his supporters, as too fundamentalist on the issue and thus as something of a liability in parliamentary terms. Secondly, as the Corrie side intended to speak little in Committee they were in less need of detailed briefs than were the pro-abortion side. As such the MPs felt that long co-ordinating or briefing meetings were less important. However because there were few such meetings the anti-abortion side did not develop a coherent strategy particularly in relation to priorities if it became necessary to drop parts of the Bill. This lack of any strategy on priorities was an important factor in the ultimate failure of the Bill.

In fact the members of the anti-abortion lobby seem to have used two tactics at the Committee Stage, which were in most senses contradictory. Initially they decided to speak as little as possible in order to ensure that the Bill's progress was speeded up. With hindsight this was a strange decision. The longer the Bill was in Committee the less time a subsequent bill would have in the Committee, and consequently the more time the Corrie Bill would have at Report Stage. Actually because the Corrie supporters introduced a number of significant amendments to the Bill in Committee, its stay there was prolonged, and the 'real' interests of the anti-abortion lobby served almost despite themselves.

Despite all this the main problem that anti-abortion MPs faced concerned the splits within their own ranks. In Committee they could not agree whether it was important to win the Minister's and DHSS's approval for the Bill, whether any compromises should be made, or which clauses were most important in the Bill. All this led to confusion and open disagreements among Corrie's supporters in Committee.

For instance while William Benyon, and to a lesser extent John Corrie, believed that it was important to win the Minister's support, many others on Committee opposed this approach. Benyon believed that Dr Vaughan could sway votes on Report and therefore he redrafted clause 1 and clause 4 of the Bill with help and advice from the Department. In contrast others, like Michael Ancram, Jill Knight and Bernard Braine, felt that the Department was strongly 'pro-abortion' and therefore that it was better to avoid its embrace. In fact the Benyon strategy prevailed although it was opposed by other Corrie supporters, and was eventually unsuccessful as the Department and Dr Vaughan withheld active support for the Bill.

The disagreement among the Bill's supporters about their priorities among its various clauses was also important. Benyon and Corrie believed that the time-limit and grounds clause (clause 1) contained important elements of the Bill. Benyon in particular felt that the main purpose of the Bill was to remove the so-called 'statistical argument' from the 1967 Abortion Act. However once again others on his side disagreed. For example Sir Bernard Braine, and to a lesser extent Jill Knight and Michael Ancram, believed the most important clause in the Bill was clause 4 dealing with the charities.

These disagreements between the Bill's sponsors were obvious particularly when the Committee was discussing clauses 1 and 4. During the summer Benyon had redrafted clause 1. Although he had left the time limit at 20 weeks he had altered the rest of the clause making it less restrictive by omitting the word 'serious' which qualified the degree of 'risk' of continuing a pregnancy. However, the more hard-line supporters of Corrie, such as Dunn and Ancram, tabled an amendment to Benyon's amendment putting the work 'serious' back into the Bill.[1] The split on this side of the Committee became apparent on the vote on this amendment which ended in a draw, six for and six against. Benyon voted with the pro-abortion MPs, and Corrie and Pollock abstained. In contrast Ancram, Braine, Dunn, Bendall, Cohen and White all voted for 'serious'. Vaughan and Rathbone, as always, abstained. To settle the matter the chairman cast his vote in favour of 'serious', which he pointed out was in keeping with the Bill as it was agreed on Second Reading.[2]

The second overt disagreement in the Committee arose over the clause dealing with the charities. The splits here were far more difficult to deal with and took some time to settle. In fact Corrie was in the middle of redrafting this clause when it was reached in Committee and as it was not ready the Committee had to stop sitting for a week. Furthermore Corrie was in a certain amount of difficulty over this clause as the Department opposed it perhaps more than any other of the clauses in the Bill. The DHSS has always resisted any form of statutory controls over the private sector, preferring to use its very wide ranging administrative controls which, it argues, are far more effective than any statutory controls it might be given. Therefore, although Corrie was looking to the Department for help in redrafting clause 4, there was reluctance to offer any such advice. Indeed the Department itself had tried to persuade the two main charities, BPAS and PAS, to prevent the need for this clause by breaking the financial links between their advisory bureaux and the nursing homes.[3]

The situation was made worse when Corrie fell ill with mumps. As there had been little or no co-ordination between him and his supporters, no one knew how he intended redrafting clause 4. Benyon alone shared Corrie's view that this clause should be changed, so he redrafted it with the help of his own draftsmen. Benyon's redraft still sought to break the financial link between the bureaux and nursing homes but tried to meet Vaughan's criticism and reduce the administrative burden on the Department. This meant that there were now two versions of clause 4, and no agreement among the Corrie supporters about which to accept; Braine and Knight preferred the original version and at first refused to accept any need to change it. Indeed so great was the confusion and disagreement on Corrie's side that at one stage an agreement was reached with the opposition not to make up a quorum at the next Committee sitting. This meant that the Committee could not sit and left Corrie's side to sort out their decision on the clause. Benyon's version was eventually accepted.

In the Benyon Committee the anti-abortion supporters had agreed priorities and decided which clauses to drop if time became short. On the Corrie Committee there was no such agreement largely because of the divisions which existed among the Bill's supporters. Thus when the Bill came out of Committee it was as broad in scope, and as radical, as when it went in. This had considerable repercussions for the Bill's future. In particular many MPs who had supported the Bill at Second Reading, believing that it would be substantially modified in Committee, felt anger and resentment at Corrie and his supporters who they thought were showing themselves to be uncompromising and incompetent. In addition, because no compromises had been made in Committee, and the Bill had not been reduced in scope, the opposition was left with plenty of opportunities to delay the Bill on Report.

A New Bill?

The Committee Stage was prolonged, particularly because of the uncertainties on clause 4, and in fact took up 17 sittings lasting for a total of 43 hours.[4] The Committee began by sitting for 2½ hours every Wednesday morning. However, the vote on clause 1 was only reached after 6 sittings and 15 hours of debate, and

Corrie expressed concern that if as much time was spent on the remaining clauses the Bill would not be ready by 8 February, the first day set aside for the Report Stage. Therefore he moved a sittings motion and the Committee was called upon to sit three mornings and three afternoons a week.[5] No time was specified for the end of the afternoon sittings so that, if necessary, the sitting could continue throughout the night. Corrie was prepared to reject this sittings motion if the opposition would agree to a timetable he had drawn up which would get the Bill out of Committee in time for its Report Stage. However no agreement was forthcoming and the sittings motion was approved.

The opponents of the Corrie Bill put down a total of 85 amendments, of which 35 were selected for debate by the chairman. However only one of these amendments, a minor amendment to clause 1, was accepted, and this only after advice from the Minister.[6] Thus the major redrafting of the Bill came not from the opposition, whose minority voting power meant they could not effect any votes, but from Corrie's own supporters.

In total: four new clauses were drafted and moved by Benyon, and accepted; five clauses were completely withdrawn; and two clauses in the original Bill, clauses 4 and 6, were voted down by supporters of the Bill themselves. By the time the Committee ended, every clause in the Bill, except the conscience clause, had either been redrafted, or dropped as they became included in new clauses. This did not mean that the four main principles were altered, but it did mean that the wording of clauses was substantially different.

Indeed the final state of the Bill was summed up accurately, if mischieviously, by Ian Mikardo in Committee:

> When it [the Bill] is finished it manifestly will not be anything like the Bill to which the House gave a Second Reading. Clause 1 has been redrafted in toto by Benyon. Clause 3 had disappeared. Clause 4, we are told, is to be redrafted in toto, and up to now the Hon. Member has no inkling of the form the redrafting will take. Clause 5 is to be redrafted in toto. Clause 6 must be redrafted in toto. Clause 7 has disappeared. Clause 8 had to be put in order by Hon. Members who oppose the Bill. Clause 9 had to be redrafted. Clause 10 has disappeared.[7]

Therefore when the Bill came back to the floor of the House of Commons for Report its main principles were intact, but it had been radically redrafted. This meant that the Bill was significantly different from that approved at Second Reading and the existence of such differences seems to have influenced the Speaker's choice of amendments at Report Stage. The Speaker appeared willing to call amendments already discussed in Committee, presumably because he felt that the whole House should have a chance to discuss thoroughly the details of this extensively redrafted Bill.

The Minister's Role during Committee

Although the Minister's official role during the Committee was to offer information he did in fact make recommendations on each of the major clauses. His words were always listened to attentively as most MPs on the Committee felt that his views would carry weight with many Conservative MPs at Report Stage. It is interesting therefore to look at how the minister acted in Committee.

Overall his attitude was very ambiguous. On the time limit he repeatedly assured the Committee that there was no evidence of a foetus surviving below 24 weeks.[8] He therefore advised the Committee to accept 24 weeks, which he said, was preferred by the overwhelming majority of the medical profession. However later, just before the Committee voted on the time-limit clause, he produced a letter which had considerable impact and which advocated 22 weeks. In fact Dr Vaughan had written to all the neonatal centres in the country asking them to comment on the time-limit clause in the Bill in the light of their experience. One of the replies he received was from Prof. Reynolds of University College Medical School, the main centre in the country dealing with very young infants. The crucial section of this letter, which Dr Vaughan released to the Committee, read:

> We occasionally admit babies born at 23 weeks gestation, and while none has yet survived, it is inevitable that one will sooner or later. Infants born at 23 weeks are, incidentally, sometimes very much alive at birth whatever you may hear to the contrary!

The letter concluded: 'I suggest that 22 weeks rather than 24 weeks be the gestational age proposed in the amendment.'[9] This letter hit the Committee like a bombshell, elating Corrie and his supporters and surprising the opposition. The Corrie supporters believed it represented a change of mind on Vaughan's part while their opponents feared it did.

In fact when the Bill left Committee no one was really sure of Dr Vaughan's views on the time limit or on the grounds clause. Vaughan obviously saw his role as providing advice and evidence to the Committee and tried to remain as neutral as possible. However this neutrality appeared to many on both sides to be a reflection of indecision, and as such, in trying to please both sides, the Minister ended up pleasing neither.

Parliamentary Lobbying

At this stage the parliamentary supporters and opponents of the Bill began to organize their whipping systems. Obviously whipping on private members' business never reaches the level of sophistication achieved by the parties on government business. However the whipping on abortion is much more sophisticated than on any other private members' issue.

Pro-abortion MPs

On this occasion Oonagh McDonald became chief whip of the pro-abortion MPs. She nominated a further nine whips who covered the various regions of the country.[10] This whipping system however only applied to Labour MPs. The lobbying of the Conservative side was conducted from outside the House by Sharon Spiers of Tories for Free Choice, although just before Report Stage one Conservative MP, Bowen Wells, did begin to lobby his colleagues.

At this stage the whips had lists of the voting on the Second Reading debate together with the voting records of those MPs who had previously voted on the issue. The whips approached all Labour MPs who were not known to be implacably opposed to abortion telling them about the progress of the Bill in Committee and asking them if they intended to attend the Report Stage debate and, if so, how they intended to vote. As we have previously mentioned the whips were helped by the fact that they could use PLP meetings as a means of keeping MPs informed of the progress of the Committee and the likely details of the Report Stage. Indeed a large number of Labour MPs we talked to commented on the efficiency of the whipping system.

Anti-abortion MPs

The anti-abortion lobby nominated 15 whips who were each given a list of 20 MPs to lobby.[11] The activities of these whips were similar to those of their opponents although they were drawn from all three political parties. They worked from the Second Reading voting records approaching all MPs not known to be strongly against the Bill and asking them for details of their intentions. However they had two disadvantages as compared to their counterparts. First, they had no equivalent forum to that provided for the other side in the PLP meetings. Secondly, because there were important splits on tactics and views among the sponsors of the Bill, the whipping was not always as conscientious or co-ordinated as it might have been. A number of anti-abortion MPs suggested that the whipping system was less effective than its counterpart on the pro-abortion side.

Extra-parliamentary Lobbying: Pro-abortion

The Labour Movement

The Labour Movement soon made clear its opposition to the Corrie Bill. At the TUC Conference on 4 July, the Labour Women's Annual Conference in June and the Labour Party Conference in September, strong resolutions attacking the Bill, and calling on all members to resist it, were passed with overwhelming majorities.

However the most significant event in which the Labour movement took the lead was the TUC National Demonstration against the Corrie Bill which was held on 28 October 1979. It is estimated that between 30,000 and 40,000 people marched through London with representatives of 24 trade unions being joined by Labour Party organizations and the pro-abortion interest groups.[12] The march achieved considerable publicity and obviously confirmed the growth of support in the country for the 1967 Abortion Act.

At the same time a number of unions printed and distributed leaflets against the Bill, while the pressure groups within the Labour Party lobbied MPs constantly. LARC sent out three mailings to Labour Party constituencies. Similarly the Women's Advisory Committee mailed MPs throughout the Bill's progress and the National Council of Working Women's Organizations (affiliated to all trade unions) wrote to all sponsored MPs, as did a number of unions including NUPE and APEX. In addition the Women's Advisory Committee also mailed 1,200 Labour Party Women's organizations on a number of occasions.

The Medical Profession

The views of the medical profession were sought during the summer by the DHSS. By the time the Committee sat again it was clear that there was little support from medical organizations for the Bill. Most agreed that the upper time limit should be lowered to 24 weeks, although the BMA wanted no change, and there was some support from the nursing organizations for a widening of the conscience clause. However all the professional organizations were against restricting the grounds for abortion, and against splitting the links between the pregnancy advisory bureaux and the nursing homes. The overwhelming majority of comments to the DHSS supported the 1967 Act as providing a reasonable framework for an unhappily necessary service. Any restrictions would, most feared, lead to a resurgence of back-street abortions, something doctors throughout the country were relieved they no longer had to deal with, and which they never wanted to see return.

As well as this formal response to the DHSS enquiries, the BMA and RCOG launched a strong attack on the Bill in the press. Indeed as early as 30 July the RCOG stated that the Bill would increase the difficulties facing doctors.[13] However it was the BMA which led the medical profession's attack against the Bill, telling the press that the Bill 'is not just putting the clock back to immediately before the 1967 Act, it is going back much further'.[14] The detailed evidence submitted by the BMA to the DHSS was published in *The General Practitioner* where it was reported as a 'swingeing and detailed attack on the main clauses of the Bill'.[15] This evidence was also sent by the BMA to all MPs on the Standing Committee.

In addition Josephine Barnes (then president of the BMA) spoke out on several occasions against the Bill and in October at an inaugural meeting of the York Medical Society's lecture season defended the 1967 Act which she said had 'abolished the terrible catastrophies that happened in back-street abortions'.[16] In fact, the BMA continued throughout the Bill's progress to lobby strongly against it and was one of the most powerful and effective of the pressure groups on the pro-abortion side.

At the same time, the doctors' organizations within the pro-abortion lobby, Doctors in Defence of the 1967 Act, the Doctors and Overpopulation Group and Doctors for a Woman's Right to Choose, were also very active. In particular speakers from these organizations appeared on many platforms and they were responsible for organizing a write-in campaign by their members to both MPs and the newspapers. Overall there can be little doubt that members of the medical profession were more hostile to this Bill than to previous bills largely because they saw it as a particularly radical reform which stood a good chance of becoming law.

Other Pressure Groups

The main pro-abortion activity at the local level was generated by NAC. They believed that the best way to campaign against the Bill was to set up a mobilizing committee which would have one aim: to defeat the Bill. In addition such an organization would attract supporters who might feel unable to agree with NAC's advocacy of abortion up to term. For this reason the Campaign Against Corrie (CAC) was formed after the Second Reading of the Corrie Bill. Within the first few months 60 CAC groups were formed. In fact NAC provided the central administration of CAC but the local groups were autonomous. CAC employed one full-time office worker and co-ordinating meetings were held once a week. The first of these meetings decided to establish a specialist committee within CAC to deal with publicity and this was particularly successful. Women journalists and other representatives from the media met regularly to produce leaflets, write press releases and generally organize publicity. As a result CAC produced 12 separate leaflets on the Corrie Bill each of which had a distribution of 15,000. In addition CAC made and distributed a short film to the independent and alternative cinemas giving information about the Bill and what people could do to campaign against it.

During this period a number of independent groups were also formed under titles like 'Women's Voice', 'Women's Aid' or 'Women's Action Group' to fight the Corrie Bill. The growth of these local campaigns was dramatic. Remarkably, perhaps for the first time during any campaign on abortion the pro-abortion groups outnumbered the anti-abortion groups. By the time the Standing Committee sat again on 24 October, the main provincial newspapers had carried news of the activities of 20 anti-abortion groups and 73 pro-abortion groups.[17] In the same newspapers there had been 43 anti-abortion letters and 65 pro-abortion ones. The pattern had changed somewhat at the end of the Committee Stage, by which time these newspapers had published 160 anti-abortion letters and 139 pro-abortion letters — although even then the activities of 129 pro-abortion groups and only 80 anti-abortion groups had been reported. Of course this does not necessarily mean that there were more supporters of pro-abortion groups than supporters of anti-abortion groups or that they were better organized. However it does indicate that the two sides were more evenly balanced in the constituencies on this occasion than ever before.

During the summer Co-ord also began to organize a campaign against the Bill. Member-organizations were delegated specific tasks according to their field of interest: CFFC sent out letters putting a Christian point of view in favour of the 1967 Act and monitored the religious press; the doctors' groups monitored the medical press; and other member-organizations performed the same function in their particular area. In the Co-ord office, briefs were prepared for the Committee Stage and information was continually sent out to member-organizations. In addition a pamphlet explaining the Bill and its contents was written and widely distributed so that all MPs received a copy before the Committee sat again. At the same time a campaigning pamphlet which listed the way MPs had voted on the Second Reading of the Bill was published by ALRA. This was launched at a press conference just before the Committee Stage began, and again was widely distributed during the winter.

Extra-parliamentary Lobbying: Anti-abortion

The Church

The help provided to the supporters of the 1967 Act by the TUC and Labour Party was matched on the other side by the efforts of the Roman Catholic Church. Indeed on 24 October 1979 a rare joint statement from Cardinal Hume of Westminster and Cardinal Gray of St Andrews, Edinburgh was issued which clearly supported the Corrie Bill. It claimed: 'We believe that, because abortion is against the law of God, individuals have an overriding duty to obey that law in all circumstances.'[18] Up and down the country support was given to the Bill by churches whose clergy urged their congregations to write to their MPs asking them to support the Bill. In addition petitions were placed in churches[19] and letters and articles published in parish magazines.[20]

SPUC and LIFE

SPUC and LIFE, like the pro-abortion campaigners, distributed to their members details of the MPs' voting on Second Reading. In addition LIFE published a booklet on the Bill's contents which had a very wide circulation. Members of SPUC and LIFE also took part in a counter march to the TUC demonstration on 28 October. Some 3,000 people marched to Downing Street and a wreath commemorating the 1.4 million unborn children legally aborted since 1967 was handed in to the Prime Minister. Similar wreaths were also presented to TUC headquarters and the DHSS's head office. The march was led by Lord Longford, a Labour Peer, who was flanked by nurses carrying wreaths, and accompanied by Prof. Jack Scarisbrick, chairman of LIFE, and Phillip Norris, president of the British section of Doctors Who Respect Human Life.

During this period SPUC and LIFE concentrated on

encouraging their members to write to their MPs and lobby them in the constituencies. In this they were successful as all but two of the MPs we interviewed reported receiving more letters from supporters of the Corrie Bill than from its opponents.[21] However there was a distinct change in the relative numbers of letters from both sides on the Corrie Bill as compared with previous occasions. All the MPs we talked to who had been in the previous Parliament (1974-9) reported that the balance between the letters from the two sides was more even on the Corrie Bill than previously. In addition most of the MPs noticed that the number of letters from opponents of the Corrie Bill increased during the Committee Stage. The point here is that while the anti-abortion groups are better organized in the constituencies they were much more successfully challenged on the Corrie Bill because of the activities of NAC and CAC.

The Media

During October and November the Bill was widely publicized in the medical journals and women's magazines. All the medical journals carried editorials opposing the main contents of the Bill, with the exception of lowering the time limit, which they thought should be put at 24 weeks. This view taken by the medical press is consistent with the view they have held on previous amending bills, but it was perhaps expressed more vociferously during Corrie than on other bills.

The majority of the national daily papers continued to oppose the bill. Initially only the *Daily Telegraph*[22] and *Sunday Telegraph*[23] carried articles giving support to the Bill and attacking the TUC support for the abortion law. However both *The Times*[24] and *Daily Mail*[25] carried articles and editorials in favour of the Bill. Again this is fairly consistent with views taken by the national press on previous bills. The provincial press reflected the growth of the pro-abortion groups and the majority of their editorials that we have been able to trace were against the Bill.

The major change in the media came from the women's magazines. During Benyon's Bill only *Women's World* and *'19'* magazine[26] carried articles against the Bill. But during Corrie's

Bill a whole range of women's magazines strongly attacked it. These included *Cosmopolitan, Company, Girl About Town, Woman's Own, Spare Rib, Good Housekeeping* and *'19'*.[27] This was a totally new phenomenon and to some extent reflected the growth of feminism in the country. The more radical journals, such as *Spare Rib,* had always opposed restrictive abortion bills and kept their readers informed of events. But the growth alongside the feminist movement of magazines such as *Cosmopolitan* and *Company* which do not invariably portray women in traditional roles provided a new outlet for issues which affect women. Some of these magazines published articles giving both sides of the argument (such as *Girl About Town*) but always came down on the side of the opposition to Corrie's Bill and often called upon readers to write to their MPs.

Most surprising was the strong attack on the Bill which came from *Woman's Own,* a magazine not known for its radical views and with a largely conservative readership. Articles were written by Claire Rayner, Dr Michael Smith (Hon. Medical Officer of the Family Planning Association) and Angela Willans, while Corrie was given the right of reply. The effect of these articles was dramatic, coming as they did from such a 'respectable' magazine. Jane Reed, then the magazine's editor, told us that the issue was talked about by the staff for some time, and that the majority of the staff thought the Bill posed a major threat to the lives and health of women. It was therefore decided to go ahead with the articles and with an opinion poll which was conducted by Gallup and published just before the Report Stage. She emphasized that 'the time was right' to take a public stand on the issue.

The women's magazines carried the pro-abortion lobby's message far more widely than ever before, and not just to the more radical women. The anti-abortion groups lacked this kind of publicity, and as previously explained, they did not find much support amongst the national daily papers.

The End of the Committee Stage

With the Committee Stage of the Bill over, both sides lined up for the crucial battle when the Bill returned to the House for its Report Stage.[28] As we have shown in this chapter the anti-abortion lobby had been unable to agree on any common strategy for the next stage of the Bill. The pro-abortion lobby, on the other hand, had planned carefully from the very beginning of the Committee for the Report Stage, which they knew would be crucial. They had campaigned hard both in Parliament and in the country and organized themselves into a very effective opposition. The next chapter will show how their strategy paid off, and led to the downfall of the Bill.

Notes

1. Tabled on 24 October 1979 (second sitting), col. 54.
2. 21 November 1979 (sixth sitting), col. 281.
3. Personal interview with Helene Grahame of PAS, 5 September 1980 and with Diane Munday of BPAS, 29 August 1980.
4. The 17 sittings were held on the following days in 1979:

25 July	4 December (afternoon)
24 October	5 December (morning)
31 October	5 December (afternoon)
7 November	12 December (morning)
14 November	12 December (afternoon)
21 November	13 December (morning)
28 November	13 December (afternoon — no quorum)
4 December (morning)	18 December (morning)
	18 December (afternoon)

5. Moved on 28 November 1979 (seventh sitting), col. 295.
6. 7 November 1979 (fourth sitting), col. 177.
7. 5 December 1979 (eleventh sitting), cols. 485-8.
8. 24 October 1979 (second sitting), col. 88; 31 October 1979 (third sitting), col. 117; 7 November 1979 (fourth sitting), col. 173.
9. 21 November 1979 (sixth sitting), col. 272.
10. The nine whips were: Jeff Rooker (West Midlands); Philip Whitehead (East Midlands); Andrew Bennett (North West); Joe Dean (Yorkshire); Alan Roberts (North West Merseyside); Ioan Davies (Wales); Giles Radice (Northern); Robin Cook, Maurice Miller and Martin O'Neil (Scottish Region); Frank Dobson (Eastern, Southern and Western).
11. John Corrie was unable to supply us with a list of these whips.
12. At the outset of the march there was some dispute between the TUC and a group of feminists who felt that women should lead the march. Ultimately the women unofficially headed the march. This dispute was the focus of much of the coverage by the media.

13. *Sunday Mirror,* 29 July 1979.
14. *British Medical Journal,* 3 November 1979.
15. *The General Practitioner,* 5 October 1979.
16. *Yorkshire Evening Post,* 11 October 1979.
17. These figures are based on the cuttings from the local press supplied to Co-ord by the press clipping bureau, Romeike & Curtice. The news agency has instructions to forward all mentions of abortions and related matters in local newspapers.
18. *Daily Telegraph,* 25 October 1979.
19. For instance a petition was placed in Ogle Street, London W1, and three churches in Langley Park, Durham (the latter was reported in the *Durham Advertiser,* 25 January 1980).
20. See *Camden Journal,* 13 July 1979; *Finchley Press,* 25 January 1980; *Enfield Gazette* and *Observer,* 7 February 1980; *Western Morning News,* 7 February 1980; *Lincoln, Rutland and Stamford Mercury,* 8 February 1979.
21. Both these MPs were strong supporters of a liberal abortion policy.
22. *Daily Telegraph,* 14 July 1979 and 6 November 1979.
23. *Sunday Telegraph,* 4 November 1979.
24. *Times,* 6 February 1980 and 7 February 1980.
25. *Daily Mail,* 8 February 1980.
26. *Womens World,* May 1977; *'19',* May 1977.
27. *Cosmopolitan,* September 1979; *Company,* November 1979; *Girl About Town,* 5 November 1979; *Woman's Own,* 10 November 1979; *Spare Rib,* published articles and news throughout the Bill's progress; *Good Housekeeping,* March 1980; *'19',* March 1980.
28. A copy of the Bill as amended in the Standing Committee is included as Appendix 3.

5
Report Stage — the Final Battle

The Report Stage of the Corrie Bill took up an unprecedented four complete Fridays. This amount of time is unique for private members' legislation and one might have thought it would have ensured the Bill's success. This was not the case, however, and after four days debate, with half its clauses withdrawn by Corrie, the Bill ran out of time. In addition neither of the two main clauses which had been debated when the Bill was withdrawn was passed by the House of Commons in the form in which it had been approved at Second Reading, or in the form in which it had been reported back by Committee. Why did the Bill have so much time available? Why, given this time, did it still fail to complete its Report Stage? Why did the MPs vote against elements in the Bill which they approved by such a large majority at Second Reading? This chapter together with the following one will try to answer these questions.

The chapter is divided into three sections. The first section looks briefly at why the Bill had so much time. The second section examines the strategy and the tactics of the lobbies both inside and outside Parliament. The final section looks in some detail at the debates and votes on the four days of the Report Stage. This provides the essential background against which the next chapter analyses both the reasons for the failure of the Corrie Bill, and the future of the abortion issue in Parliament.

The Time Factor

There are several reasons why the Bill managed to gain four days on Report. First, as it was the first of the private members' bills it went into and came out of Committee first. This meant that until the second private member's bill, Neil Carmichael's Seat Belts Bill, had completed its Committee Stage, Corrie could have each available Friday for his Bill. The only way such a situation can be avoided is if the government makes available a second committee room to allow other Bills to progress more quickly. This is in fact what happened with David Steel's Bill.

The government had set aside six days for Report and Third Reading of private members' bills. Corrie was assured of the first two available Fridays, 8 and 15 February, because it was unlikely that Carmichael's Bill would be out of Committee that soon. There was no evidence of any filibustering in this Committee by anti-abortion MPs, and the Seat Belts Bill came back for its first day on Report on 22 February. However, because the Seat Belts Bill itself was strongly opposed it did not complete its final stages on that day, and therefore it also took the fifth Friday available, 7 March. Even so the Seat Belts Bill never reached the statute book as it was filibustered and much of it had not even been discussed when its second day on Report was completed. All this meant that the Corrie Bill got a third day on Report on 29 February.[1]

The further day was made available when Robert Taylor (Conservative Member for Croydon North-west) withdrew his Bill (Affiliations Orders Aliments Annual Uprating Bill) before its Report Stage. Taylor, a strong supporter of the Corrie Bill, was approached by anti-abortion MPs and received a large postbag asking him to withdraw his Bill. However, he did not withdraw for those reasons but because Lord Hailsham, the Lord Chancellor, informed him that because the government opposed his Bill they would ensure that it would be defeated in the House of Lords either by putting a whip on Conservative peers to oppose it, or by organizing a filibuster of the Bill.[2] Taylor was therefore faced with the choice of continuing with the Bill and seeing it defeated in the Lords or allowing the whole matter to be referred to the Law Commission. He decided to withdraw the Bill, a course which had at least the advantage that the Corrie Bill, which he supported, would then have an extra day as no other bill had come out of Committee by that time.

The Strategy and Tactics of the Lobbies

At this stage of the Bill most of the work had to be done by the MPs in the House and both sides stepped up the lobbying of their colleagues. Although it makes the pressure groups outside Parliament feel frustrated there is little they can do to influence events once the Bill reaches a Report Stage. In the later stages of a bill the initiative lies almost entirely in the hands of the MPs.

The Pro-abortion Lobby – Inside Parliament

At the Report Stage the tactics of those opposing Corrie were very different from those employed in the Committee. Unlike the Committee Stage, time at the Report Stage is limited. The major aim of the pro-abortion lobby was, therefore, to prevent the Bill completing its Report Stage by delaying it. However, anxious not to be accused of filibustering, the lobby organized numerous speakers who were willing to make short but frequent speeches; indeed the longest any MP spoke for on this side was half an hour. The pro-abortion lobby was also fortunate in that it was able to call upon several Members of the Shadow Cabinet and former Ministers of Health and Law Officers to speak on clauses. Obviously it was hoped that speeches coming from Members who had been intimately involved with the working of the law would sway any Labour waverers. In fact a total of 24 MPs spoke against the Bill (seventeen Labour, six Conservative and one Liberal). Six of these spoke from, or had been on, the Labour frontbenches, while the Liberal was David Steel, leader of the Liberal Party.

As we have already noticed, one of the major tactics of the pro-abortion lobby was to keep back substantial amendments and new clauses for Report. No fewer than 80 amendments were tabled for consideration at the Report Stage, in the hope that the Speaker would have no choice but to select a number of these amendments and that considerable time would be taken up in debating them. This tactic was extremely successful. On the first day of the Report Stage the Speaker selected over 50 amendments, which were put into 28 separate groupings (amendments dealing with the same sections of a bill are grouped together). This meant that there had to be a debate and vote on each of these 28 groups, a fact which ensured extensive debate.

Indeed as soon as Ian Mikardo saw the Speaker's selection of amendments for that first day he was confident for the first time the Bill was doomed.[3] The only way that it could be saved was if its supporters realized the implications of the Speaker's selection and dropped large parts of the Bill straight away. They did not do this.

Actually the pro-abortion lobby was well aware that the Bill's sponsors might at some stage withdraw clauses and for that reason used the ingenious tactic of ensuring that a pro-abortion MP attached his name to any amendments put down by Corrie or his supporters. This meant that even if the anti-abortion lobby wished to withdraw an amendment they could not do so unilaterally. This tactic proved important on the third day's debate on Report when, although the sponsors wished to withdraw the second half of their Bill, that section had to be considered and voted upon, because certain pro-abortion MPs had their names associated with those clauses. This tactic used up considerable time.

The preparations of the pro-abortion whips for the Report Stage debates were thorough. Oonagh McDonald as chief whip issued letters to all pro-abortion Labour MPs before each debate informing them of the Bill's progress and calling upon them to be present at each debate. When voting got complicated, and timing was crucial, on the fourth and last day on Report, suggestions on how to vote on each clause were sent out. In addition Parliamentary Labour Party meetings continued to be used regularly to lobby MPs, and the individual Labour whips approached all MPs and produced a list of who would attend on each day and how they would vote.

Lobbying on the Conservative side inside Parliament improved greatly at this stage when Bowen Wells took on the job. Up to this time the lobbying of Conservative MPs on the Corrie Bill had been carried out by Tories for Free Choice. MPs, however, are always likely to respond more openly to fellow MPs rather than to external pressure groups, so the efforts of Bowen Wells were important. It is clear, however, that a major weakness in the pro-abortion parliamentary lobby was that it was composed exclusively of Labour MPs. The lobbying on this side overall proved highly effective. A large number of MPs attended each day's debate. But more important, they used the parliamentary procedure available to them extremely intelligently. This superior knowledge and use of procedure was acknowledged by the anti-abortion MPs as one of the major reasons for the Bill's failure. But, it must be said again, they were helped considerably by the fact that they were fighting a defensive campaign, a much easier task than fighting to change legislation.

The Pro-abortion Lobby – Outside Parliament

By the time the Report Stage was reached the Co-ord parliamentary group had had meetings with the five MPs who opposed the Bill during Committee and agreed upon the amendments to be tabled. In addition several new clauses were drafted, and briefs were prepared and distributed to approximately 100 MPs. The Co-ord group discontinued its weekly meetings after the first day on Report but individual members of the group kept in close contact with the MPs, and two sat under the public gallery of the House of Commons throughout the Bill's Report Stage, so that MPs could seek advice whenever it was needed. Several organizations within Co-ord wrote individually to all MPs calling upon them to be present during the Report Stage and most urged MPs to vote against the Bill. These included BCC, LARC, DWCA and ALRA. Co-ord itself wrote to all MPs and to the Prime Minister and Norman St John-Stevas, calling upon them not to provide any extra time for the Bill.

The pressure groups within the Labour movement also stepped up their activity. In January an invitation to a meeting was sent to Labour MPs from NJCWWO, LWAC and LARC. Speakers at the meeting included Marie Patterson (TGWU), Bill Birtles (barrister and in the Co-ord team of advisers) and David Paintin (consultant obstetrician at St Mary's Hospital). The NJCWWO and LWAC also mailed MPs before each day's debate and Joyce Gould, secretary of both these organizations, sat under the public gallery, in order to keep an eye on Labour MPs. Some members looked genuinely worried at the sight of her closely watching events as they knew that she would soon question them if they did not vote according to Labour Party policy — as passed at Conference. In fact she was a continual reminder to Labour MPs that abortion was party policy, and this may have gone some way to sway waverers.

The activity on this side of the lobby culminated in a number of demonstrations. On 4 February the National Union of Students called for a week of action against the Bill, while on the weekend before the first day on Report NAC organized activity in the north which was sponsored by the Northern Regional TUC. In London the biggest rally against the Bill took place on 5 February. It was organized by CAC and sponsored by the South-east Regional TUC. It drew the support of 15,000-20,000 people who heard speeches from David Steel, Tony Benn and Jo Richardson as well as Dr John Marks and Dr Frank Wells of the BMA. Approximately 7,000 people lobbied their MPs that day, and if they did not see their MP they were provided with pen and paper by ALRA, who organized this side of the event, so that they could hand in a letter.

The Medical Profession

The views of the BMA were perhaps the most influential of all among the pro-abortion pressure groups. Their condemnation of the Bill now attracted considerable publicity. The most direct attack on the Bill came from 70 leading doctors, surgeons and professors of obstetrics and gynaecology. In a letter to *The Lancet* on 1 February, seven days before the first day on Report, they launched into a fierce attack on the Bill which they regarded as 'a most swingeing attack [on the 1967 Act] which would, according to one of its supporters, cut abortions by two thirds and destroy the charities'. It would, they went on, result in a return to the 'scourge' of septic abortion, which had been greatly reduced by the 1967 Act. The signatories included Sir George Godber, former chief medical officer at the DHSS, Sir Richard Doll, Professor of Medicine at Oxford University, Dame Josephine Barnes, president of the BMA, and the presidents of all but one of the Royal Colleges of Medicine.[4]

This devastating attack on the Bill probably had considerable influence on the voting of MPs at Report Stage. It was referred to again and again during the debates and was used by Dr Vaughan as a justification for his recommendations on the time-limit and grounds clause. What is more, many of the MPs we spoke to listed it as one of the reasons for the Bill's failure.

The Anti-abortion Lobby – Inside Parliament

The main tactic of those supporting Corrie was to speak as little as possible during the Report Stage in order to get the Bill completed as quickly as possible. Only eight MPs spoke for the Bill during this stage, five Conservatives, two Labour and one Official Ulster Unionist. The urge to promote the Bill at times overwhelmed particular MPs, notably Sir Bernard Braine, who on one occasion spoke for half an hour and on another for a quarter of an hour. On the whole, however, they kept a very low profile.

Nevertheless, members of the anti-abortion camp made a major mistake in not withdrawing part of their Bill at an early stage. Although they withdrew half of the Bill before the third day of the Report Stage, by then it was too late. If the Bill's sponsors had taken such action before the Report Stage, or even after the first day's debate, then it is almost certain that part of the Bill would have obtained a Third Reading. Why didn't they do so? The reason is simple. There was no agreement among the sponsors of the Bill or between them and the extra-parliamentary lobby about the need for, or the basis of, such a compromise.

As we saw in the last chapter the sponsors of the Bill disagreed about their priorities. In particular Bernard Braine, Jill Knight and Michael Ancram were reluctant to drop clause 4 which dealt with the charities. In addition the extra-parliamentary lobby was consistently urging Corrie and his fellow sponsors not to compromise or drop any of the Bill. In fact during the passage of the bill Corrie received 8,000 letters from SPUC and LIFE members to this effect.[5] This indicates just how difficult it is for the promoter of a private member's bill on an issue like abortion. If he attempts too much he cannot succeed because of procedural constraints, if he is more realistic he cannot guarantee the support of his fellow sponsors, or the extra-parliamentary lobby. Corrie was caught in a cleft stick and with hindsight was probably too indecisive in his response. At any rate there can be no doubt that this inability to accept compromises which resulted from the splits within the Corrie side, at the right time, was a major factor leading to the Bill's failure.

At the same time the whipping by Corrie and his supporters was not as effective as the pro-abortion lobby's whipping. Although they sent out letters before each day's debate, on the final day they were seriously caught out. Like their opponents they did not know until the last minute that Taylor was going to drop his Bill and make way for Corrie's Bill to be debated for a fourth day. However, unlike the pro-abortion lobby they assumed that there would not be another day's debate and thus did not send out any whips urging MPs to be present on that day. When they did learn Taylor was dropping his Bill they had only one day in which to rally support, and in some cases they were too late as MPs had made other engagements. This was a major tactical blunder. The pro-abortion lobbyists had whipped their MPs and therefore won several crucial votes on the last day, notably the vote on the closure motion during discussions of the Silkin amendment.

In addition the anti-abortion MPs' whipping system was undermined by the dissension that existed among the whips. The whips did not always agree on tactics or even on how their MPs should vote on all amendments. The most notable example of this dissent occurred before voting on the amendment to include 'serious' in the grounds clause when William Benyon, one of the main whips, told a large number of MPs that it did not matter if they voted on that amendment. Such lack of unity was reflected in the fact that their whipping was less detailed and thorough than that of the pro-abortion lobby.

The Anti-abortion Lobby – Outside Parliament

The activity on this side of the campaign culminated in a national demonstration and mass lobby of the House of Commons organized by SPUC on 29 January. Coaches and buses arrived from all over the country bringing 15,000-18,000 people, in one of the largest mass lobbies in the history of the House of Commons. The demonstrators lobbied their MPs throughout the day and the scenes in the Central Lobby were unprecedented. In the nearby Methodist Central Hall they were addressed by John Corrie who told them, rather surprisingly in the light of some of his other statements, that his Bill did not go far enough to amend the abortion law, but went as far as possible at the present time.[6] Other speakers included Cyril Smith (Lib. Rochdale), James Hamilton (Lab. Bothwell), Sir Bernard Braine (Con. Essex, South-east), Michael Ancram (Con. Edinburgh, South) Mrs Elaine

Kellett-Bowman (Con. Lancaster), and Alan Beith (Lib. Berwick-upon-Tweed).

SPUC and LIFE were primarily involved in the period leading up to the Report Stage debates in organizing this mass lobby. At the same time they continued to encourage their members to write to MPs. LIFE in particular requested its members to write to Corrie and other sponsors of the Bill urging them not to withdraw any of it nor to compromise with its opponents.

The Churches

The Roman Catholic Church now threw all its weight behind the Bill. On 21 January it was reported in the *Guardian* that the Church Union, the largest organized body of opinion in the Church of England, had posted 10,000 individual letters to Anglican priests and churchmen throughout England. All were urged to support the mass lobby of Parliament organized by SPUC. Two days later there was an unprecedented display of unity when seven Roman Catholic archbishops, representing England, Wales and Scotland, issued a joint statement in the name of 48 bishops.[7] This statement was part of a 4,500-word document in which the bishops set out the case for human rights against abortion, which they referred to as a 'massive and growing trivialisation of human life by the community'.[8]

Catholic priests were not alone in their support of the Corrie Bill although there were certainly more divisions within the Church of England. Indeed in response to the Roman Catholic statement the executive committee of the Board of Social Responsibility of the Church of England explained that, while they had no authority to speak for the Church as a whole, they believed that abortion could only be justified when a woman's life or health was seriously threatened.[9] In addition five Scottish church leaders representing four denominations travelled down for the SPUC demonstration in an interdenominational delegation.[10] As Bishop Contin, Roman Catholic Bishop of Aberdeen commented: 'It is the first time we have come together on an issue. I think it is fair to say that it is unique.'[11]

It is clear then that the Roman Catholic Church campaigned strongly for the Corrie Bill and that many clergy from other churches were also strong advocates of legislation to amend the

1967 Act. However there was some criticism of the role of the churches in the campaign from within the Church of England. Indeed a letter in *The Times* from the Bishop of Durham informed readers that not all Christians were deeply involved 'in the vigorous campaign in favour of Mr. Corrie's Bill. I believe it ought to be said publicly that this campaign does not represent the only Christian view on the matter.' He went on to refer to an 'element of emotional blackmail in language which refers to the murder of thousands of babies...' and called for a 'code of practice' between doctors to deal with any 'proven abuses', rather than further legislation.[12]

The Medical Profession

The major medical organizations no longer supported moves to amend the 1967 Abortion Act. As such the anti-abortion lobby found it difficult to mobilize support within the profession, particularly among doctors. After the letter from 70 senior doctors and consultants attacking the Corrie Bill appeared in *The Lancet,* for example, the only response was a letter to *The Times* from six doctors and consultants supporting the Bill.[13]

The Media and the Public Opinion Polls

The Report Stage of the Bill was exceptional in the amount of publicity it created. All the medical journals, national daily papers and Sunday papers carried editorials on the Bill. The great majority condemned the Bill, although they did support the lowering of the upper time limit to 24 weeks. The only exceptions were *The Times* which, under the headline 'A Moderate Bill' wrote that the Bill 'deserves success',[14] and the *Daily Mail* which felt that Steel's Act had gone too far in practice, and that 'Parliament now has the chance for second thoughts, MPs should not fumble that opportunity.'[15]

In addition to the extensive coverage the issue was receiving in the press, television now took up the debate. On Sunday, 31 January 'Credo' a religious affairs programme on London Weekend Television looked at the pressure groups on both sides of the campaign. Similarly on 9 February 'Panorama' reported on the activities of the interest groups in the run up to the debate. In each case, the programmes attempted to present a balanced picture of the debate rather than to influence opinion.

In the week before the first day of the Report Stage two more opinion polls were released. The first, conducted by Gallup on behalf of *Woman's Own*, was the more interesting and influential.[16] It found that nearly two-thirds (65 per cent) of men and women in the 25-34 age group, felt that abortions should not be made more difficult to obtain, whilst 81 per cent of women questioned felt that the choice as to whether to continue with a pregnancy should be left to the woman in consultation with her family doctor. More striking was the finding that 80 per cent of women said that if legal abortions were more difficult to obtain then women would seek other avenues to terminate an unwanted pregnancy. The poll also sought the opinions of Roman Catholics and found that more than half (57 per cent) agreed that abortion should be a matter of personal and medical choice while only 20 per cent disagreed entirely with abortion. In addition the poll also showed that Conservative supporters were as much in favour of maintaining the present abortion law as Labour supporters.

This poll was sent by *Woman's Own* to all MPs before the debate began on Report. It is difficult to judge its effect but Ian Mikardo listed it as one of the reasons the Corrie Bill eventually failed. He felt that the finding that 80 per cent of women would resort to other methods of abortion if denied easy legal abortions, was especially important, and brought home to MPs the real impact the Bill would have on the lives of women.[17]

The second poll, conducted by MORI for the *Sunday Times*, also found that the majority of the public was against Corrie's Bill.[18] The survey questioned 1,090 people over 15 years of age throughout Britain. They found that 54 per cent of those questioned agreed with the statement: 'Abortion should be made legally available for all who want it.' Rather surprisingly the survey also found that only 33 per cent of the public knew that a bill to restrict the abortion law was going through Parliament. This suggests that while some people are very concerned with the issue, the majority are uninvolved and know little about the subject.

The Debates and Votes on Report

The First Day of Report – 8 February

On the first day of the Report Stage it appeared that the pro-abortion lobby's tactics of keeping back amendments to use at the Report Stage had been successful. The Speaker's selection list was extremely long, covering over 50 amendments placed in 28 separate groups. However there may have been other reasons why the Speaker selected so many amendments. First, the Bill had been substantially redrafted in Committee and new clauses had been introduced which had not previously been debated on the Floor of the House. Although these amendments had not altered the four main principles of the Bill the Speaker may have thought the whole House should be given a chance to debate these substantially redrafted clauses. Secondly, the vote on inclusion of the word 'serious' had ended in a draw in Committee. Given such a close vote the Speaker obviously felt the House itself should debate and decide the issue. Lastly, the Speaker may have considered that because the Bill came out of Committee with considerable drafting problems the House should be given the opportunity of tidying it up. Whatever the justification the number of amendments selected by the Speaker proved to be one of the most crucial factors in the Bill's downfall. Indeed during the first day's debate only two clauses out of twenty-eight were fully discussed.

As with all abortion debates the speeches were highly emotional, interruptions were frequent and often abusive, and the House was unusually well-attended. When the House is considering private members' business, which mostly takes place on a Friday, there are rarely more than about 50 MPs present except when a vote is imminent. Indeed, many private members' bills fall because less than the statutory 100 MPs are present to vote on a closure to allow a vote on the Second Reading of a bill. During the Report Stage of the Corrie Bill, not only was the House at all times at least three-quarters full but the public gallery was packed and noisy. Trouble broke out on the first day when twelve women unfurled a banner which read 'Women will not obey your Bill', and shouted 'We want women's rights'. They were abruptly and unceremoniously thrown out by the attendants of whom there were an unusually large number. Obviously trouble had been expected.

David Ennals (Lab. Lewisham, East) moved the first amendment which was one of the new clauses drafted by Corrie's opponents.[19] It lowered the upper time limit to 24 weeks by altering the Infant Life (Preservation) Act 1929, and tried to clarify the meaning of the words in that Act, 'capable of being born alive', words which had earlier led to allegations that foetuses had been born alive. The new clause attempted to define more precisely the point at which a foetus may show signs of life but be incapable of sustaining independent life.

However, this new clause was defeated for a number of reasons. First, the DHSS, in a letter to Corrie that was read out by Willie Hamilton during the debate, advised that it was virtually impossible to redraft more precisely the section in the 1929 Act defining viability, and suggested the Act be left alone.[20] Secondly, David Steel pointed out that the new clause set the time limit at 24 weeks with no presumption of viability below that limit.[21] This would mean there would be no protection for a viable foetus under 24 weeks. It was for these reasons rather than because it included a 24-week upper limit that the new clause was voted down after 2½ hours' debate by 256 to 179 votes, a majority of 77.

Another new clause was then moved by Jo Richardson.[22] The first section of the clause provided for one doctor to perform an abortion if the woman was under six weeks pregnant, regardless of grounds. The aim was to allow very early abortions, by menstrual regulation, to be carried out quickly without the woman having to seek a second doctor's opinion. The second section included a provision whereby the doctor could not be prosecuted if his intention was to terminate a pregnancy but it turned out the woman was not pregnant. The aim of this part of the clause was to clarify the legal position on very early abortions by menstrual regulation, and relatively new abortifacient devices, such as IUDs and various post-coital pills. At present, under the 1967 Act, a doctor must know that a woman is pregnant before he can perform an abortion; however the above devices can act as abortifacients before it is known whether the woman is pregnant. The clause was withdrawn when two doctors, Dr Maurice Miller (Lab. East Kilbride)[23] and Dr Roger Thomas (Lab. Carmarthen),[24] pointed out that it might mean that an abortion could be carried out without a doctor being present.

The House then went on to debate three separate amendments to lower the upper time limit: to 27 weeks, moved by Jo Richardson; to 24 weeks, moved by Charles Morrison (Con. Devizes); and to 22 weeks, moved by Douglas Hogg (Con. Grantham) and supported by Leo Abse (Lab. Pontypool). After 40 minutes of debate the House adjourned for the day and no vote was taken.

After five hours of debate only one vote had been taken. Yet Corrie and his supporters remained determined that no compromises were necessary. With the probability of a further two days debate they felt optimistic about the Bill's chances of success. However at the same time there was constant pressure from both sides of the lobby, respectively urging the government to provide or to withhold any extra time.

The Second Day of Report – 15 February

The evening before the debate continued five Privy Councillors from all parties circulated a letter calling for opponents of Corrie to support a compromise and accept 24 weeks as the time limit. In return they called upon Corrie and his sponsors to withdraw the remainder of the Bill. They urged 'all sides to accept this as a proper and reasonable solution to what could become a protracted, perhaps unseemly, certainly bitter, conflict...'. It was signed by Rt Hon. Peter Bottomley (Con. Middlesbrough); Rt Hon. Edward du Cann (Con. Taunton); Rt Hon. Jo Grimond (Lib. Orkney and Shetland); Rt Hon. Fred Mulley (Lab. Sheffield Park); and Rt Hon. Sir Derek Walker-Smith (Lab. Hertfordshire East). However when the debate resumed that day it was clear that neither side was prepared to make any compromises.

The debate continued on the time limit. In one of the first debates of the day Corrie stated he was not prepared to compromise in the way suggested by the five Privy Councillors. However, he did acknowledge that 20 weeks might not be acceptable, and recommended that Members vote instead for an amendment lowering the time limit to 22 weeks.[25]

In fact Corrie's speech does not seem to have been as significant in influencing the vote on the time limit as two others made later. First, Nicholas Fairburn (Con. Kinross and W. Perthshire, and Solicitor General for Scotland) advised against imposing any time limit on Scotland which had never had any time limit, and suffered no ill effects from not having one.[26] More important, Dr Vaughan recommended a time limit of 24 weeks. In reaching this decision he pointed to all the difficulties a lower limit would impose, and told the House that the overwhelming advice from the medical profession was for 24 weeks.[27]

With such a strong recommendation for 24 weeks it was fairly predictable that the amendment for 24 weeks was carried by a majority of 103 (275 to 172). However, a surprisingly large number of MPs, in fact 120, voted for a time limit of 27 weeks. Since this was more or less a vote to leave the time limit where it stood it could be taken as an indication of the number of MPs who wished to see no change to the 1967 Act. However, 298 voted against 27 weeks which meant that it fell by a majority of 178.

The vote may also have been influenced by a number of other factors. First, Willie Hamilton put on record the facts concerning various allegations made in the course of the previous year claiming that foetuses had survived abortions. MPs should be aware, he said, that even if the time limit was lowered the anti-abortion groups would not cease to attack the 1967 Act. In a memorable phrase he went on, 'The opponents of the 1967 Act want to destroy it by salami tactics — slice by slice.'[28]

Secondly, Renée Short made an important, and unexpected, intervention during the debate. She told the House that she had received a note from Prof. Reynolds of University College Hospital, whose evidence had been used so widely to support a 22- or 20-week limit. Part of this note read: 'I would still gladly settle for 24 weeks, provided the rest of the Bill was thrown out.'[29]

The debate on the time limit took up nearly three hours. Eight separate speeches were made by those opposing Corrie, but apart from Corrie's short speech at the beginning of the day, no speeches were made in favour of the Bill. The debate then moved on to amendments to the grounds for abortion, but no vote was reached before the House adjourned. With a further 20 separate groups of amendments to debate it was clear that Corrie must make major concessions.

The compromise eventually came three days before the third

day of the Report Stage. In a statement issued to the opposition MPs and the press Corrie and his sponsors said they were now prepared to drop the conscience clause and the clause relating to the charities. In addition they would accept any 'reasonable amendments' to the exemptions to the upper time limit. However the pro-abortion lobby scented victory and saw no reason to compromise. Moreover Corrie found that he could not simply drop these clauses because MPs on the pro-abortion side had attached their names to all these amendments.

The Third Day of Report – 29 February

When the debate on the third day began several Members queried the way in which the Speaker had grouped the amendments to delete large sections of the Bill.[30] Essentially the Speaker had selected four single amendments and one group of amendments. The group itself deleted two major and two significant clauses from the original Bill. Furthermore he had linked all these amendments together which meant that they would not be debated and voted upon separately. Obviously this decision was very important to the pro-abortion lobby. By grouping the amendments together in this way the Speaker had ensured that the proceedings would be speeded up, which would have given the truncated Bill a much greater chance of success.

Eric Deakins (Lab. Waltham Forest) was the first to challenge the Speaker's selection. He pointed out that amendments are usually grouped together 'when they relate to one clause, to one subject, or to a group of subjects which are in themselves related one to another'. He could not see how any of these considerations applied to the Speaker's grouping of amendments.[31] This argument was taken up by Michael Foot, a former Leader of the House and in no sense an activist on the abortion issue.[32] Initially the Speaker was reluctant to alter his selection, but after a major challenge from George Cunningham (Lab. Islington and Finsbury)[33] he conceded and allowed separate votes on each of the four amendments which deleted the major sections of the Bill. However, he stuck to his original ruling that the amendments must be debated together.

The debate continued on restrictions to the grounds for abortion, and this took up almost the entire day. One speech, by

Michael Ancram, had been made in support of restricting the grounds for abortion on the second Friday on Report,[34] but on this, the third Friday, not one speech was made in its favour. In fact there were five major speeches against restricting the grounds, including significantly two from former Law Officers of the Crown, Alex Lyon and Peter Archer, one from the Shadow Minister of Health, Stan Orme, and one by the former Minister of Health, Roland Moyle.[35] In addition two Conservative Members spoke against the restrictions, Sheila Faith, who spoke on the previous Friday, and Nigel Forman.[36]

Despite this the evidence of Dr Vaughan was probably most significant. He recommended that Members who wanted to ensure that the wording of the criteria was not capable of a purely 'statistical' interpretation (i.e., to allow 'abortion on demand') should vote for the inclusion of the word 'substantial', and against 'serious'. He had, he said, been advised by the Attorney-General, Sir Ian Percival, that the inclusion of both was unnecessary.[37] The vote which followed took note of this advice but by an extremely narrow majority. The amendment to delete the word 'substantial' from the grounds clause was defeated by only three votes (180 to 177). In contrast the amendment to delete the word 'serious' was passed by a majority of 56 (201 to 145).

With only half an hour left of the day's proceedings voting began on the large group of amendments to delete part of the Bill. The only vote reached was to leave out the statutory instrument clause. This was accepted by a majority of 26 (175 to 149). This was against the advice of the Minister, but in accordance with Corrie's recommendation. After the third day Corrie thought his Bill would have no further days for debate. However, as explained, unknown to him or to his supporters Taylor withdrew his Bill to provide Corrie with another day.

The Fourth Day of Report – 14 March

A further surprise lay in store for both sides when they arrived for the fourth day's debate. They found that a new clause which had been drafted by Sam Silkin (former Labour Attorney-General) had been tabled and accepted by the Speaker. This clause referred back to the clause relating to the grounds which had been voted on the previous Friday. It provided that if a doctor, in assessing whether a woman qualifies for an abortion or not, judges her case solely on the statistical probability that it is safer for her to have an abortion than go to term, then the doctor must be sure that the risk is 'substantial'. Where a doctor does not use the statistical factor, the word 'substantial' could be ignored.

Giving his reasons for moving the amendment Silkin argued that the inclusion of the word 'substantial' had been voted for by a majority of only three. He believed that Members had voted for that word to be included

> on the basis that all the Minister and Attorney-General had meant was that the use of the word 'substantial' was a way of avoiding the difficulties in the minds of some Conservative Members... by what is known as the statistical argument.

This being so he had drafted an amendment to meet these 'difficulties' more precisely, and without doing the damage that simply incorporating the word 'substantial' would cause. He did not believe the House had fully realized the repercussions this word would have if it remained in the Bill. He said it would put the life of a foetus above that of the preservation of the life of the pregnant woman. The amendment offered, he concluded, 'the last possible chance for the House to agree to a compromise that in my view would satisfy the majority on both sides of the argument'.[38]

The case was cogently argued, but it is difficult to understand why the Speaker saw fit to select Silkin's amendment for debate given that the House had already taken a decision, even if a bad decision, on the issue. Two factors may be relevant here. First, Silkin as a former Attorney-General was bound to be listened to sympathetically by the Speaker. Certainly Silkin went to see the Speaker before the last day's debate and argued that a point of law was involved and that the amendment covered new ground. Evidently the Speaker accepted his arguments. Secondly, the Speaker may have been more willing to take advice after the successful challenge to his previous selection list.

After only one and a half hours' debate on this new clause

Benyon, seriously misjudging the mood of the House and the number of Corrie supporters available, moved the closure.[39] For the first time during the whole of the four days' debate this was lost, by a majority of seven. It was reported the next day that one of the reasons for this narrow defeat was that Irish Members travelling down for the day's debate arrived too late to vote. Their plane had apparently been delayed.[40] Whatever the reason, it proved a major tactical error for Corrie's side and debate on Silkin's amendment continued for a further two and a quarter hours.

Many of those speaking for the amendment pleaded for a compromise to be reached so that a law could be passed, with a 24 week time limit, which would, they felt, prevent the issue returning again and again to Parliament. However, it was far too late for compromise even if both sides had wanted it. The Bill's opponents in particular were convinced that it was a false hope to think the issue would not return to Parliament if the time limit was reduced.

Before the vote Sir George Young, Under-Secretary for Health and Social Security, advised Members to vote for the Silkin amendment.[41] Perhaps appropriately the last to speak on the Bill was Jo Richardson who said she supported Silkin's amendment because it went some way towards ameliorating the damage the Bill would cause.[42] Voting then began on all the remaining clauses. Silkin's amendment was taken first, and accepted by a majority of 35 (157 to 122). The votes deleting the remainder of the Bill were complicated as Members were voting tactically. For instance, on clause 3, the conscience clause, the pro-abortion lobby had decided to call upon as many of their supporters as possible to vote to leave the clause in the Bill. This would enable them to move their amendments to the clause and take up more debating time. The whole point was to have something left to talk about in order to prevent the Bill completing its Report Stage. On the other side Corrie's supporters were voting down clauses they had previously wholeheartedly supported, simply to get the Bill completed as soon as possible.

Before the voting on all these clauses could be completed the House adjourned. At last opponents of Corrie knew they had won. There was only one more day on which the Bill could be debated (4 July) but this seemed extremely unlikely as other bills would by then be out of Committee and take precedence over Corrie. However, the pro-abortion campaigners did not relax completely until John Corrie formally withdrew his Bill on 25 March, admitting there was simply no more time available.[43] The pro-abortion lobby were elated. As Willie Hamilton commented: 'It has been a great funeral. A lot of people will breathe a sigh of relief that the bill is finally dead'.[44] In a similar vein, Marie Patterson, chairwoman of the TUC Women's Conference, declared it 'A great victory for women in the whole country.'[45] In contrast of course the anti-abortion lobby was disillusioned but not downhearted.

As if to illustrate how volatile abortion is as a parliamentary issue the pro-abortion lobby had hardly had a chance to savour its success when another bill was introduced. David Alton, Liberal Roman Catholic MP for Liverpool, Edge Hill, decided to introduce a ten-minute rule bill to reduce the time limit for abortion to 24 weeks. Because it was a ten-minute rule bill it had little hope of success but the pro-abortion lobby feared it might receive overwhelming support, which might encourage a future private member's bill. They need not have worried: Alton's Bill was undermined by the anti-abortion lobby. Alton had, of course, consulted prominent anti-abortionists in Parliament and talked to SPUC. However his Bill met with little enthusiasm from the politicians and none at all from SPUC, who had little interest in a Bill dealing solely with the time limit, particularly if that Bill only reduced the time limit to 24 weeks.

SPUC's view was that if a one-clause bill was to be introduced it should deal with the grounds for abortion or possibly with the question of conscientious objection to carrying out abortions. For this reason SPUC urged its supporters in Parliament to oppose the Alton Bill. A number of MPs who support restrictions to the abortion law approached Alton in an effort to persuade him to withdraw his Bill. Alton went ahead nevertheless and introduced his Bill on 22 April 1980.[46] His ten-minute speech was weak and was replied to by Alex Lyon of the pro-abortion lobby who, in contrast, gave a strong and impressive speech. However as no vocal support was given to the Bill at the appropriate time there was no vote and the Bill automatically fell.

The Alton Bill was a non-event and something of a parliamentary debacle. Nevertheless it did reveal the new direction in which the anti-abortion lobby was moving. Given their experience on the Corrie Bill they advocated the introduction of single-clause bills to change the 1967 Abortion Act, though they were not interested in a bill on the time limit alone, a point to which we shall return in the next chapter.

In Conclusion: The Report Stage in Perspective

The Corrie Bill fell ultimately because it ran out of time and the reasons for that failure are examined in detail in the next chapter. However, it should also be clear by now that even if the Bill had passed in its final form it would have been a very different Bill from the one which was given a Second Reading by the House of Commons and approved in Standing Committee. Not only was the second half of the Bill dropped in an effort to salvage something, but also the two major clauses approved by the House were markedly different in content to those originally proposed by Corrie. On the time limit the House had voted for a 24-week upper time limit instead of the 20 weeks which had originally been proposed. As far as the grounds clause was concerned Parliament had approved the inclusion of 'substantial' but rejected the inclusion of 'serious'. What is more the passing of the Silkin amendment went some way towards negating the vote on 'substantial'. In fact the Bill was so emasculated that a number of prominent anti-abortion MPs, including two members of the Standing Committee, told us that they would have voted *against* the Bill on Third Reading if it had got that far. This means that the next chapter also examines why Parliament implicitly rejected so much of the original Bill at the Report Stage.

Notes

1. Second Reading, HC Debs., 20 July 1979, vol. 970, cols. 2199-290; Report Stage, HC Debs., 22 February 1980, vol. 979, cols. 815-912; ibid., 7 March 1980, vol. 980, cols. 853-86.
2. Personal interview with Robert Taylor, 5 February 1981.
3. Personal interview with Ian Mikardo, 19 June 1979.
4. The letter was not signed by Sir Anthony Alment, president of the RCOG.

5. Personal interview with John Corrie, 8 July 1979. John Corrie confirmed this in the *Guardian,* 1 December 1980.
6. *Times,* 31 January 1980.
7. The Archbishops were: Cardinal Hume of Westminster; Cardinal Gray of St Andrews and Edinburgh; Archbishop Murphy of Cardiff; Archbishop Worlock of Liverpool; Archbishop Dwyer of Southwark; Archbishop Winning of Glasgow.
8. *Times,* 24 January 1980.
9. *Times,* 30 January 1980.
10. The five church leaders were: Rev. James Scott, Moderator of the Presbytery of Aberdeen; Bishop George Sessford, Episcopal Bishop of Moray Ross and Caithness; Bishop Mario Conti, Roman Catholic Bishop of Aberdeen; Canon James Alexander, Convenor of the Episcopal Social Services Board and representing Bishop of Aberdeen and Orkney; Rev. Graham Bruce, Convenor of the Public Question Committee of the United Free Church.
11. *Times,* 30 January 1980.
12. *Times,* 30 January 1980.
13. *Times,* 4 February 1980.
15. *Times,* 6 February 1980.
15. *Daily Mail,* 8 February 1980.
16. *Woman's Own,* 9 February 1980.
17. Personal interview with Ian Mikardo, 19 June 1979.
18. *Sunday Times,* 3 February 1980.
19. HC Debs., 8 February 1980, vol. 978, col. 931-9. On 31 October Parliament agreed a change in procedure to allow the House to sit from 9.30-2.30 on Friday. This came into force in January 1980.
20. Ibid., col. 942.
21. Ibid., cols., 965-8.
22. Ibid., cols. 979-82.
23. Ibid., cols. 987-9.
24. Ibid. cols. 991-2.
25. HC Debs., 15 February 1980, vol. 978, cols. 1937-40.
26. Ibid., cols. 1944-8.
27. Ibid., cols. 1965-8.
28. Ibid., cols. 1948-55.
29. Ibid., cols. 1953-4.
30. These were Ian Mikardo, Stan Orme, Michael Foot, Alex Lyon and Eric Deakins (all Labour MPs), HC Debs., 29 February 1980, vol. 979, col. 1716.
31. Ibid., cols. 1716-17.
32. Ibid., col. 1719.
33. Ibid., cols. 1743-7.
34. HC Debs., 15 February 1980, vol. 978, col. 2004-11.

35. Ibid., cols., 1996-2004; HC Debs., 29 February 1980, vol. 979, cols. 1726-9; ibid., cols. 1762-7; ibid., cols. 1720-5.
36. HC Debs., 15 February 1980, vol. 978, cols., 2015-19; ibid., 29 February 1980, vol. 979, col. 1768.
37. Ibid., cols. 1725-6.
38. HC Debs., 14 March 1980, vol. 980, cols. 1748-58.
39. Ibid., col. 1768.
40. *Morning Star,* 15 March 1980.
41. HC Debs., 14 March 1980, vol. 980, cols. 1800-1.
42. Ibid., cols. 1806-11.
43. *Times,* 26 March 1980.
44. *Guardian,* 15 March 1980.
45. *Morning Star,* 15 March 1980.
46. HC Debs., 22 April 1980, vol. 983, cols. 221-8.

6

The Failure of the Corrie Bill

On 25 March 1980 John Corrie withdrew his Abortion (Amendment) Bill and the war was over. Why did the Bill fail? That may be a most important question, but it is certainly not the only one. We must not forget that the voting at Report Stage reflects a definite move against the Bill after Second Reading: this has considerable implications for any analysis of the likely parliamentary future of the abortion issue. In fact as we have seen *none* of the clauses in the Bill as it emerged from Standing Committee was passed at Report Stage without serious amendment. Therefore we must also ask how this apparent change in the views of MPs can be accounted for.

This chapter is consequently divided into three sections. The first section looks at the reasons for the failure of the Bill. The second section offers an explanation of the changes in the pattern of parliamentary voting during the Corrie Bill. The final section speculates on the future of the abortion issue in Parliament in the light of our analysis of the Corrie Bill.

Why did the Corrie Bill Fail?

It is not always easy for someone not versed in the idiosyncracies of Parliament to understand how a bill which receives overwhelming support in principle at Second Reading, and is debated at length in Parliament, can fail to become law. In the case of the Corrie Bill the answer at one level is simple; the Bill ran out of time. However this answer merely begs another question: Why did it run out of time? As we have shown, it had more time than any other private members' bill that we have been able to trace. It was debated for 5 hours on Second Reading, 43 hours in Committee and 20 hours at Report. This meant that it had more parliamentary time than most successful *government* bills. In other words it is not enough simply to conclude that it did not have sufficient time. It is more accurate to say that when the Bill came back to the House of Commons it had insufficient time to complete its stages given a number of factors: the scope and content of the Bill; the strength and organization of the opposition to it; and the government's refusal to give it time. Each of these factors is worth some discussion in the light of our preceding analysis. In addition we look at the role of John Corrie himself; many of our interviewees on both sides of the debate thought he was at least partially responsible for the failure of his Bill.

The Scope and Content of the Bill

When the Bill came back to the House from the Standing Committee it was not reduced in scope. It still contained eight clauses and represented a very radical attempt to amend the 1967 Abortion Act. This had a number of consequences. First, the large number of clauses meant that its opponents had ample opportunity to put down a wide variety of amendments. Indeed 80 amendments were put forward at Report Stage. Obviously not all of them were chosen for debate by the Speaker but he selected a total of over 50 amendments in 28 separate groupings. If the Bill had been reduced in scope at the Committee Stage, or even after the first day's debate on the Report Stage then such a truncated Bill might well have succeeded. In fact it was not until just before the third day's Report Stage debate that John Corrie and his supporters withdrew part of the Bill, and by that time it was too late.

What is more, the Bill actually came out of Committee considerably altered, and altered in such a way that it made the opposition's task in fighting it easier rather than more difficult. Almost all of the clauses in the original Bill were amended, totally redrafted, or withdrawn. So when the House of Commons saw the Bill again it was significantly changed. This allowed the opposition to claim that it was a different, although no less radical, Bill. More important, it appeared to influence the Speaker's choice of amendments for Report Stage. The Speaker called amendments which had already been debated and decided upon in Committee. One obvious, although unstated, justification for that decision was that the House itself should have a chance to debate the major clauses in a Bill which had changed so substantially since they had approved it in principle at Second Reading. The Speaker's choice of a large number of amendments for debate virtually ensured that the Bill, in the form it came out of Committee, could not complete its Report and Third Reading stages in the time available.

The Bill's contents influenced its fate in one other way. There is little doubt that many MPs who supported the Bill on Second Reading did so because they favoured a reduction in the time limit for abortions. They did so in the belief that many of the other elements in the Bill would be removed in Committee; that a compromise would be reached between pro- and anti-abortionists. It is difficult to understand how MPs could have taken this view given that there was ample evidence of the strength of feeling on both sides, and therefore no obvious basis for compromise. However so many of our interviewees reported this as their view, or the view of other MPs they knew, that there can be little doubt this was a popular misconception, particularly among MPs newly elected to Parliament. Such MPs were therefore surprised when the Bill returned to the floor of the Commons with no evidence of compromise and all of its radical elements intact. What is more John Corrie and his supporters were blamed by these MPs for failing to compromise or, as one MP put it: 'There can be little doubt that the supporters of the bill were held responsible for not responding to the obvious desire of the House for compromise and as such for being politically inept.'[1]

Of course we are still left with the question: Why was there no compromise? As we have said, there was in fact little basis for compromise. The main supporters of the Abortion Act in Parliament might have been willing to compromise on a bill which merely reduced the time limit for abortion to 24 weeks, but they would accept no change in the grounds for abortion. In contrast the anti-abortion MPs were most anxious to change radically the grounds for abortion and remove the so-called 'statistical argument'. There was therefore no way that there could be a compromise between the two sides. However the Bill's supporters could have unilaterally dropped some of the clauses of their Bill, in Committee or before Report, in order to improve the chances of getting the rest of it through. Why did they not do so?

As we have seen, the second half of the Bill was only withdrawn by its sponsors when it was too late. They did not do so before partly because some of them initially believed that they could get all the Bill through, and partly because there was no obvious basis for compromise among the Bill's supporters. There appears little doubt that there was some complacency among the parliamentary supporters of the Bill both because of its overwhelming success at Second Reading, and because there was considerable private members' time available for its consideration on Report. With hindsight it is easy to see this was a mistake, but until the Corrie Bill no amending legislation had ever reached Report Stage, and so neither side had a clear impression of what would happen. Indeed when the Report Stage began many of the pro-abortion MPs themselves thought that the Bill would go through in some form.

At the same time however the anti-abortion MPs had no contingency plans nor had they drawn up a coherent strategy on what to concede if necessary. The major reason for this was the divisions which existed on the anti-abortion side. For example John Corrie and William Benyon were most anxious to amend the grounds for abortion, and less concerned with the licensing clause and the restriction of the operation of the charities. In contrast Jill Knight, Michael Ancram and Sir Bernard Braine were much more concerned with the licensing clause, and were therefore reluctant to drop it. In addition the MPs were constantly under pressure from the extra-parliamentary anti-abortion lobby to hold firm to their principles and not drop sections of the Bill. This meant that it was difficult for the anti-abortion MPs to agree a strategy, a problem which was further compounded by John Corrie's illness during the Committee Stage. Indeed the absence of cohesion or a coherent strategy was the most important reason for the failure of the Bill's sponsors to rescue it at Report Stage.

The Strength and Organization of the Pro-abortion Lobby

One noticeable feature of the lobbying on the Corrie Bill as compared with that on the previous amending bills was the growth of the extra-parliamentary pro-abortion lobby. The activities of NAC and CAC meant that there was a much more even balance between the efforts and visibility of the two lobbies in the country. This was reflected by the large growth in the number of pro-abortion groups during the period and by a much more equal distribution between pro- and anti-abortion letters in MPs' postbags than had occurred on previous bills. In addition the pro-abortion lobby was greatly assisted by the efforts of the TUC, the Labour Party and the British Medical Association. The TUC organized the large pro-abortion march while the Labour Party, through its Women's Officer and LARC, put considerable pressure on Labour MPs. The continued and outspoken support of the BMA was especially important as MPs obviously take particular note of the medical profession on issues of this sort.

Despite this, however, the battle outside Parliament was fairly finely balanced given the continued widespread support for, and local activities of, SPUC and LIFE. It was inside Parliament that the battle was really won by the strategy, effort and organization of the pro-abortion lobby. Of course it had the advantage at Report Stage in that there was limited time available, a fact which works in favour of the side fighting a defensive action. In such circumstances the lobby defending the status quo merely has to delay and filibuster so that a bill runs out of time. Nevertheless such delaying tactics, while effective, are not easy to organize, nor are they inevitably successful. The achievement of the parliamentary pro-abortion lobby was that it drafted enough legitimate amendments to ensure extended debate; that it provided and briefed enough speakers to produce a sophisticated filibuster; and that it organized its supporters so that the voting on Report was always close, and on a number of occasions the Corrie side was defeated. Why was this lobby so effective?

As we have said the parliamentary pro-abortion lobby had an easier task because it was fighting a defensive campaign and as such it could be successful without necessarily having to be victorious in the division lobbies. It merely needed to use tactics to delay a decision and ensure the Bill fell through lack of time. In other words the pro-abortion parliamentary lobby did not need to be more effective than the anti-abortion side — although we would argue that they were — they only needed properly to organize their forces and effectively use parliamentary delaying tactics. However, that is easier said than done. In this case the parliamentarians were successful because they were cohesive, tactically skilful and industrious, and because they were given great moral and practical support by the extra-parliamentary lobby. The bulk of the parliamentary work was done by the five pro-abortion members of the Standing Committee but they were helped by a hard core of other MPs and by the efforts of certain outsiders.

It is difficult to apreciate how much work was involved in organizing the parliamentary lobbies on both sides. The Committee sat for 43 hours and the MPs who sat on it were also involved in strategy meetings, in organizing the whipping of their parliamentary supporters, and in speaking and writing to thousands of outside supporters. However the situation was much worse for the pro-abortion Members of the Standing Committee for two reasons. First, there were only five of them as compared to the ten supporters of the Corrie Bill. More important, however, it was the pro-abortion side which made most of the running in Committee, speaking much more frequently, and putting down many more amendments, all of which had to be discussed and drafted. As we have seen earlier, the five pro-abortion Members were willing to work hard and all took on different and complementary roles. This commitment and unity among the parliamentarians was matched by the efforts of the extra-parliamentary lobby. The Co-ord advisers were constantly on hand to help with drafting amendments, and the Co-ord office was continually preparing briefs for MPs, and keeping the extra-parliamentary lobby in touch with what was going on at Committee and Report Stage. This unity among the MPs, and between the MPs and the extra-parliamentary supporters, was a notable and crucially important factor in the success of the pro-abortion lobby.

However unity and effort would have had little effect without the skilled use of parliamentary tactics. The five MPs included two, Jo Richardson and Oonagh McDonald, who were extremely knowledgeable on the issue and had had the experience of sitting on the Benyon Standing Committee. They were hardened campaigners on the issue but they were aware that they needed colleagues on the Committee who were not only willing to work hard, but who also had a detailed grasp of parliamentary procedure and the use of parliamentary tactics. It was for this reason that they approached Ian Mikardo, one of the House's acknowledged experts on procedure, to serve on the Committee. They were also helped by the fact that Willie Hamilton, another long-serving parliamentarian, asked to join them. Obviously, right from the outset the pro-abortion lobby was aware that it was going to be largely a battle of parliamentary tactics and there can be little doubt that the lobby proved adept in that battle. In Committee it introduced a series of amendments to ensure extended discussion with the aim of educating MPs as to the radical nature of the Bill. At the same time, and more crucially, it kept back for Report Stage a series of amendments which could have been brought forward at Committee. The most notable of these was an amendment to introduce a time limit of 24 weeks for abortions rather than the 20 weeks included in the Corrie Bill. The aim of this tactic of course was to ensure that the Speaker would call that amendment at Report Stage, which he might not have done if the amendment had been moved and defeated in Committee.

Despite this all these efforts in Committee would have been of little use if the pro-abortion lobby could not have ensured extended debate and close votes at Report Stage. At this stage it obviously aimed to put down a large number of amendments and filibuster the Bill. While it kept back a number of amendments, the Co-ord lawyers drafted a great many more. Even so there was an extended series of debates on Report, and as such a lot of time to fill, particularly as the Bill's supporters were committed to speeding up proceedings by speaking briefly and infrequently. What is more the Speaker was obviously alert to the possibility of filibustering. The usual private members' filibuster consists of long speeches by a few opponents of a bill. In this case however the filibuster was less obvious but more effective because it involved a large number of short speeches. In fact 24 MPs spoke against the Bill on Report: the average length of the speeches was only 15 minutes. Some of these MPs relied fairly heavily on briefs prepared by Co-ord, but one of the strengths of the pro-abortion parliamentary lobby was that it could rely on so many MPs who were willing to attend and speak.

The other aspect of the pro-abortion parliamentary lobby which was important was its whipping system. We have already described the whipping on both sides at length. Both had a very sophisticated and effective whipping system for a private member's issue. However the pro-abortion side was better organized and this fact stood it in particularly good stead on the fourth day of the Report Stage. For reasons we discussed earlier it was not until very late that either side knew for certain that there would be a fourth day's debate. However the pro-abortion side had assumed there would be, and had sent out a whip urging its supporters to attend. In contrast the Bill's supporters had assumed there would not be a fourth day, had not sent out a whip, and had told their supporters they were free to fulfil other engagements. When finally it became clear that there would be a debate the pro-abortion lobby was left to try to repair the damage. For this reason fewer of Corrie's supporters turned up on the final Friday and the Corrie side lost an important closure vote on debate on the Silkin amendment. This partly reflected the poor attendance by Corrie supporters which in turn resulted from limitations in the organization of its whipping.

One other aspect of the pro-abortion lobby's parliamentary whipping deserves particular mention. It whipped only Labour MPs, leaving the canvassing of Conservative MPs to one or two individual Conservative members, notably Bowen Wells, and to Tories for Free Choice. In one way this was an important weakness in its parliamentary organization as there was not a great deal of contact between the pro-abortion wings of the two main parties. However any deficiency in this sense was more than made up for by the fact that the Labour pro-abortion parliamentarians could use the PLP meetings as a major channel of communication with its Labour supporters. During the Committee Stage the PLP meetings were used to tell pro-abortion supporters of the progress in the Committee, and at the Report Stage PLP members were given an outline of the business and votes likely to occur on the following Friday. The anti-abortion MPs had no equivalent forum. The very fact that such announcements were made at PLP meetings reminded wavering Labour MPs that defence of the 1967 Act was party policy.

The general conclusion here must be that once the anti-abortion parliamentarians had decided not to withdraw sections of their Bill before Report its fate lay to a large extent in the hands of the pro-abortion parliamentary lobby. If the lobby organized itself effectively it could defeat the Bill given the time constraint. It was notably well organized and this was a major reason for the eventual defeat of the Bill.

The Government's Attitude

As we said in looking at the history of the issue, David Steel's original Bill was successful largely because it was given government time. Indeed all the major controversial social/moral legislation passed in the 1960s received government time. Needless to say if the Conservative Government had been willing to give the Corrie Bill time it would have got through largely intact if substantially amended. Therefore the fact that the government was unwilling to give time played a crucial role in deciding its fate.

Unfortunately we do not have access to Cabinet meetings, but nevertheless it does appear that the question of time for the Bill was discussed at Cabinet. Certainly there was a report of a Cabinet meeting in the *Guardian*[2] and many of the MPs and pressure group activists we talked to claimed they knew of such a meeting. All these reports suggest that the issue was brought up by Norman St John-Stevas, then the Leader of the House and a strong parliamentary campaigner against abortion.

The Cabinet might have been expected to be sympathetic to the idea of granting time for a number of reasons. First, a number of its members, including Margaret Thatcher, Norman St John-Stevas and chief whip Michael Joplin, supported the idea of amending the 1967 Abortion Act. Secondly, the government and particularly the Department of Health would probably prefer to see some minor amending legislation passed in order to defuse the issue and remove it, temporarily at least, from the parliamentary arena. Thirdly, the Bill had been overwhelmingly supported at Second Reading and some of its clauses had received considerable subsequent support, so members of Cabinet might well have felt that the House should have a chance to state its view on the final Bill. However despite this the Cabinet rejected the idea of granting the Bill time for two reasons. First, Conservative governments, unlike Labour governments, have traditionally not given private members' bills time except under very unusual circumstances. In addition the Cabinet believed that if it made an exception for one private member's bill, then this would set a precedent and others, which had even wider support among Conservative backbenchers, would justifiably feel entitled to time.

The Role of John Corrie

In our interviews with MPs and interest group activists in both lobbies the role of John Corrie was always mentioned. Most of our respondents saw him as at least partially responsible for the failure of the Bill. He was widely described by both lobbies as 'weak', 'politically inept' and 'well meaning but no expert on the subject'. How far are such judgements valid?

Certainly Corrie was not initially an expert on the subject and had no real history of involvement in the issue. However he did consult a number of MPs with more experience, and various outside interest groups, before introducing his Bill. It is also fair to say that he is not as skilled a parliamentarian, or as well versed in parliamentary tactics, as some of his opponents. But few MPs are as 'parliamentarily wise' as Ian Mikardo and Willie Hamilton. Certainly then Corrie made mistakes which are clear, particularly with hindsight, but it is far from certain that such mistakes were avoidable, or that other MPs would have avoided them.

In fact he made two crucial and clearly related mistakes. The Bill as he introduced it was too long, and he failed to withdraw sections of it early enough to ensure that some of the Bill was salvaged. However, in both cases it is an obvious oversimplification to see the decisions either as solely John Corrie's or as a result of his poor political judgement. Throughout Corrie had to retain as far as possible the support of both his fellow sponsors in Parliament and the anti-abortion lobby outside Parliament.[3] Yet as we have seen many of his fellow sponsors, and even more of the extra-parliamentary lobby took a more fundamentalist view on abortion than he did. This meant that organizations like SPUC and LIFE, and MPs such as Jill Knight and Michael Ancram, wanted a tougher 'grounds clause' than Corrie, and were very anxious to persevere with the 'licensing clause' in the Bill. Corrie might have stood firm against this by insisting on a briefer bill, or later, by withdrawing parts of it in Committee; but in doing so he would have alienated a large section of his support, without necessarily ensuring ultimate success. It was not an easy choice. Indeed although with hindsight Corrie made choices which did much to ensure the failure of the Bill his decisions were ones which most other MPs would probably have taken. The most accurate conclusion is probably that he might have done better, and probably would do better given another chance.

The Votes at Report Stage: a Changing Pattern

The pattern of parliamentary voting on the Corrie Bill certainly changed considerably between Second Reading and Report Stage. There was a clear movement away from support for the Corrie Bill (see Table 6.1). Indeed as we have said only the vote on the

Table 6.1: Parliamentary Voting on the Corrie Bill

Vote	Voting (expressed as % of those voting) for*	against	Majority	No. of MPs voting
Second Reading vote (1979)	71 (N 242)	29 (N 98)	+144	340
Report Stage (1980) — amendment to change 20 weeks to 24 weeks	62 (N 275)	38 (N 172)	+103	447
Report Stage (1980) — amendment to delete 'serious' from grounds clause	58 (N 201)	42 (N 145)	+56	346
Report Stage (1980) — amendment to delete 'substantial' from grounds clause	50 (N 177)	50 (N 180)	-3	357
Report Stage (1980) — Silkin amendment	56 (N 157)	44 (N 122)	+35	279

This table, together with Table 1.1, are the only two tables reported in this book which do not include Tellers.

*Voting for the Second Reading and against all the amendments on Report is an anti-abortion vote.

amendment to withdraw 'substantial' from the grounds clause of the Bill reflects a victory for its supporters. This means, as Table 6.2 indicates, that the voting on Second Reading is a good but far from perfect predictor of voting at Report Stage, although the relationship is much stronger if we concentrate only on those MPs who voted (Table 6.3).

Table 6.2: Inter-relationship between Votes on the Corrie Bill (all MPs)

Votes				
Second Reading				
24 weeks	0.243*			
'Serious'	0.177*	0.356*		
'Substantial'	0.277*	0.360*	0.834*	
Silkin	0.159*	0.170*	0.340*	0.391*
	Second Reading	24 weeks	'Serious'	'Substantial'
	Votes			

* All relationships significant at 0.001 level.

Note: The statistics reported in this table are *Lamda symmetrical,* and are based upon three by three tables. More details of the basis of this analysis can be obtained from David Marsh.

Table 6.3: Inter-relationship between Votes on the Corrie Bill (only those MPs who voted on the two votes concerned)

Votes				
Second Reading				
24 weeks	0.609*	—		
'Serious'	0.679*	0.752*	—	
'Substantial'	0.843*	0.703*	0.814*	
Silkin	0.816*	0.741*	0.830*	0.942*
	Second Reading	24 weeks	'Serious'	'Substantial'
	Votes			

* All relationships significant at the 0.001 level.

Note: The statistics reported in this table are *Lambda symmetrical,* and are based upon two by two tables. More details of the basis of this analysis can be obtained from David Marsh.

If we look at the votes in more detail it is evident that the MPs who voted against the Corrie Bill at Second Reading were subsequently much more likely to vote consistently pro-abortion than were the MPs who voted for it at Second Reading to vote consistently anti-abortion (see Table 6.4). However, because there were so many more MPs who supported the Bill at this stage, the Corrie side would have been successful in all the votes at Report Stage unless there had been other changes. In fact there were three key elements in the pattern of changing votes. Some MPs who had voted for the Bill at Second Reading did oppose it later. In particular of course a considerable number of MPs who had initially supported Corrie later opposed the more radical elements in the Bill. So 34 MPs in this position voted for the amendment to 24 weeks, while 21 voted for the amendment to remove 'serious' from the grounds clause (see Table 6.4). Nevertheless two other movements were more significant. First, there were a large number of MPs who voted for a Second Reading but subsequently did not vote on various amendments at Report (see Table 6.4). Secondly, an equally large number of MPs who had not voted at Second Reading voted against the Corrie Bill on Report (see Table 6.5). We can go further than this however. It is clear from Table 6.6 that this first group was composed largely, although not exclusively, of Conservatives. In contrast Table 6.7 reveals that the second group consisted mainly of Labour MPs.

Table 6.4: Continuity of Voting on the Corrie Bill of MPs who Voted at Second Reading

	Pro-abortion (N 100)				Anti-abortion (N 244)			
Vote	For amendment*	Against amendment	Not voting	Index of continuity**	For amendment*	Against amendment	Not voting	Index of continuity**
24 weeks	81	0	19	81%	52	139	53	57%
'Serious'	72	0	28	72%	34	114	90	47%
'Substantial'	75	0	25	75%	14	140	90	57%
Silkin	72	1	27	72%	15	104	125	43%
				Average level of continuity 75%				Average level of continuity 51%

*Voting for each amendment is a pro-abortion vote.

**The number of MPs who voted consistently expressed as a percentage of the number of MPs who had voted on that side at Second Reading. The percentages are unweighted.

Table 6.5: Report Stage Voting Patterns of MPs who did not Vote at Second Reading (N 289)

Vote	For amendment %	Against amendment %	Not voting %
24 weeks	50 (N 144)	12 (N 34)	38 (N 111)
'Serious'	34 (N 97)	11 (N 33)	55 (N 159)
'Substantial'	31 (N 90)	15 (N 42)	54 (N 157)
Silkin	25 (N 72)	7 (N 19)	65 (N 198)

Overall, then, most of the movement between Second Reading and Report was in one direction; away from support for the Corrie Bill, with a particular growth of opposition to its most radical elements. More specifically, two groups appear especially important — a group of Conservative MPs who voted for Corrie on Second Reading but subsequently did not vote, and a group of Labour MPs who had not voted at Second Reading but later opposed the Bill at Report. How can we explain these changing voting patterns and in particular the voting of these two groups of MPs?

In fact it would be inaccurate on the basis of our figures to assert that a large number of MPs changed their minds. Indeed the apparent discrepancy in voting is to a considerable extent a reflection of the fact that Second Reading votes on private members' bills provide an inadequate indication of the views of MPs on an issue. In this case it is clear that many MPs who voted for the Second Reading of the Corrie Bill, and many others who did not vote on Second Reading, were always opposed to its more radical elements. Therefore they voted against these elements of the Bill on Report. Certainly this interpretation is confirmed by the fact that the most radical elements — the reduction of the time limit to 20 weeks, and the inclusion of 'serious' in the grounds clause — were most clearly defeated in the voting on Report.

Table 6.6: Continuity of Voting on the Corrie Bill of MPs who Voted at Second Reading, by Party

(a) Anti-abortion MPs (N 244)

	Labour (N 54)				Conservative (N 190)			
Vote	For	Against	Not voting	Index of continuity*	For	Against	Not voting	Index of continuity*
24 weeks	13	32	9	59%	39	95	46	50%
'Serious'	13	26	15	48%	21	81	78	43%
'Substantial'	9	31	14	57%	5	102	73	54%
Silkin	8	24	22	44%	7	76	97	40%
				Average 52%				Average 47%

(b) Pro-abortion MPs (N 100)

	Labour (N 86)				Conservative (N 14)			
Vote	For	Against	Not voting	Index of continuity*	For	Against	Not voting	Index of continuity*
24 weeks	71	0	15	83%	8	0	6	57%
'Serious'	64	0	22	74%	6	0	8	43%
'Substantial'	68	0	18	79%	6	0	8	43%
Silkin	66	1	19	77%	5	0	9	36%
				Average 80%				Average 44%

* The number of MPs who voted consistently expressed as a percentage of the number who had voted on that side at Second Reading. The percentages are unweighted.

Table 6.7: Report Stage Voting of MPs who did not Vote at Second Reading, by Party

	Labour (N 130)			Conservative (N 196)		
Vote	For %	Against %	Not voting %	For %	Against %	Not voting %
24 weeks	67 (N 87)	8 (N 11)	25 (N 32)	34 (N 50)	14 (N 20)	52 (N 76)
'Serious'	52 (N 67)	8 (N 10)	40 (N 53)	16 (N 24)	14 (N 20)	70 (N 102)
'Substantial'	54 (N 70)	8 (N 10)	38 (N 50)	10 (N 14)	20 (N 29)	70 (N 103)
Silkin	45 (N 54)	3 (N 4)	52 (N 67)	8 (N 11)	8 (N 12)	84 (N 124)

In effect then much of the 'change' among both the groups we identified was a product of our definition of change. Many MPs in both groups had not changed their position but rather their detailed view on abortion was better expressed by the Report Stage voting. Unfortunately our quantitative material does not show which MPs fall into this category and which MPs actually altered their opinions during the Bill's progress. Nevertheless it is clear from our interviews that many MPs in both the groups we have identified did in some sense alter their views during the Corrie campaign. Our interviews also suggest a number of explanations of these changes, some of which apply to both groups and some of which are particular to one.

The majority of the MPs we are dealing with who altered their views were MPs who had little knowledge of, or interest in, the abortion issue prior to the Corrie Bill. Many of these MPs were newly elected and voted, or did not vote, at Second Reading when they had little knowledge of the details of the Bill, or of the issues and questions involved. The publicity and the lobbying associated with the Corrie Bill did much to politicize them.

In particular two aspects of the lobbying seem to have been important. First, some MPs only realized after the Second Reading how radical the Bill was: they had previously believed that it dealt mainly with the time limit for abortions. This new understanding owed much to the letters and lobbying of the extra-parliamentary pro-abortion lobby. In addition however the pro-abortion MPs on the Standing Committee lobbied extensively at this stage in order to emphasize the Bill's radical elements. Secondly, the role of the professional medical organizations was important. As we have seen the BMA and the RCOG have opposed all the abortion amendment bills since the White Bill. However, before Corrie, many MPs had not been aware of the strength of the medical profession's opposition to any major changes to the 1967 Abortion Act. On the Corrie Bill the BMA in particular was much more overt in its opposition and there is little doubt that in the light of the opposition, which was only clearly expressed after Second Reading, some MPs rethought their position on some elements in the Bill. As one Conservative MP told us:

> There can be little doubt that the medical profession's opposition to the Bill influenced the votes of many MPs at the Report Stage. I personally would have voted for a change in the grounds for abortion if it hadn't been clear that the bulk of the medical profession opposed such a change.[4]

If we look particularly at the Labour MPs who did not vote on Second Reading but opposed the Corrie Bill on Report then two factors appear to be particularly important in explaining their changing votes. As we said when considering the Second Reading Vote there is little doubt that some MPs voted for the Corrie Bill or did not vote because they had given their electors an understanding that they would not oppose an abortion amendment bill on Second Reading. These MPs, having fulfilled their commitment, asserted their opposition to the Corrie Bill on Report. More significantly a larger number of uncommitted Labour MPs who had not voted at Second Reading opposed the Bill at Report as a result of the intensive lobbying which took place in the Labour Party during the period prior to the Report Stage. A whole series of factors pushed Labour MPs in the direction of opposition to the Corrie Bill. A pro-abortion position was Labour Party policy; most Labour Party constituency general management committees were committed to that policy; the majority of the PLP was firmly pro-abortion, and PLP meetings were used to proselytize on behalf of that position; in addition the Labour Party Women's Organizer was always ready to chastise MPs who voted for the Corrie Bill. Against such a background it would have been surprising if many Labour MPs who were uncommitted on the issue had not voted against the Corrie Bill on Report.

The Conservative MPs who voted with the Corrie side at Second Reading and subsequently opposed it were probably particularly influenced by the lobbying of the medical profession. However one other factor may have played some part. The Minister of Health, Dr Gerard Vaughan, showed no enthusiasm for the Bill on Report, and recommended that Parliament adopt a 24-week time limit and accept the inclusion of 'substantial', while rejecting the inclusion of 'serious' in the grounds clause. This lack of enthusiasm may well have caused some Conservative MPs who voted for the Bill at Second Reading to reconsider their support for it, and abstain on Report.

Our analysis then would suggest that while many MPs who voted differently at Second Reading and Report did not in fact alter their views, other uncommitted MPs did change their voting intentions. In most cases such MPs changed from voting for the Corrie Bill to abstaining, or from abstaining to voting against it. Only 14 MPs who had supported the Bill at Second Reading subsequently opposed it consistently, voting for all the four major amendments we have considered. Of course many more MPs who voted for Second Reading voted against the Corrie side on the two most radical amendments. Those MPs who did actually alter their views were obviously influenced by the campaign, and in particular it would appear by the lobbying of the professional medical organizations. More specifically Labour MPs who altered their intentions were affected by the fact that the pro-abortion position was in many senses legitimized within the Labour Party.

The Future of the Abortion Issue

Obviously abortion remains a live political issue. There will be another amending bill introduced as soon as an MP with very strong anti-abortion views wins a prominent place in the private members' ballot. All this raises two immediate questions: Why is abortion such a live political issue? And what are the chances of an amending bill being successful in the future?

Of course there are other social and moral issues which have been the subject of frequent debates in Parliament, the most notable being capital punishment. However none of these issues generates anything like as much interest and activity in and around the Chamber as does abortion. Why is abortion such a unique private members' issue?

There are a number of reasons. In the first place, abortion involves potentially conflicting moral and social values. To many people believing the sanctity of human life is paramount, life is seen as beginning at conception. Those people believe that abortion at any stage, and under almost any circumstances, is immoral and should be illegal. Others place emphasis on the belief that a woman has a right to exercise control over her own body, and thus should have the final responsibility for deciding whether or not to have an abortion. We can conceptualize these two positions as opposite ends of a continuum between which there are a variety of positions, most of which are justified by those who hold them in moral as well as practical terms. There are two separate but related points here. First, compared with capital punishment, the moral issues involved are more complex and much more open to argument and debate. Secondly, there are numerous solutions to the moral dilemmas involved. An individual can favour abortion on demand up to term as NAC does, or oppose abortion under almost all circumstances as LIFE and SPUC do. At the same time if one favours abortion under some circumstances, or at some stages of pregnancy, then there are an infinite variety of answers one could give to the questions, under what circumstances, and at what stages? The issue of capital punishment is by comparison clear cut. Most people either advocate or oppose capital punishment. The only compromise position is one which promotes the use of the death penalty in certain restricted cases — usually for terrorists, or for murderers of policemen or prison officers. There can be little doubt that the complexity of the moral issues involved and the variety of positions possible have helped to make the abortion issue a more contentious, volatile and live issue in parliamentary terms. This is reflected in the fact that individual MPs have changed their voting patterns much more on abortion than on capital punishment.

Despite this the issue would probably not be such a political one if there were not a number of institutions and movements which keep the issue near the centre of debate. Most obviously the Roman Catholic Church and the variety of pro- and anti-abortion interest groups play an important role here. The doctrine of the Catholic Church has had considerable influence upon the views of Roman Catholic MPs and has given a boost to the activities of the anti-abortion interest groups. Similarly the activities of the extra-parliamentary lobbies do much to ensure that the issue remains in the minds of MPs and the public. Perhaps more contentiously however it also appears to us that the abortion issue has been directly related to the growth of feminism in Britain. The major organization promoting the 'woman's right to choose' argument, NAC, is overtly feminist. Indeed in both Parliament and the country the issue has been taken up by women as an important symbolic one as well as a crucial practical one. This association of abortion with feminism has helped ensure it remains a live topic.

The last point stems fairly obviously from what has gone before. In every year since 1975 abortion has been a significant issue in Parliament. The interest groups developed in number, size, organization, and political expertise during the 1970s. Once a topic develops such a momentum with strong groups pushing for reform and other groups opposing it, the process becomes almost inexorable. The anti-abortionists will not stop unless there is a major reform, while the supporters of the Abortion Act will oppose any major reform and would fight to repeal it if such a reform were passed. Everyone is politicized, feelings run high and the issue remains in the forefront.

Both the parliamentary and the extra-parliamentary arms of the anti-abortion lobby learnt from their defeat on the Corrie Bill. They had suffered a setback, but almost at once their thoughts turned to the next campaign. Their analysis of the defeat emphasized two factors and that analysis had an immediate effect. First, nearly everyone in the anti-abortion camp was convinced that in future a step by step approach should be adopted, that is, introducing a series of one-clause bills rather than another wide-ranging bill like Corrie's. It was clear, in the light of experience, that given the current private members procedure and the strong and organized opposition, any broad bill would be defeated. Secondly, many people in the lobby believed that it was essential to establish better liaison and planning both among anti-abortion MPs, and between them and their extra-parliamentary supporters. As a result, when the 1980-1 parliamentary session opened, a group of 10 to 15 MPs decided to form an *ad hoc* committee which would meet regularly to discuss strategy and tactics. They also agreed to invite to the meeting representatives of the main interest groups SPUC and LIFE.

This response to defeat indicated once again the depth of commitment in the abortion lobby. There are about 20 or so MPs who would seriously consider introducing an abortion bill if they drew a high place in the private members' ballot. As such there are certain to be other abortion amendment bills. When the ballot for the 1980-1 session was drawn on 27 November 1980 three of the successful MPs expressed an interest in promoting such a bill. Timothy Sainsbury (Con. Hove), who drew first place[5] and Charles Morrison (Con. Devizes),[6] who drew fifth place, both claimed to be considering a bill to reduce the time limit. Donald Stewart (SNP Western Isles) seemed in contrast to favour a more radical bill probably restricting the grounds for legal abortion.[7] In the end none of the MPs took an abortion bill but it is noteworthy both that so many were interested, and that they all had in mind one-clause bills. Indeed Sainsbury told a press conference after the ballot that he believed that earlier attempts at reform had failed because they were too broad.[8]

There can be little doubt given the voting on the Report Stage of the Corrie Bill that there is strong support in the House for a reduction in the time limit to 24 weeks. If such a bill was introduced by an MP with a high place in the ballot it would be very likely to be successful. However it appears unlikely that such a bill will be introduced because the anti-abortion lobby, inside and outside Parliament, would have little interest in such a bill. In fact Sainsbury himself implied this when he explained why he had finally decided not to introduce an abortion bill. He argued:

> SPUC are now pressing for implementation of the Infant Life (Preservation) Act, 1929, under which it is an offence to destroy a child capable of being born alive. That could be taken to be a foetus younger than 22 weeks [Sainsbury had a time limit of 20 or 22 weeks in mind] and therefore an upper limit could be a disadvantage.[9]

In other words SPUC and LIFE hope to use the Courts to reduce the upper time limit below 28 weeks.

However this is only part of the picture. SPUC and LIFE have little interest in marginally reducing the time limit as this would have a relatively small effect on the number of abortions performed. They are much more interested, as a first step, in a radical reform of the 'grounds' clause which would remove the statistical argument and bring about a major reduction in the level of abortions. In effect this means that no MP would receive support from SPUC or LIFE for a bill merely dealing with the time limit. In fact LIFE made no approach to Sainsbury as they were not interested in the type of bill he was considering. In contrast SPUC made considerable efforts by direct approaches to Sainsbury, through letters from its members, and by pressure from sympathetic MPs to persuade Sainsbury not to take a time limit bill, but to consider a bill on the grounds.[10] It was unsuccessful partly because Sainsbury is not a strong anti-abortionist, and partly because he was aware of the opposition such a bill would generate. However SPUC did make it clear to him that he would not receive its support on a time-limit bill and this must have been a major reason why he did not promote such a bill. Sainsbury also realized that any attempt to restrict the 1967 Abortion Act would be, what he termed, 'fanatically' opposed. Given the strength of this opposition he doubted whether he could even lower the upper time limit to 20 or 22 weeks.

Any future bill then is almost certain to be a one-clause bill, and is most likely to be a bill dealing with the grounds for legal abortion. However such a bill would not necessarily receive a Second Reading. In their voting on the Report Stage of the Corrie Bill MPs approved the inclusion of the word 'substantial' in the 'grounds' clause by a majority of three, and rejected the inclusion of the word 'serious' by 56 votes. In addition the Silkin amendment which would have reduced the likely effect of the inclusion of 'substantial' was passed by a majority of 35. This implies that if there is a parliamentary majority for a change in the 'grounds' clause it is a narrow majority, and it involves support for a moderate, rather than a radical, change. Given this precarious balance on the issue a radical clause would almost certainly be defeated, while a more moderate clause might just pass on Second Reading. Even so the fate of such a bill at Report Stage would be problematic as there would be ample opportunity for amendments to be put, which would make it easier to filibuster than a one-clause bill on the time limit. All this would suggest that a 'grounds' clause would be unlikely to succeed given the current composition of Parliament. A similar view was in fact put forward by Donald Stewart when he gave his reasons for not taking an abortion bill. He argued: 'I do not believe a [major] reform will be possible until there is a change in the composition of the House.'[11]

In effect it seems that a radical reform of the Abortion Act is only likely to be achieved if there is a considerable change in parliamentary opinion. Given the relationship between party and vote this might happen if a Conservative Government was elected with a very large majority. At the same time it might result from a change in public and parliamentary attitudes to abortion as a result of some conservative or moralistic reaction to liberal social policies. At present the first eventuality appears more likely, but even if it happened, the procedure for private members' bills could still prevent a large bill being successful.

One other point needs to be emphasized. After the saga of the Corrie Bill most uncommitted MPs are tired of the issue. They wish it would go away although they know it will not. This view was in evidence after the private members' ballot in December 1980 when one prominent Labour backbencher was searching the lobbies for Donald Stewart. When asked why, he replied: 'I must persuade him not to introduce an Abortion bill, I couldn't stand to go through all that again.' This antipathy is common and while it will not be enough to prevent a strong anti-abortionist from introducing a bill, it may sway a waverer, and it may influence voting patterns on Second Reading at least for the rest of the life of this Parliament.

Notes

1. Personal interview, 15 July 1980.
2. *Guardian,* 5 March 1980.
3. *Guardian,* 1 December 1980.
4. Personal interview, 19 June 1980.

5. *Guardian,* 28 November and 1 December 1980 and *Daily Mail,* 28 November 1980. Sainsbury finally decided to take an Indecent Displays (Control) Bill, see the *Times,* 14 January 1980.
6. *Swindon Evening Advertiser,* 27 November 1980 and *The Lancet,* 6 December 1980. Morrison finally decided to take a Horserace Betting Levy Bill.
7. *General Practitioner,* 5 December 1980 and *The Lancet,* 6 December 1980. Stewart finally decided to take a Gaelic (Miscellaneous Provisions) Bill.
8. *Times,* 14 January 1981.
9. *Times,* 14 January 1981.
10. *Times,* 2 March 1981. John Smeaton, general secretary of SPUC wrote in a letter to the *Times*: 'SPUC could not support a Bill which introduced a 22 or 20-week age-limit for abortion'.
11. *Times,* 14 January 1981.

7
In Conclusion — Some Wider Implications of this Case Study

Our case study of the Corrie Bill, while interesting in its own right, can also help to answer a number of wider questions of concern to students of British politics. Our aim in this chapter is to examine four wider questions, which we raised in the introduction, in the light of our case study of the Corrie Bill: Do private members' bills have a useful role to play in the legislative process? Which strategy and tactics are most efficacious for parliamentary interest groups? How important is feminism in British politics? What factors influence MPs' voting on unwhipped issues?

The Usefulness of Private Members' Bills

In the nineteenth and early twentieth century private members' bills were often highly controversial, and indeed were sometimes used by opposition parties as a means of publicizing their own legislative proposals. In this way the Irish Nationalists used the procedure to introduce a series of Home Rule bills at the end of the nineteenth century, and even in the 1920s and 1930s the Labour Party used it to bring forward a series of radical proposals.[1]

Nevertheless as Bromhead has shown, the twentieth century has seen a decline in the number of controversial bills introduced. In the period between 1900 and 1955 there was a continuing increase in the number of bills passed without a division on Second Reading,[2] and a decline in the number of divisions taken in Committee and at the Report Stage on private members' bills.[3] In fact, most of the bills introduced in the period were minor technical bills, often suggested to private members by a government department. Indeed Bromhead, after a very thorough study of private members' business up to the mid-1950s, was far from convinced of its usefulness. He argued that in a period when the government was faced with increasingly complex problems it should have more time to legislate to solve them at the expense of increasingly irrelevant private members' business.[4]

The period of Labour Government between 1964 and 1970 appeared to contradict Bromhead's view. This period saw the passage of a whole series of liberal reforms in the fields of capital punishment, homosexuality and divorce as well as abortion.[5] However all these bills received government time, and none would have been successful without it. In fact between 1964 and 1970 the Labour Government gave assistance to 23 private member' bills which became law. The support was given to MPs of all parties and usually took the form of the provision of help at the Committee Stage.[6]

In contrast, the 1970-4 Conservative Government gave assistance to only one bill. During this period 46 private members' bills were successful but none of these could be described as controversial. Indeed there was only one vote at Second or Third Reading on any successful private member's bill and on that occasion the vote was 75 to 1 in its favour. At the same time 35 of the 46 successful bills (76 per cent) were minor or technical.[7]

The return of a Labour Government in 1974 did change the pattern slightly and the government granted time to seven bills. In this period 98 private members' bills received the Royal Assent but 67 (69 per cent) were minor and technical. There was no parliamentary division on any of these bills at Second or Third Reading. The general pattern then is clear. Since 1970 no controversial legislation has been passed on private members' business in the sense that the House has divided only once on a successful private member's bill in that period. In addition the vast majority of the successful legislation introduced by private members is minor and technical and in *no sense* contentious. Of course these legislative changes may affect considerable numbers of people but they most often involve small administrative changes. Private members' business obviously serves some role in promoting such changes but it is a relatively low key political role.

Of course issues like abortion are very different from the normal run of private members' issues. Indeed by any definition this is the most controversial issue discussed in private members' time. There have been 13 bills introduced since 1953. The debates are heated, well attended and with large votes. Our analysis of the Benyon and Corrie Bills indicates the great difficulty of achieving any legislative change on such a controversial issue through private members' business.

The Benyon Bill received a majority of 38 at Second Reading, but it was late going to Committee because Benyon had only won fifth place in the ballot for private members' bills. The pro-abortion MPs on the Committee, although nothing like as well organized as they were to become on the Corrie Bill, managed to prevent the Bill returning for a Report Stage debate by putting a large number of amendments down for debate in Committee and by filibustering the debate. The pattern on the Corrie Bill was different but the result was the same. Here the Bill received even more support at Second Reading, came out of Committee in good time but was prevented from achieving a Third Reading when the pro-abortion side tabled a large number of amendments at Report Stage and organized a substantial filibuster of the debate. In both cases a small, well-organized group of parliamentarians, admittedly with considerable support inside and outside the House of Commons, managed to prevent the bills becoming law.

Of course this presents only part of the picture. As we have pointed out the Corrie Bill was very wide in scope and a smaller bill, perhaps including a time-limit clause and a grounds clause, might have got through in some form, although significantly amended. However it must be remembered that the Corrie Bill drew first place in the ballot and had four days at Report Stage. It is always possible that another MP may draw first in the ballot and promote a smaller abortion bill, but it is unlikely that such a bill would get more than two days on Report. In that case a one-clause bill dealing with the time limit would probably get through, as there is strong support for it in Parliament. In contrast it seems to us that it is quite possible that a one-clause bill to change the grounds on which abortions could be carried out, even if it was supported by a majority of MPs, would be successfully filibustered by pro-abortion MPs. They would have scope for amendments and plenty of speakers to filibuster the debate.

It is not only on abortion that this pattern emerges. Another excellent example was provided in the same session by the Seat Belts Bill. This Bill received a Second Reading by 134 votes to 59. It was delayed in Committee not so much by direct filibustering as by the threat of it. Neil Carmichael, the Bill's sponsor, knew from the outset that it had little, if any, chance of success because it would be strongly opposed by a group of 12 to 15 MPs on the grounds that it infringed personal liberty with its stress on compulsion. In fact the Bill had two days on Report during which it was efficiently filibustered largely through the efforts of two men, Ivan Lawrence (Con. Burton), and Ronald Bell (Con. Beaconsfield). Indeed by the end of these two days less than half of the Bill's clauses had been discussed and it was effectively talked out.[8] Here again a Bill which received considerable support at Second Reading was defeated by a well-organized small group of opponents. Indeed it is difficult to see any seat belts bill being successful under the current procedure unless it were granted government time.

The aggregate figures thus show a decline in controversial bills. Our detailed study of the abortion issue reveals how easy it is to use parliamentary procedure to prevent a bill which receives wide support in principle from becoming law, even in a much amended form. All this suggests that private members' bills have limited utility. They certainly cannot be used to introduce large-scale controversial legislation without help from the government. Even less radical, yet still contentious legislation, has little chance of passing because a few MPs can successfully filibuster it. This means that most successful private members' bills are minor and technical. At the same time of course because Labour governments have been willing to give time to such bills while Conservative governments have not, then Members who sponsored 'liberal' reforms have been favoured. The Labour Party and Labour MPs have tended to promote 'liberal' causes and so have supported controversial 'liberal' proposals. The Conservative party and Conservative MPs have tended to be less open to change on such issues but Conservative governments have been unwilling to grant time. This is obviously crucial in the abortion case. David Steel could not have got his legislation through without considerable support from the Labour Government, while John Corrie would have been successful in getting some conservative amendment to the Abortion Act through if he had been granted similar facilities by a Conservative government.

Where does this leave us? Private members' business evidently serves a purpose for the introduction of minor and technical bills to amend legislation. However, current procedure is inappropriate for dealing with contentious legislation. It would seem misguided to abandon private members' bills, not only because they can be used to tidy up existing legislation, but also because governments, for party political reasons are unwilling to introduce bills to deal with a wide range of social, moral or contentious issues. Apart from abortion, issues like freedom of information, seat belts, blood sports and obscenity concern many people, and are only likely to be raised and legislated upon through private members' bills. Yet there is no point in Parliament wasting time and money continually debating the same issues because parliamentary procedure does not allow these issues to be resolved. What is needed is a change in procedure to allow Parliament to come to a final decision on such bills. This means that more time needs to be provided.

There are problems of course; one would need to reduce the number of such private members' bills introduced each session so as to ensure that they did not monopolize too much parliamentary time. In addition one would need to prevent a bill dealing with the same issue being introduced in each session. Perhaps a rule which allowed only one bill on each issue per Parliament would be most appropriate. Such a procedure would certainly appeal to most of the MPs we talked to who found the current procedure intellectually challenging but practically inappropriate. It would also make the procedure much more understandable to the general public. At present many MPs and professional lobbyists find it difficult to appreciate its complexities, and most members of interest groups find it incoherent and inexplicable.

Parliamentary Interest Groups

Most, although by no means all, studies of British interest groups concentrate upon economic interest groups. As such, and given the dominance of the executive in British politics, they are concerned with the groups' contacts with Whitehall and to a lesser extent with the political parties. Little attention is paid in such studies to Parliament as it is assumed, quite rightly, that most policy is made by Ministers and civil servants and merely legitimized by Parliament. What is more, large economic interest groups themselves pay little attention to Parliament as they are equally aware of the facts of British political life. Of course the pattern is very different on so-called conscience issues, where the government coyly steps aside and allows MPs to make up their own minds. Here Parliament makes the decisions and therefore interest groups devote much of their effort to influencing MPs and persuading them to promote or defend legislation. As such it is on conscience issues that we can see most clearly the tactics and strategies used in parliamentary, as distinct from departmental, lobbying.

Once again abortion provides us with an unusually good case study. It is an issue which has persisted and one where there are a variety of cause and economic interest groups involved, almost exclusively attempting to influence MPs. At the same time the process is heightened by the fact that the level of politicization of both the interest groups and the MPs far exceeds that on other issues. In such circumstances do any interest groups have much influence, or do MPs make up their minds unaffected by such pressure? Which are the most effective tactics an interest group can use? Our case study, especially if examined together with a number of other books written about the abortion issue to which we shall be referring below, throws considerable light on these questions.

It is clear from our study that interest groups have had considerable influence on this issue. In some senses this merely confirms the impression given by both Simms and Hindell[9] and Richards.[10] In fact as we saw earlier Richards after his study of all the conscience issues of the 1960s concluded that ALRA was the most influential of the interest groups which he examined. Yet the pattern of interest group activity on the issue and the influence of the various groups involved have changed considerably since the 1960s. ALRA is no longer an important force, although some individuals who were members of it at the time of the Steel Bill are still influential. In fact the 1970s saw first the growth of the anti-abortion groups to a stage where they were the dominant groups involved, followed by a reaction in which the pro-abortion lobby developed a two-pronged attack through the efforts of NAC and Co-ord.

There is little doubt then that interest groups have played an influential role on the abortion issue, or that different groups have been important at different times. At the same time our analysis clearly indicates that certain strategies and tactics are most appropriate in attempting to influence Parliament. The first conclusion is obvious but can hardly be too strongly emphasized. It is much easier to defend existing legislation than to promote new legislation. This is largely because of the limitations of the procedure for private members' bills which we discussed earlier. So any interest group intending to change legislation needs either to persuade the government to give it time, or to promote gradual change and smaller bills. As only the Labour Party appears willing to give time to private members' bills then groups promoting 'conservative' policies have to be circumspect in their aims. In fact on the abortion issue the anti-abortion groups have learnt that lesson and are now committed to a step-by-step approach to reform, rather than to the grand design of the Corrie Bill.

It is also evident from our study that the anti-abortion lobby has over-emphasized extra-parliamentary activity. Of course any interest group attempting to influence MPs must have support from the country, and in the case of the White Bill and the Benyon Bill, SPUC and LIFE's orchestrated write-in campaigns to MPs were effective. However such efforts were less effective on the Corrie Bill. This was partly because these efforts were increasingly matched by those of NAC from the pro-abortion side, and partly because MPs, inundated with constituents' letters, quickly became punch-drunk and alienated by the efforts of both sides.

On the Corrie Bill there is no doubt that the balance struck by the pro-abortion side was much more appropriate for a parliamentary interest group. The pro-abortionists emphasized the necessity for a strong organization within Parliament which was well co-ordinated with the extra-parliamentary forces. This side was a united whole. The efforts of the extra-parliamentary groups were co-ordinated through Co-ord which also provided important liaison between those groups and the MPs. It is true that they were helped by the fact that any policy differences between the groups could be subsumed within the common cause of defending the 1967 Act, but nevertheless the stress on co-ordination and planning was a direct response to the problems they had experienced on the Benyon Bill. In contrast the Corrie side was in disarray. There was insufficient co-ordination between the extra-parliamentary and the parliamentary branches of the lobby, and little real discussion of strategy. Once again the anti-abortion side has learnt from this experience. We have already noted that, at the beginning of the 1980-1 session, a number of MPs established an *ad hoc* committee to discuss both the lessons to be learnt from that experience and the future strategy and tactics to be adopted. Representatives of both SPUC and LIFE will be invited to all this Committee's meetings. Such co-ordination and strategy is crucial to any parliamentary interest group.

The Corrie Bill also shows how important a knowledge of parliamentary procedure is for parliamentary interest groups. The pro-abortion side was better versed in procedure, and on most occasions better at using it. They made one mistake by delaying matters in Standing Committee, but MPs from both sides whom we interviewed emphasized their 'superior' political and procedural skills. This is important not only because it allows the side with such knowledge to benefit from its use, but also because such skill is admired by MPs. In the case of the Corrie Bill some MPs may even have voted against some of its provisions at Report because its supporters were regarded as politically inept. Certainly it is crucial for any interest group promoting a private member's bill to have detailed knowledge of procedure, and parliamentary supporters with a similar appreciation of such complexities.

One final point is clear. In the case of a social or medical issue like abortion there is considerable advantage to having the support of the appopriate professional associations. When David Steel piloted the original Bill through Parliament he made important concessions to the BMA and the RCOG in order to minimize their opposition. Subsequently both the BMA and the

RCOG have become strong defenders of the current legislation. While this appeared to have little effect on voting on the White, or the Benyon Bills it did have considerable effect on voting at Report Stage on the Corrie Bill. On the Corrie Bill for the first time MPs seemed to appreciate the strength of medical opposition to any radical amendment of the Abortion Act, and a large number of MPs told us that they believed this was a crucial factor in influencing the votes of uncommitted MPs at Report Stage. Certainly one of the weaknesses of the anti-abortion interest groups in future is likely to remain their failure to gain support from such professional bodies.

Feminism

It would be wrong of course to claim that abortion is just a feminist issue. It is a moral issue and women take positions on both sides. Nevertheless it appears to us to be a feminist issue in at least three ways. First, it is unusual in parliamentary terms because it is the issue on which Labour women first united as a group. As Elizabeth Vallance has said in a study of women in Parliament:

> it is the Labour women, and specifically the Labour women of the 1974 Parliament, who have developed a strong group sense. This was probably largely the result of the threats to the 1967 Abortion Act which drew them together in support of the already existing liberal legislation.[11]

Certainly Labour women have played a crucial role in the defence of the Abortion Act. Of the six pro-abortion members of the Benyon Standing Committee five were Labour women although at the time there were 27 women, 18 of them Labour MPs, in Parliament. On the Corrie Bill the two most active MPs were Jo Richardson and Oonagh McDonald. There can be no doubt that it has been an issue on which women in Parliament have played the main role, and it is an issue which has helped to politicize and unify Labour women in Parliament.

The abortion issue has played a similar role outside Parliament. As Vallance says:

> Abortion focussed attention on a particular issue and has, inside and outside the House, concentrated women's aspirations and self awareness on one issue — rather as the sufragettes did in earlier days. Both gave women a focus, something precise and specifiable and central to their developing self-consciousness.[12]

In fact one of the most notable aspects of the lobbying since the Benyon Bill in 1977 has been the growth of the extra-parliamentary activities of the supporters of the 1967 Act. This growth, as we have seen, resulted largely from the efforts of NAC which was formed in 1975. NAC is a strongly feminist organization and indeed the vast majority of its active members are women and feminists. Without the efforts of NAC the balance between the two sides on the Corrie Bill would have been less even, so once again there is a significant feminist element here.

The feminist movement has also been important in relation to the media coverage of the abortion issue. In the run-up to the Second Reading Debate upon the White Bill in 1975 the press comments on abortion were evenly balanced. By 1977 and the Benyon Bill the pattern had changed, with the majority of the national newspapers who commented upon the issue opposing amending legislation while a minority still supported it. On the Corrie Bill almost all press comment was unfavourable to the Bill. In particular there was a significant change among both the provincial newspapers and the women's magazines. This seems to have resulted from two related factors. First, there has been an increase in the number of women journalists and a greater willingness among these women to dispute the editorial line if it is anti-abortion. Secondly, feminist views have become respectable enough for even fairly conservative women's magazines to regard taking a stand against the Corrie Bill as acceptable and uncontentious.

This growth in the acceptability of the feminist viewpoint also had a considerable effect on thinking in the Labour Party and among liberal MPs. As we saw the change in Labour Party and TUC policy to overt support for liberal abortion law owed much to the efforts of women within these organizations and had some effect on the voting of Labour MPs on the Corrie Bill. More generally the idea of women's rights has become an important aspect of a 'liberal' political perspective. Liberal abortion law is associated with women's rights and so some liberal MPs voted to defend the 1967 Abortion Act even if they had little interest in, or knowledge of, the issue.

It is clear then that feminism has had a significant effect on the abortion issue. This does not mean that feminism is an important political force generally. There are so few women in Parliament that even if they were united across parties, which they are not even on abortion, they could have little effect. However what the abortion issue does suggest is that the feminist viewpoint has been incorporated, at least in some form, into the liberal ideological perspective. In addition, and perhaps more importantly, it indicates what a well organized group of women, inside and outside Parliament, can achieve if they are united.

Parliament without Party Discipline

Although Britain is a parliamentary democracy the existence of strong party discipline means that in most circumstances policy is made by government and merely legitimated by Parliament.[13] It is true, as Norton has documented, that there has been a significant increase in dissent on the floor of the House of Commons with many more MPs willing to defy the whip on frequent occasions.[14] Nevertheless any government can be sure of a majority on almost all elements in its legislative programme. This tight, if slightly slackening, party discipline means that on all whipped votes most MPs toe the party line and as such are not influenced by other factors. It is thus only on unwhipped issues that we can see more directly the effect of other factors such as ideology, religion, constituency pressures and lobbying on MPs' votes. Among these unwhipped issues abortion is an unusual and useful case because we have a whole series of votes which we can analyse in relation to such factors.

It might be argued of course that as there are relatively few free votes in the House of Commons there is little point in examining the factors which affect MPs voting under such circumstances. This view seems shortsighted. MPs retain their consciences and ideological positions, and are subject to constituency and interest group pressure on whipped issues although such factors are normally subsumed under the all-pervasive strictures of party discipline. However as party discipline decreases, as the signs show it is doing, these factors will become more significant. Given such a development an analysis of the factors which influence MPs in circumstances of free voting may well offer insights into the wider pattern of parliamentary voting in the future.

What factors influence MPs voting in free-vote situations? We have concentrated upon four sets of factors: the party identification and ideological position of the MP; the personal background of MPs; constituency characteristics and pressure; and the political environment within which MPs are voting.

Party Identification and Ideological Position of the MP

The best study to date of MPs' voting on conscience issues is George Moyser's analysis of parliamentary voting in the 1960s on divorce, capital punishment, abortion, homosexuality and Sunday entertainment.[15] He found that despite the fact that the issues were unwhipped, party was the best predictor of voting. On these issues, the Conservative MPs overwhelmingly opposed liberal reform, while Labour MPs consistently supported the liberal position.[16] In addition, Moyser's data indicated that there was a general liberal/conservative ideological dimension at work so that a liberal stance on one issue was related to a liberal stance upon another, and likewise a conservative stance on one issue was related to conservative stances upon others.[17]

Moyser's work however only deals with the 1960s and indeed, when considering abortion, only looks at the Second and Third Reading votes on the Steel Bill. In contrast, we have data on all the abortion, capital punishment and homosexuality votes which occurred in the 1960s and 1970s.[18] How far does Moyser's conclusion hold true for the later period?

It is clear from our material that the relationship between party and voting on these three moral issues continued into the 1970s (see Table 7.1). Labour MPs supported the liberal position while Conservative MPs took the conservative position. However, the relationship, while persistent and significant, is a far from perfect one particularly if we consider all MPs. This is largely because party is not a good predictor of non-voting on the issues. As

Table 7.1: Relationship between Party and Voting on Social Issues

(a) Abortion, 1966-80

Vote	Strength of relationship: All MPs of all parties	Strength of relationship: Labour & Conservative MPs who voted
Steel Bill Second Reading (1966)	0.043us	0.000**
Steel Bill Third Reading (1967)	0.000us	0.305*
St John-Stevas Bill (1969)	0.184us	0.543*
White Bill, Second Reading (1975)	0.007us	0.000*
Benyon Bill, Second Reading (1977)	0.007us	0.484*
Braine Bill (1978)	0.006us	
Corrie Bill, Second Reading (1979)	0.102us	0.306*
Report Stage, 24-week amendment (1980)	0.109us	0.114*
'Serious' amendment (1980)	0.174us	0.365*
'Substantial' amendment (1980)	0.199us	0.616*
Silkin amendment (1980)	0.099us	0.556*

usChi Square unstable.
*Chi Square significant at 0.001 level.
**Chi Square significant at 0.05 level.

Note: The statistic used in all three parts of the table (a, b, c) is *Lambda B*. In the case of the left-hand column it is based on eight by three tables and in the right-hand column on two by two tables.

Table 7.1 also indicates, if we exclude the non-voters and the minor party MPs from the appropriate divisions, then the relationship is much closer.

The data also reveals a number of interesting differences between the relationship of party to abortion voting, and its relationship to voting on capital punishment and homosexuality. Moyser found that in the 1960s party was a better predictor of voting on abortion and divorce than of MPs' votes on other social issues. In contrast, in the later period our results indicate that party is a much better predictor of voting on capital punishment

Table 7.1 (continued)

(b) Capital Punishment, 1965-79

Vote	All MPs	Only those Labour & Conservative MPs who voted
Murder (abolition of death penalty) Bill, Third Reading (1965)	0.000[us]	0.711*
Sandys's motion concerning re-introduction of capital punishment (November 1966)	0.342[us]	0.689*
Murder (abolition of death penalty) Bill (June 1969)	0.382[us]	0.667*
Government affirmative motion on capital punishment (December 1969)	0.235[us]	0.727*
Anti-capital punishment amendment to government affirmative motion on capital punishment (December 1974)	0.556[us]	0.676*
Government affirmative motion on capital punishment (July 1979)	0.515[us]	0.576*

[us]Chi Square unstable.
*Chi Square significant at 0.01 level.

(c) Homosexuality, 1967-80

Vote	All MPs	Only those Labour & Conservative MPs who voted
Third Reading, Sexual Offences Bill (1967)	0.000[us]	0.000*
Vote on Criminal Justice (Scotland) Bill (homosexuality law reform for Scotland) (1980)	0.088[us]	0.237*

[us]Chi Square unstable.
*Chi Square significant at 0.01 level.

than it is of voting on abortion or homosexuality. The relative weakness of the relationship on abortion results from the fact that the Labour Party has been split on abortion but very cohesive on the other issues. In contrast it is the split in the Conservative Party which weakens the relationship as far as homosexuality and capital punishment are concerned (see Table 7.2). How can we explain these patterns?

It is clear both from Moyser's results, and from our analysis that there is a liberal/conservative ideological dimension operating here, a fact which is confirmed by the strong relationships which exist between voting on the three issues, particularly if we exclude non-voters (see Tables 7.4 and 7.5). In the case of the Labour Party the liberal position on social issues has been endorsed by Conference decisions, strongly supported by most constituency parties and at times legitimized by discussions in PLP meetings. In other words, although these are not party issues, in the Labour Party there is a clear liberal ideology which is reinforced by practical political pressures. In effect, this means that the more interesting problem is to explain the division in the Labour Party, on abortion, rather than its cohesion on other social issues.

Even within the Labour Party there appears to be a relationship between ideology and voting on the abortion issue. The members of the Tribune Group are consistently much more likely to oppose amending legislation than their party colleagues. This pattern is clear in Table 7.5. Tribune Group MPs are more likely to oppose amending legislation, less likely to support it and much less likely not to vote on the issue than their Labour colleagues. This pattern persists throughout the voting on the Corrie Bill and also exists when we consider all the votes of Labour MPs in the 1974-9 Parliament. Obviously there is a relationship among Labour MPs between support for socialist economic policies and liberal views on abortion. The pattern does not appear on the other issues because the Labour Party is so united in its support of the liberal position on both capital punishment and homosexuality reform.

Actually as Table 7.2 indicates, there has been greater intraparty cohesion in the Labour Party on some of the abortion votes. It was most split on the Second Reading votes on the White Bill and on the Corrie Bill. As we said earlier, the voting on the White

Bill was very much influenced by the late abortion stories in the press immediately prior to the vote.[19] In addition, for reasons we dealt with at some length in the last chapter the voting at Report Stage on the Corrie Bill was a more accurate reflection of the views of MPs on the Bill than the Second Reading vote, and the Labour Party was more unified on these votes. In effect then, the split within the Labour Party is not as great as those two votes at first suggest. nevertheless, there is a significant division to explain. Obviously, the split is partly due to the voting of Roman Catholic MPs. Indeed, of the 20 Labour MPs who voted for the Corrie Bill in all the five major divisions we have considered, 40 per cent (8) were Roman Catholics, whereas Roman Catholics only make up 8 per cent of the PLP as a whole. However, given these figures it is clear that the Catholicism of MPs does not totally explain the split in the PLP. What is more, there is no evidence that Labour MPs with a large Roman Catholic element in their constituencies are more likely to support amending legislation. Indeed if anything an opposite pattern exists, as we shall see below.[20]

In fact, the other main element in the explanation applies not only to Labour MPs. It probably also goes some way to explaining the anti-abortion voting of some Conservative MPs who are liberal on other issues. Abortion is unlike capital punishment and homosexuality, in that there are potentially two liberal values involved which are somewhat contradictory. Many liberals support abortion because they see a woman's right to choose abortion as a basic human right. Such liberals would argue that the foetus does not have rights until it is viable, or for some of them, until it is born. In contrast however, if the liberal sees human life as beginning at conception then he is faced with a choice between the competing rights of the mother and the child. Thus while there is little doubt that the majority of liberals favour a liberal abortion policy, whilst conservatives advocate at most limited abortion, there are contradictory moral values involved which make it difficult to locate positions on the issue along with a simple liberal/conservative ideological dimension. Certainly some Labour MPs, amongst whom Leo Abse is probably the most notable, who are liberal on other social issues are strong opponents of abortion, a position which they would defend by reference to liberal values.

Table 7.2: Intra-party Cohesion and Inter-party Differences on Social Issues (MPs who voted)

(a) Abortion, 1966-80

		Conservatives			Labour		
Voted	Inter-party difference %	Pro-** %	Anti-*** %	Intra-party cohesion* %	Pro-** %	Anti-*** %	Intra-party cohesion* %
Steel Bill, Second Reading (1966)	12	80	20	60	92	8	84
Steel Bill, Third Reading (1967)	51	34	66	32	85	15	70
St John-Stevas Bill (1969)	58	20	80	60	78	22	56
White Bill, Second Reading (1975)	42	4	96	92	46	54	8
Benyon Bill, Second Reading (1977)	55	15	85	70	70	30	40
Braine Bill, ten-minute rule bill (1978)	48	23	77	54	71	29	42
Corrie Bill, Second Reading (1979)	47	8	92	84	55	45	10
Report Stage, 24 week amendment	34	46	54	8	80	20	60
'Serious' amendment	48	38	62	24	86	14	72
'Substantial' amendment	62	16	84	68	78	22	56
Silkin amendment	66	24	76	52	90	10	80

*Measured by subtracting those supporting a bill from those who oppose it within the party — perfect cohesion is therefore 100% and occurs when all MPs of the party vote in the same way. Intra-party difference is arrived at by subtracting the percentage of Conservative supporters from the percentage of Labour supporters. It can range from 0% to 100%.

**Here, as throughout, a vote for the Steel Bill and against the Amendment Bills.

***Here, as throughout, a vote against the Steel Bill and for the Amendment Bills.

(b) Capital Punishment, 1965-79

Vote	Inter-party differences %	Conservatives Pro-* %	Conservatives Anti-** %	Conservatives Intra-party cohesion %	Labour Pro-* %	Labour Anti-** %	Labour Intra-party cohesion %
Murder (abolition of death penalty) Bill, Third Reading (1965)	77	77 (N 76)	23 (N 23)	54	0 (N 0)	100 (N 157)	100
Sandys' motion concerning re-introduction of capital punishment (November 1966)	74	81 (N 147)	19 (N 34)	62	7 (N 17)	93 (N 244)	86
Murder (abolition of death penalty) Bill (June 1969)	79	81 (N 105)	19 (N 25)	62	2 (N 5)	98 (N 212)	96
Government affirmative motion on capital punishment (December 1969)	74	76 (N 163)	24 (N 51)	52	2 (N 5)	98 (N 257)	96
Anti-capital punishment amendment to government affirmative motion on capital punishment (December 1974)	78	80 (N 198)	20 (N 60)	60	2 (N 6)	98 (N 290)	96
Government affirmative motion on capital punishment (July 1979)	70	71 (N 228)	29 (N 95)	42	1 (N 3)	99 (N 251)	98

*See note to Table 7.2 (a) on intra-party cohesion.

**An 'aye' vote in November 1966, June 1969 and December 1974 and a 'no' vote on the other occasions.

***An 'aye' vote in 1965 and July 1979 and a 'no' vote in June and December 1969 and December 1974.

Table 7.2 continued

(c) Homosexuality, 1967-80

Vote	Inter-party difference %	Conservatives Pro- %	Conservatives Anti- %	Conservatives Intra-party cohesion* %	Labour Pro- %	Labour Anti- %	Labour Intra-party cohesion* %
Sexual Offences Bill, Third Reading (1967)	21	50 (N 14)	50 (N 14)	0	71 (N 200)	39 (N 80)	42
Amendment to Criminal Justice (Scotland) Bill (1980)	54	43 (N 53)	57 (N 71)	14	97 (N 139)	3 (N 5)	94

* See note to Table 7.2 (a) on intra party cohesion.

Note: More information on these votes is contained in note 18 to this chapter.

Table 7.3: Relationship between Voting on Abortion, Capital Punishment and Homosexuality, 1979-80 (all MPs)

Votes on Corrie Abortion Bill	Relationship with vote on homosexuality	Relationship with vote on capital punishment
Second Reading	0.067	0.091
24 week amendment	0.040	0.100
'Substantial' amendment	0.080	0.094
'Serious' amendment	0.074	0.096
Silkin amendment	0.032	0.077

Note: Chi Square is unstable in all these cases. The statistic used here is *Lambda symmetrical.*

Table 7.4: Relationship between Voting on Abortion, Capital Punishment and Homosexuality, 1979-80 (MPs who voted on all issues)

Votes on Corrie Abortion Bill	Relationship with vote on homosexuality	Relationship with vote on capital punishment
Second Reading	0.027*	0.138*
24 week amendment	0.179*	0.141*
'Substantial' amendment	0.262*	0.417*
'Serious' amendment	0.204*	0.338*
Silkin amendment	0.213*	0.353*

*Chi Square is significant at the 0.001 level. The statistic used here is *Lambda symmetrical.*

The other question posed by this data is: why is the Conservative Party split on homosexuality and, to a slightly lesser extent, on capital punishment, yet more cohesive on abortion? In fact, our results make it clear that there is a distinctly liberal/conservative division within the Conservative Party on the other two moral issues with one-third of the Conservatives who vote adopting a liberal stance, and two-thirds taking a conservative position (see Table 7.2). It seems likely to us that the

Table 7.5: Relationship between Tribune Group Membership and Voting on Second Reading of the Corrie Bill

Voting	Tribune Group membership	Other Labour MPs
For	9 (N 5)	23 (N 49)
Against	56 (N 30)	25 (N 54)
Not voting	35 (N 19)	52 (N 112)
Total:	100%	100%

existence of this liberal wing in the Conservative Party owes a great deal to the general liberal intellectual climate on social, sexual and moral issues which has developed in Britain since the beginning of the 1960s. Indeed it would be surprising if some Conservative MPs, who after all are overwhelmingly drawn from middle-class backgrounds and are university educated, had not been influenced by this liberal climate, which in itself was reinforced by the passage of liberal social legislation in the 1960s. Once again however, abortion is the exception to the general picture as here the Conservative Party is more cohesive. As we have already suggested, it may be that because abortion does not involve a simple liberal/conservative dimension, the group of liberal Conservatives are split in their views and votes on this issue, in a way which they are not on the other issues, so that some of them vote for amending legislation.

Two other patterns in the data deserve attention. First, as we have already said, there is a significant inter-relationship between voting on capital punishment and voting on homosexuality reform. In contrast, the relationship between abortion voting and voting on capital punishment is weaker, but still fairly strong, while that between abortion and homosexuality reform voting is weakest (see Table 7.3). The explanation of that pattern is clear from our prevous discussion. The Labour Party splits on abortion and is cohesive on the other two issues, while the Conservative Party is cohesive on abortion and split on the other issues. As such there is an obvious symmetry between the voting on capital punishment and homosexuality reform. Secondly there is a relationship between non-voting and party which is not strong but is nevertheless revealing. On all the social issues, Conservative MPs are more likely not to vote than their Labour colleagues (see Table 7.4). This has great significance for the results of the votes. As Conservative MPs generally favour the conservative position, then this differential abstention decreases the likelihood of a successful amendment to the 1967 Abortion Act, or a return to capital punishment.

We have seen that party is a good predictor of voting on these issues especially if we only consider those MPs who vote. At the same time it is evident that there is a significant inter-relationship between voting on these moral issues. As such, there appears to be a conservative/liberal ideological dimension which parallels party and which underpins voting on these issues.

Personal Background of MPs[21]

Moyser found that the only factor apart from party which was significantly related to an MP's vote was religion.[22] In particular, and not surprisingly, he found a strong relationship between Roman Catholicism and the adoption of a conservative stance on moral issues. In contrast he found that social class, educational background, age and sex were relatively insignificantly related to voting patterns.[23] Are these results confirmed in the analysis of the later period?

Our study totally confirms Moyser's findings. There is no consistent relationship between social class, age, date elected to Parliament, level of secondary education or level of tertiary education, and voting on any of the three social issues (see Tables A.3 to A.10). The results with regard to sex and religion are more informative and worthy of brief consideration.

Religion.. At first glance there appears to be no strong association between religion and voting on social issues (see Tables A.3 and A.4). It does not matter whether one compares those MPs who have an identifiable religious denomination with those who do not, or Roman Catholic MPs with all other MPs — there is no apparent association. Of course the problem with using these summary statistics to describe the relationship is that there are relatively few Catholics (in 1979 there were 41 (6 per cent)) and a large number of MPs with no known religious affiliation in the House of Commons (45 per cent).

Despite this there is obviously some relationship between religion and voting, particularly on the abortion issue. Roman Catholics overwhelmingly support amending legislation whilst MPs with no known religious affiliation tend to support the liberal position (see Table 7.6). If we approach the same problem from the other direction and consider the groups of strong anti-abortionists in the House of Commons, then the effect of religion is clear. Among the 56 strong anti-abortionists (that is MPs who voted for the Corrie Bill in all the five key divisions we have analysed) there were more strong Catholics (30 per cent compared with 6 per cent in the entire House of Commons), fewer Anglicans (18 per cent as compared with 33 per cent), and fewer MPs whose religion was unknown (36 per cent as compared with 45 per cent) than among parliamentarians as a whole. In contrast, if we consider the 53 strong pro-abortionists (those MPs who voted against the Corrie Bill on the same five occasions) there were fewer Catholics (2 per cent), fewer Anglicans (6 per cent) and more MPs with no acknowledged religion (68 per cent), than in the House generally. In addition, it is interesting that Anglicans are found more frequently, and MPs with no religious affiliation less frequently than one would expect among those who do not vote.

Overall then, while religion is not a good predictor of voting on these social issues, Roman Catholicism is strongly related to opposition to liberal social reforms, and absence of religious identification is fairly strongly related to voting for such reforms. In contrast Anglicans are more likely to remain out of the division lobbies. It is not surprising of course that Catholic MPs are so strongly opposed to abortion, while the apathy or indecision of Anglicans may reflect their Church's mixed feelings on the issue. It is difficult to say much about the pattern among MPs with no religious affiliation as we have no real way of knowing their actual views. However it may be that many of these MPs are in a broad sense humanists, unidentified with any religious denomination; as such one might expect a connection between such values and a liberal stance on social issues.

Table 7.6: Religion and Votion on Abortion, 1966-80 (numbers)

	Roman Catholics			Anglicans			No known affiliation		
Votes	Pro-	Anti-	No vote	Pro-	Anti-	No vote	Pro-	Anti-	No vote
Steel Bill, Second Reading (1966)	0	14	17	52	7	94	134	8	225
Steel Bill, Third Reading (1967)	0	20	11	38	23	92	95	36	236
St John-Stevas Bill (1969)	0	23	8	43	60	50	93	128	146
White Bill (1975)	0	30	11	13	81	155	46	55	114
Benyon Bill (1977)	1	26	14	29	84	136	65	38	113
Braine Bill (1978)	1	22	18	43	85	121	81	41	94
Corrie Bill, Second Reading (1979)	1	33	7	18	81	110	99	58	131
Report Stage, 24 week amendment (1980)	4	29	8	80	52	77	141	70	77
'Serious' amendment (1980)	3	26	12	44	49	116	117	55	116
'Substantial' amendment (1980)	3	27	11	29	68	112	111	67	110
Silkin amendment (1980)	2	22	17	25	40	144	100	46	142

Table 7.7: Women and Voting on Abortion, 1966-80 (numbers)

Vote	Pro-	Anti-	No vote
Steel Bill, Second Reading (1966)	13	2	10
Steel Bill, Third Reading (1967)	9	4	12
St John-Stevas Bill (1969)	10	6	9
White Bill, Second Reading (1975)	12	3	12
Benyon Bill, Second Reading (1977)	13	6	8
Braine Bill, (1978)	13	4	10
Corrie Bill, Second Reading (1979)	6	6	7
Report Stage, 24 week amendment (1980)	9	3	7
'Serious' amendment (1980)	7	4	8
'Substantial' amendment (1980)	8	4	7
Silkin amendment (1980)	9	4	6

Sex. As there are so few women MPs (only 19 after the 1979 election) sex could not be a major explanatory variable (see Table A.10). However, there is no relationship between sex and voting on these issues. In fact as Table 7.7 shows, women MPs are split on all these issues including abortion. What is more the split almost always exactly follows party lines. So on the Corrie Abortion Bill, no Labour women supported the Corrie Bill at any time, although four or five of the eleven fairly consistently abstained. In contrast, no Conservative woman opposed the Bill at Second Reading, although one, Sheila Faith, did consistently oppose it on Report, while three of the eight abstained. Of course these statistics do hide the fact that two Labour women, Jo Richardson and Oonagh McDonald, provided the core of the pro-abortion lobby while two Conservative women, Jill Knight and Elaine Kellett-Bowman were active on the anti-abortion side.

Constituency Characteristics and Pressure. One of the major limitations of Moyser's work is that he has no data on the MPs' constituencies. Obviously certain constituency characteristics, such as the religious or class composition of the constituency, may have an effect on voting patterns. In particular one might

Table 7.8: Relationship between Party and Voting on Abortion, Controlling for Marginality (Labour and Conservative MPs who voted)

Vote	Relationship between party and vote for MPs in safe seats	Relationship between party and vote for MPs in marginal seats
Steel Bill, Second Reading (1966)	0.000[ns]	0.000*
Steel Bill, Third Reading (1967)	0.098*	0.512*
St John-Stevas Bill (1969)	0.326*	0.760*
White Bill, Second Reading (1975)	0.000*	0.242
Benyon Bill, Second Reading (1977)	0.405*	0.612*
Braine Bill (1978)	0.358*	0.516*
Corrie Bill, Second Reading (1979)	0.051*	0.692*
Report Stage, 24 week amendment (1980)	0.141[ns]	0.857*
'Serious' amendment (1980)	0.267*	0.654*
'Substantial' amendment (1980)	0.313*	0.750*
Silkin amendment (1980)	0.312*	0.882

*Relationship significant at 0.001 level.
[ns]Relationship not significant.

Note: The statistic used here is *Lambda B*. In this case it is based upon two by two tables similar to that reported above see p. 106.

expect MPs with a strong Roman Catholic element in their constituency to be especially vulnerable to constituency pressure and, as the anti-abortion groups are so well organized in many constituencies, to be more likely to vote for amending legislation.

There is in fact a persistent relationship between marginality and voting on abortion. MPs in marginal constituencies are much more likely to vote on the issue than their colleagues in safe seats.[24] In addition, as we indicated in Chapter 3, Labour MPs in marginal constituencies are much more likely to support the 1967 Act, while Conservative MPs in marginal constituencies are slightly more likely to support amending legislation. The association between marginality, party and voting on abortion is clear in Table 7.8, and is to be found on all the votes on the Corrie Bill that we examined, and on most of the preceding votes on abortion.

If we look at the same question from another perspective, all of the 20 Labour MPs who were strongly anti-abortion — that is who voted for Corrie on the five key votes we have examined — held safe seats, although only 68 per cent of the PLP as a whole were in such a position. In contrast, many more of the 33 Conservative MPs who were strongly anti-abortion came from marginal constituencies (45 per cent as compared with 29 per cent in the Parliamentary Party as a whole). It is clear from all these figures that marginality has a persistent effect on voting on abortion.

On homosexuality reform and capital punishment voting a similar although considerably weaker pattern exists with Conservative MPs in marginal constituencies being more likely to oppose liberal reforms.[25] However as so few Labour MPs oppose the liberal position on these two issues marginality has no explanatory power as far as they are concerned.

How can we explain these patterns? There is no doubt that, particularly as far as abortion is concerned, MPs in marginal constituencies are more likely to vote than their colleagues in safe seats. This suggests that MPs in such constituencies are under more pressure from their constituents or local party organizations. However the exact nature of the pressure is obviously different in Conservative and Labour marginal seats. In Labour seats MPs are influenced to vote for a liberal abortion law while in Conservative seats MPs are more likely to be persuaded to support amending legislation. This may result from the fact that anti-abortion groups tend to be more prominent and better organized in Conservative constituencies, while NAC concentrates its efforts in Labour constituencies. At the same time however it may result more from the different views of the local party organization (with Labour GMCs often being liberal or radical and Conservative conservative) than from the action of interest groups, or the views of constituents. After all MPs have much closer contacts, and a more important political relationship with their local party activists than with their constituents as a whole.

The Religious Composition of the Constituency

We must be particularly careful about interpreting these results because the data on the religious composition of the constituencies have two major weaknesses. First, they represent the churches' reports of their membership and as such may be inaccurate. Secondly, we do not have data on the religious composition of constituencies but only on the churches' membership in the counties of which the constituencies are part. As such we have had to make the dubious assumption that there is a close relationship between the religious composition of all constituencies in a given county. In addition the data only deal with English counties, and not with Scottish, Welsh or Northern Irish counties. Nevertheless despite their grave weaknesses these are the best data available and they do reveal some interesting patterns.

There is no obvious uni-dimensional statistical relationship between the religious composition of the constituency and voting on these issues. We had hypothesized that all MPs with a high proportion of Roman Catholic constituents would be more likely to vote for amending legislation on abortion. No such pattern emerges. In fact, while MPs in such constituencies are usually between 15 to 20 per cent more likely to vote than MPs in constituencies with lower Catholic populations, there are distinct differences between the voting behaviour of Labour and Conservative MPs. On the Corrie Bill Labour MPs in constituencies with a higher proportion of Catholics (over 10 per cent) are between 10 and 20 per cent more likely to support liberal abortion policy than are MPs with a lower proportion of Catholics (under 6 per cent) in their constituencies, depending on which of the votes we consider. In contrast Conservative MPs in constituencies with a higher concentration of Roman Catholics are between 5 and 15 per cent more likely to support amending legislation than their colleagues. What is more these relationships persist regardless of the size of the majority in the constituency,[26] although the relationship is not strong enough to show up in the summary statistics. How can we explain this pattern?

It appears likely that MPs with constituencies with larger Roman Catholic elements are more likely to vote because abortion is a more contentious issue in such constituencies and MPs are therefore more politicized upon it. However, the differential effect on Labour and Conservative MPs is harder to explain. Indeed the only explanation we can suggest is based on two, at best plausible, assumptions. If we assume firstly that the majority of Roman Catholics in Labour consitituencies are working class while in Conservative constituencies they are middle class, and secondly that working-class Catholics are more likely to support abortion than middle-class Catholics (because they are more likely to be faced with the practical possibility of abortion); then we would expect the pattern we have identified to occur. Unfortunately because at present we have no data on the class composition of constituencies we cannot attempt to test this new hypothesis.

The Political Environment

It is evident from our analysis that one cannot explain voting on any of these three issues merely by reference to social structural variables. Party and ideology are related and an important explanatory factor, while the two constituency factors we identified also play some role, particularly on abortion. However it is also clear that other factors which we cannot quantify are important. In particular, as our case study of the Corrie Bill has shown, three factors must be emphasized. First, the influence of lobbying outside and especially inside Parliament is obviously crucial. So to take just one example there is no doubt that many Labour MPs were swayed in their voting on the Report Stage of the Corrie Bill by the actions of the persistent and well organized pro-abortion whipping system within the Labour Party. Secondly, on some votes on abortion, particularly for example in the cases of the vote on James White's Bill in 1975 and the Second Reading vote on the Corrie Bill in 1979, the media's coverage of the issue, and especially of late abortion cases prior to the voting, had an effect. Thirdly, there can be little doubt given our analysis that Second Reading votes, and votes on ten-minute rule bills, are not accurate tests of the feeling of the House of Commons on an issue, as many MPs vote to allow a bill to proceed even if they intend to oppose it later. In other words MPs tend to be predisposed to support a bill at Second Reading unless they violently object to it.

Overall then in analysing such issues in Parliament we should not merely concentrate on party, personal or constituency variables to explain votes. Such an approach gives at best a partial picture.

Notes

1. P. Bromhead, *Private Members Bills,* London, Routledge & Kegan Paul, 1956, pp. 48-52.
2. Ibid., pp. 50-2, 81-5.
3. Ibid., pp. 76-81.
4. Ibid., pp. 41, 168-72.
5. See P. Richards, *Parliament and Conscience,* London, Allen & Unwin, 1970.
6. P. Richards, 'Private Members' Legislation' in S. Walkland and M. Ryle (eds.), *The House of Commons in the Twentieth Century,* Oxford, Clarendon Press, 1979.
7. See D. Marsh and M. Read, 'Private Members' Business, 1970-80', University of Essex, mimeo 1981.
8. See HC Debs., 22 February, vol. 979, col. 845, and 7 March, vol. 980, cols. 853-86.
9. M. Simms and K. Hindell, *Abortion Law Reformed.*
10. Richards, 'Parliament and Conscience'.
11. Elizabeth Vallance, *Women in Parliament,* London, Athlone Press, 1979, p. 75.
12. Ibid., p. 92.
13. See G. Dewry, 'Legislation', in S. Walkland and M. Ryle, *The Commons in the 70s,* London, Martin Robertson, 1977.
14. P. Norton, *Dissention in the House of Commons, 1945-74,* London, Macmillan, 1975; P. Norton, *Dissention in the House of Commons, 1974-79,* Oxford, Clarendon Press, 1980; P. Norton, *Conservative Dissents: Dissents within the Parliamentary Conservative Party 1970-4,* London, Temple Smith, 1978.
15. G. Moyser, 'Voting Patterns on "Moral" Issues in the British House of Commons, 1964-69', paper delivered at the Political Studies Association Conference, 1980.
16. Ibid., p. 11.
17. Ibid., pp. 6-8.
18. Before the data can be analysed, however, it is essential to have some idea about what MPs were voting on when each of the issues was debated. The situation is simplest in the case of the homosexuality issue. In this instance only two votes are concerned. The first was on the Third Reading of the Sexual Offences Bill in 1967 which legalized homosexual relations between consenting adults in private. The second vote concerns an amendment to the Criminal Justice (Scotland) Bill in 1980. The House supported this by 202 to 78 and thus legalized homosexuality in Scotland.

    The situation is rather more complicated when considering the issue of capital punishment. The original Murder (Abolition of

Death Penalty) Bill was passed in 1965. It contained a provision, reluctantly accepted by the sponsors, which limited its life to five years unless during that time there was an affirmative resolution by Parliament. However, the issue was debated and voted upon before the first five-year period expired. In November 1966, Duncan Sandys sought leave to introduce a bill which would have reintroduced the death penalty for murders of police or prison officers in the execution of their duty. The motion was lost by 292 votes to 170. Subsequently, in June 1969, Sandys again requested leave to introduce a bill to return the situation to one in which a new bill would have had to be introduced to abolish capital punishment. Leave to introduce such a bill was refused by 156 votes to 125 votes. The government chose to introduce an affirmative resolution in December 1969. However, Sir Harry Legge-Burke (Con. Isle of Ely) introduced a motion which criticized the government for introducing such a motion earlier than necessary. This motion took priority procedurally and a whip was imposed by both parties. The resolution was defeated and the affirmative resolution was introduced the next day and passed by 343 to 185. The vote on the procedural motion is excluded from consideration here as it was whipped and was not directly on the issue of capital punishment. Since 1969 the issue has been debated and voted upon in December 1974 and in July 1979. In both cases the government introduced affirmative resolutions. There was no whip imposed and upon each occasion amendments were introduced which would have prevented the life of the 1965 Act being extended. In December 1974 the amendment was defeated by 369 votes to 217, and in July 1974 by 362 votes to 243. So here we are examining the votes on: the Third Reading of the original Act in 1965; the Sandys motion in November 1966; the Bill to prevent the extension of the original Act in June 1969; the affirmative motion in December 1969; and the amendments to the affirmative motions in 1974 and 1979.

The relevant Hansard reports of the Debates are:

Homosexuality

1967: Sexual Offences Bill, Third Reading, 3 July 1967 vol. 749, cols. 1501-26; 1980: amendment to Criminal Justice (Scotland) Bill, 22 July 1980, vol. 989, cols. 283-322.

Capital Punishment

1965: Murder (Abolition of Death Penalty) Bill, Third Reading, 13 July 1965, vol. 716, cols. 407-66; 1966: Duncan Sandys's motion to reintroduce capital punishment, 22 November, vol. 736, cols. 1409-18; 1969: motion for leave to introduce a ten-minute rule bill, 24 June 1969, vol. 785, cols. 1228-36; 1969: vote on government affirmative motion on capital punishment, 15 December, vol. 793, cols. 1148-298; 1974: vote on anti-capital punishment amendment to government motion on capital punishment, 11 December, vol. 883, cols. 518-640; 1979: vote on government affirmative motion on capital punishment, 19 July, vol. 970, cols. 2019-126.

19. See above, pp. 26-7.
20. See below, pp. 210-12.
21. The data on the background characteristics of MPs and their majorities were collected from the appropriate editions of *The Times Guide to the House of Commons,* which is published by Times Books after each election. In addition, for data on the 1974-9 period we used M. Hulke (ed.), *Cassell's Parliamentary Directory,* London, Cassells, 1975.
22. Moyser, 'Voting Patterns on "Moral" Issues', pp. 12-14.
23. Ibid., pp. 15-17.
24. Copies of all the tables on which this analysis is based are available from D. Marsh, Department of Government, University of Essex.
25. Ibid.
26. *Prospects for the Eighties,* from a census of the Churches in 1979 undertaken by the Nationwide Initiative in Evangelism, The Bible Society, 1980.

Appendix 1: Statistical Tables

Table A.1: Total Legal Abortions in England and Wales, 1968-79

Year	Total	Residents	Non-residents*
1968**	23,600	22,300	1,300
1969	54,800	49,800	5,000
1970	86,600	76,000	10,600
1971	126,800	94,600	32,200
1972	159,900	108,600	51,300
1973	167,100	110,600	56,600
1974	163,100	109,400	53,700
1975	140,500	106,600	33,900
1976	127,900	101,000	26,900
1977	133,000	102,200	30,800
1978	142,343	112,055	30,288
1979	147,451	119,028	28,423

*Non-residents include women from Scotland, Northern Ireland and the Irish Republic.
**Figures given for 1968 refer to the eight months when the Abortion Act was in force.
Source: Office of Population Censuses and Surveys Monitors, Legal Abortions.

*More details of the tables on which the analysis in Tables A.3 to A.10 is based can be obtained from David Marsh, Department of Government, University of Essex.

Table A.2: Public Opinion on the Abortion Issue (percentages)

(a) The Abortion Act has been in operation since April 1968. Do you think the law should be:

	1970		1972		1973		1980*	
Left as it is?	40	55	30	47	34	48	37	50
Made easier?	15		17		14		13	
Made more difficult?	38		44		35		29	
Don't know	7		10		17		21	
Majority for existing or easier Abortion Act	+17		+3		+13		+21	

(b) How strongly do you agree or disagree with the following statement: 'Abortion should be made legally available for all who want it.'

	1975		1976		1979		1980*	
Agree very strongly	5		11		10		15	
Agree strongly	9	52	12	55	11	56	10	54
Agree	38		32		35		29	
Neither/Don't know	14		14		15		11	
Disagree	25		14		15		17	
Disagree strongly	5	34	10	31	6	29	8	36
Disagreee very strongly	4		7		8		11	
Majority who agree	+18		+24		+27		+18	
Feeling very strongly either way	9		18		18		25	

*Conducted by Market and Opinion Research International on 18-19 January 1980 among an interlocking quota sample of 1,090 people aged 15 and over throughout Great Britain. Figures for earlier years come from surveys by National Opinion Polls.

Table A.3: Relationship between Religion and Voting on Abortion, 1966-80 (all MPs) (comparing MPs with known religious affiliations with those whose affiliations are unknown or who are agnostic/atheist)

Vote	Strength of Relationship
Steel Bill, Second Reading (1966)	0.000*
Steel Bill, Third Reading (1967)	0.000*
St John-Stevas Bill (1969)	0.000*
White Bill, Second Reading (1975)	0.000[us]
Benyon Bill, Second Reading (1977)	0.000*
Braine Bill (1978)	0.000*
Corrie Bill, Second Reading (1979)	0.000*
Report Stage, 24 week amendment (1980)	0.000**
'Serious' amendment (1980)	0.036*
'Substantial' amendment (1980)	0.044*
Silkin amendment (1980)	0.000*

[us]Chi Square unstable; *Chi Square significant at 0.001 level; **Chi Square significant at 0.05 level.

Note: The statistic reported is *Lambda B*, based in this case upon a three by two table.

Table A.4: Relationship between Religion and Voting on Abortion, 1966-80 (all MPs) (comparing Roman Catholics with all other MPs)

Vote	Strength of Relationship
Steel Bill, Second Reading (1966)	0.000*
Steel Bill, Third Reading (1967)	0.032*
St John-Stevas Bill (1969)	0.038*
White Bill, Second Reading (1975)	0.065[us]
Benyon Bill, Second Reading (1977)	0.040*
Braine Bill (1978)	0.012*
Corrie Bill, Second Reading (1979)	0.000*
Report Stage, 24 week amendment (1980)	0.070*
'Serious' amendment (1980)	0.017*
'Substantial' amendment (1980)	0.017*
Silkin amendment (1980)	0.000*

[us]Chi Square unstable; *Chi Square significant at 0.001 level.

Note: The statistic reported is *Lambda B*, based in this case upon a three by two table.

Table A.5: Relationship between Secondary Education and Voting on Abortion, 1966-80 (all MPs)

Vote	Strength of Relationship
Steel Bill, Second Reading (1966)	0.000us
Steel Bill, Third Reading (1967)	0.000*
St John-Stevas Bill (1969)	0.054*
White Bill, Second Reading (1975)	0.000us
Benyon Bill, Second Reading (1977)	0.000*
Braine Bill (1978)	0.000*
Corrie Bill, Second Reading (1979)	0.000*
Report Stage, 24 week amendment (1980)	0.030*
'Serious' amendment (1980)	0.029*
'Substantial' amendment (1980)	0.046*
Silkin amendment (1980)	0.028*

usChi Square unstable; *Chi Square significant at 0.001 level; **Chi Square significant at 0.05 level.

Note: The statistic reported is *Lambda B,* based in this case upon a three by three table.

Table A.6: Relationship between Occupation and Voting on Abortion, 1966-80 (all MPs)

Vote	Strength of Relationship
Steel Bill, Second Reading (1966)	0.000*
Steel Bill, Third Reading (1967)	0.000*
St John-Stevas Bill (1969)	0.000*
White Bill, Second Reading (1975)	0.000us
Benyon Bill, Second Reading (1977)	0.000**
Braine Bill (1978)	0.000**
Corrie Bill, Second Reading (1979)	0.000*
Report Stage, 24 week amendment (1980)	0.024**
'Serious' amendment (1980)	0.000*
'Substantial' amendment (1980)	0.037*
Silkin amendment (1980)	0.000*

usChi Square unstable; *Chi Square significant at 0.001 level; **Chi Square significant at 0.05 level.

Note: The statistic reported is *Lambda B,* based in this case upon a four by three table.

Table A.7: Relationship between Tertiary Education and Abortion, 1966-80 (all MPs)

Vote	Strength of Relationship
Steel Bill, Second Reading (1966)	0.020*
Steel Bill, Third Reading (1967)	0.004*
St John-Stevas Bill (1969)	0.054**
White Bill, Second Reading (1975)	0.000^{us}
Benyon Bill, Second Reading (1977)	0.000**
Braine Bill (1978)	0.007*
Corrie Bill, Second Reading (1979)	0.063**
Report Stage, 24 week amendment (1980)	0.000*
'Serious' amendment (1980)	0.074*
'Substantial' amendment (1980)	0.123*
Silkin amendment (1980)	0.038*

^{us}Chi Square unstable; *Chi Square significant at 0.001 level; **Chi Square significant at 0.05 level.

Note: The statistic reported is *Lambda B,* based in this case upon a three by three table.

Table A.8: Relationship between Age and Voting on Abortion, 1966-80 (all MPs)

Vote	Strength of Relationship
Steel Bill, Second Reading (1966)	0.000**
Steel Bill, Third Reading (1967)	0.000*
St John-Stevas Bill (1969)	0.061**
White Bill, Second Reading (1975)	0.000^{us}
Benyon Bill, Second Reading (1977)	0.000^{ns}
Braine Bill (1978)	0.000^{ns}
Corrie Bill, Second Reading (1979)	0.023^{ns}
Report Stage, 24 week amendment (1980)	0.006**
'Serious' amendment (1980)	0.000^{ns}
'Substantial' amendment (1980)	0.000^{ns}
Silkin amendment (1980)	0.000^{ns}

^{us}Chi Square unstable; *Chi Square significant at 0.001 level; **Chi Square significant at 0.05 level; ^{ns}Not significant.

Note: The statistic reported is *Lambda B,* based in this case upon a four by three table.

Table A.9: Relationship between Date of First Election and Voting on Abortion, 1966-80 (all MPs)

Vote	Strength of Relationship
Steel Bill, Second Reading (1966)	0.030*
Steel Bill, Third Reading (1967)	0.000*
St John-Stevas Bill (1969)	0.097*
White Bill, Second Reading (1975)	0.000^{us}
Benyon Bill, Second Reading (1977)	0.000**
Braine Bill (1978)	0.000**
Corrie Bill, Second Reading (1979)	0.058*
Report Stage, 24 week amendment (1980)	0.020*
'Serious' amendment (1980)	0.017*
'Substantial' amendment (1980)	0.000*
Silkin amendment (1980)	0.000*

^{us}Chi Square unstable; *Chi Square significant at 0.001 level; **Chi Square significant at 0.05 level.

Note: The statistic reported is *Lambda B,* based in this case upon a four by three table.

Table A.10: Relationship between Sex and Voting on Abortion, 1966-80 (all MPs)

Vote	Strength of Relationship
Steel Bill, Second Reading (1966)	0.012^{ns}
Steel Bill, Third Reading (1967)	0.000^{ns}
St John-Stevas Bill (1969)	0.003^{ns}
White Bill, Second Reading (1975)	0.000^{us}
Benyon Bill, Second Reading (1977)	0.009*
Braine Bill (1978)	
Corrie Bill, Second Reading (1969)	0.000^{ns}
Report Stage, 24 week amendment (1980)	0.000^{ns}
'Serious' amendment (1980)	0.000^{ns}
'Substantial' amendment (1980)	0.000^{ns}
Silkin amendment (1980)	0.000^{ns}

^{us}Chi Square unstable; ^{ns}Chi Square not significant; *Chi Square significant at the 0.05 level.

Note: The statistic reported is *Lambda B.*

Appendix 2: Abortion (Amendment) Bill — Original Bill

A

B I L L

TO

Amend the Abortion Act 1967; to make further provisions with respect to the termination of pregnancy by registered medical practitioners; and for connected purposes. A.D. 1979

BE IT ENACTED by the Queen's most Excellent Majesty, by and with the advice and consent of the Lords Spiritual and Temporal, and Commons, in this present Parliament assembled, and by the authority of the same, as follows:—

Amendment of section 1 of principal Act.

1. Section 1 of the principal Act shall be amended in subsection (1)—

(*a*) by adding after the words "in good faith" the words "that the pregnancy has lasted for less than twenty weeks and—"; and

(*b*) by leaving out paragraph (*a*) and substituting therefor the words—

"(*a*) that the continuance of the pregnancy involves:—

(i) grave risk to the life of the pregnant woman; or

(ii) substantial risk of serious injury to the physical or mental health of the pregnant woman or any existing children of her family; or."

Amendment of section 4 of principal Act.

2. Section 4 of the principal Act shall be amended—

(*a*) in subsection (1) by—

(i) adding after the word " objection " where it first occurs the words " on religious, ethical or any other grounds." ; and

(ii) leaving out the proviso ; and

(*b*) by leaving out subsection (3).

Amendment and extension of Infant Life (Preservation) Act 1929.

1929 c. 34.

3. The Infant Life (Preservation) Act 1929 shall be amended—

(*a*) in subsection (2) of section 1, by leaving out the word " twenty-eight " and substituting therefor the word " twenty " ; and

(*b*) in subsection (2) of section 3 by leaving out the words " Scotland or ".

Licensing.

4.—(1) A licence shall be required under this Act for premises which are used for—

(*a*) the provision, for payment, of consultation with a medical practitioner with a view to his signing a certificate under the Abortion Regulations or to his subsequently terminating the pregnancy of the person attending the consultation ;

(*b*) the provision, for payment, of an advisory service in relation to treatment for the termination of a pregnancy ;

(*c*) the provision, for payment, of a service of testing whether or not a woman is pregnant.

(2) An application for a licence in relation to premises under this Act shall be made to the Secretary of State, and shall be accompanied by a fee.

(3) Subject to subsection (4) of this section, the Secretary of State shall, on receiving an application under subsection (2) of this section, issue to the applicant a licence in respect of the premises.

(4) The Secretary of State shall refuse to issue a licence to an applicant in relation to premises if he is satisfied—

(*a*) that the applicant, or any person employed or proposed to be employed by the applicant at the premises, is not a fit person (whether by reason of age or otherwise) to carry on, or be employed at, such premises ; or

(*b*) that, for reasons connected with situation, construction, state of repair, accommodation, staffing or equipment, the premises are not, or any premises used in connection therewith are not fit to be used for any of the purposes mentioned in subsection (1) of this section ; or (*c*) that the premises, or any premises used in connection therewith, are used or proposed to be used for purposes which are in any way improper or undesirable in the case of such premises ; or

(*d*) that the standard of medical advice offered at the premises in relation to the use in respect of which a licence under this section is required, is not likely to be adequate in the circumstances ; or

(*e*) that, in the case of the applicant, the occupier of the premises or any person associated or proposed to be associated with the use in respect of which a licence under this section is required on those premises, there is a financial arrangement or other relevant agreement with persons associated with a place approved for the purpose of section 1 of the principal Act.

(5) The Secretary of State shall refuse to issue a licence to an applicant in relation to premises unless he is satisfied that the premises shall be under the care and management of a registered medical practitioner or a qualified nurse.

(6) Subject to subsection (7) of this section, a licence under this section shall remain in force until revoked.

(7) The Secretary of State may at any time revoke a licence under this section in relation to premises—

(*a*) on any ground which would entitled him to refuse application for a licence under this section in relation to those premises ;

(*b*) on the ground that the applicant for the licence has been convicted of an offence against the provisions of the principal Act or this Act, or on the ground that any other person has been convicted of such an offence in respect of those premises ;

(*c*) on the ground that the applicant has been convicted of an offence against regulations made under Section 5 of this Act.

(8) It shall be an offence—

(*a*) for the occupier of any premises to use them for any of the purposes mentioned in subsection (1) of this section, or to permit them to be so used unless he holds a licence in relation to those premises under this section, or

(*b*) for any person other than the occupier to use any premises for any of the purposes mentioned in subsection (1) of this section unless the occupier holds a licence in relation to those premises under this section.

(9) Nothing in this section shall require premises to be licensed because of the use of those premises—

(*a*) by a registered medical practitioner for the purposes of his general practice ; or

(*b*) as a hospital vested in the Secretary of State under the National Health Service Acts ; or

(*c*) in accordance with an approval of the Secretary of State under section 1 of the principal Act ; or

(*d*) for the termination of a pregnancy in a case to which subsection (4) of section 1 of the principal Act applies ; or

1968 c. 67.

(*e*) by a registered pharmacist, provided those premises are registered under section 74 of the Medicines Act 1968.

(10) A person guilty of an offence under subsection (8) of this section shall be liable on summary conviction to a fine not exceeding £1,000 and in the event of a second or subsequent conviction to such a fine together with a fine not exceeding £100 in respect of each day on which the offence occurred or continued after the last conviction.

Regulations relating to premises.

5.—(1) The Secretary of State may make regulations with respect to the licensing of premises under section 4 of this Act and in particular with respect to prescribing fees to accompany applications for such licence and with respect to appeals in England and Wales to Magistrates' Courts and, in Scotland, to the Sheriff, against refusal to issue or revocation of a licence.

(2) Regulations made under this section shall be made by statutory instrument which shall be subject to annulment in pursuance of a resolution of either House of Parliament.

Counselling.

6.—(1) Organisations which offer counselling and advice to pregnant women may apply to the Minister to be included in a list compiled and maintained by him for the purposes of this section.

(2) The Minister shall from time to time distribute copies of such list to all registered medical practitioners.

(3) Before a registered medical practitioner issues a certificate under section 1 of the principal Act or when such medical practitioner refuses, for any reason, to issue such certificate, he shall inform the woman of the existence of such list and make a copy available to her.

Severely handicapped children.

1929 c. 34.

7. Notwithstanding anything in section 1 of the Infant Life (Preservation) Act 1929, where two medical practitioners certify in good faith that from the evidence of tests it appears to them that the child will be born severely handicapped then the pregnancy may be terminated at any time until the twenty-eighth week of the pregnancy and so much of section 1 of the principal Act as refers to twenty weeks shall not apply.

8. Where an offence under the Offences against the Person Act 1861, the Infant Life (Preservation) Act 1929, the principal Act, or this Act or against any regulations made under those Acts, which has been committed by a body corporate is proved to have been committed with the consent or connivance of, or to be attributable to any neglect or misrepresentation on the part of any director, manager, secretary or other similar officer of the body corporate or any person who was purporting to act in any such capacity he, as well as the body corporate, shall be guilty of that offence and shall be liable to be proceeded against and punished accordingly.

Offences by bodies corporate.
1861 c. 100.
1929 c. 34.

9. Summary proceedings in respect of any offence under subsection (3) of section 2 of the principal Act or subsection (8) of section 4 of this Act may, in England and Wales, notwithstanding anything in the Magistrates' Courts Act 1952, and in Scotland, notwithstanding anything in the Criminal Procedure (Scotland) Act 1975, be commenced at any time not later than three years from the date of commission of the offence.

Time limit for commencement of proceedings.
1952 c. 55.
1975 c. 21.

Provided that nothing in this section shall affect the application of those Acts in respect of offences alleged to have been committed before the passing of this Act.

10. In this Act unless the context otherwise requires—

Interpretation.

"tests" means investigations the results of which for medical reasons are not conclusive until after the twentieth week of pregnancy; and "principal Act" means the Abortion Act 1967.

1967 c. 87.

11.—(1) This Act may be cited as the Abortion (Amendment) Act 1979, and this Act and the principal Act may be cited together as the Abortion Acts 1967 and 1979.

Short title, citation, extent and commencement.

(2) This Act does not extend to Northern Ireland.

(3) Section 4 of this Act shall come into force at the expiration of six months beginning with the date of the coming into force of the remainder of this Act.

Appendix 3: Abortion (Amendment) Bill — as Amended by Standing Committee C

A

B I L L

[AS AMENDED BY STANDING COMMITTEE C]

TO

Amend the Abortion Act 1967; to make further provisions with respect to the termination of pregnancy by registered medical practitioners; and for connected purposes. A.D. 1979

BE IT ENACTED by the Queen's most Excellent Majesty, by and with the advice and consent of the Lords Spiritual and Temporal, and Commons, in this present Parliament assembled, and by the authority of the same, as follows:—

Amendment of section 1 of principal Act.

1.—(1) In subsection (1) of section 1 of the principal Act (medical termination of pregnancy) for paragraphs (*a*) and (*b*) there shall be substituted the following paragraphs—

" (*a*) that the pregnancy has lasted for less than 20 weeks; and

(*b*) that the continuance of the pregnancy would involve risk to the life of the pregnant woman, or of serious injury to the physical or mental health of the pregnant woman or any existing children of her family, substantially greater than if the pregnancy were terminated.".

(2) In subsection (2) of that section for the words " paragraph (*a*) " there shall be substituted the words " paragraph (*b*) ".

(3) In subsection (3) of that section—

(*a*) for the words from the beginning to " carried " there shall be substituted the words " This section applies only where the treatment for the termination of the pregnancy is "; and

(*b*) for the word " section " in the second place where it occurs there shall be substituted the word " Act ".

(4) For subsection (4) of that section there shall be substituted the following subsection—

" (4) The Secretary of State may by order made by statutory instrument substitute a lower number for the number of weeks for the time being specified in paragraph (*a*) of subsection (1) of this section; but no such order shall be made unless a draft of the order has been laid before Parliament and approved by resolution of each House of Parliament."

Termination of pregnancy without regard to time limit under section 1 in certain grave cases.

2.—(1) The following sections shall be inserted after section 1 of the principal Act—

" Medical termination of pregnancy to preserve mother's life, etc.

1A.—(1) Subject to subsection (3) of this section, a person shall not be guilty of an offence under the law relating to abortion or child destruction when a pregnancy is terminated by a registered medical practitioner if two registered medical practitioners are of the opinion, formed in good faith,—

(*a*) that the termination is necessary to preserve the life or to prevent grave permanent injury to the physical or mental health of the pregnant woman; and

(*b*) where the method of termination used is one which would necessarily involve or be likely to involve the destruction of the life of a child which is or may be capable of being born alive, that the use of any other method of termination would involve substantially greater risk to the life or of injury to the physical or mental health of the pregnant woman.

(2) The opinion of two registered medical practitioners shall not be required for the purposes of subsection (1) of this section in any case where the registered medical practitioner terminating the pregnancy is of the opinion, formed in good faith,—

(*a*) that the termination is immediately necessary for any purpose mentioned in paragraph (*a*) of that subsection; and (*b*) where paragraph (*b*) of that subsection applies, that the use of any other method of termination would involve such a risk as is mentioned in that paragraph.

(3) Section 1(3) of this Act shall apply for the purposes of this section, except in a case within subsection (2) of this section.

Medical termination of pregnancy to prevent birth of handicapped child.

1B.—(1) Subject to subsection (2) of this section, a person shall not be guilty of an offence under the law relating to abortion when a pregnancy is terminated by a registered medical practitioners if two registered medical practitioners are of the opinion, formed in good faith,—

(*a*) that there is a substantial risk that if the child were born it would suffer from such physical or mental abnormalities as to be seriously handicapped; and

(*b*) that, where the termination takes place in Scotland, the pregnancy has lasted for less than 28 weeks.

(2) Section 1(3) of this Act shall apply for the purposes of this section."

(2) In section 2(1)(*a*) of that Act, for the words " section 1 " there shall be substituted the words " any of the preceding provisions ".

(3) In section 3(1) of that Act, for the words " section 1 " there shall be substituted the words " sections 1 to 1B ".

(4) In section 5(1) of that Act—

(*a*) at the beginning there shall be inserted the words " Except as provided by section 1A of this Act "; and

(*b*) at the end there shall be added the words " and nothing in that section shall be taken as prejudicing the operation of the proviso to section 1 of that Act ".

(5) In section 5(2) of that Act, the words " section 1 of " shall be omitted.

(6) In section 6 of that Act, after the definition of " the law relating to abortion " there shall be inserted the following definition—

" " the law relating to child destruction " means section 1 of the Infant Life (Preservation) Act 1929.".

Amendment of section 4 of principal Act.

3. Section 4 of the principal Act shall be amended—

(*a*) in subsection (1) by—

(i) adding after the word " objection " where it first occurs the words " on religious, ethical or any other grounds."; and

(ii) leaving out the proviso; and

(*b*) by leaving out subsection (3).

Withdrawal of approval of premises.

4.—(1) If the Secretary of State is satisfied that a person is carrying on a service of providing counselling or advice to pregnant women or is employed by such a person and—

(*a*) is, or has been at any time within a period of six months previously, carrying out treatment for the termination of pregnancy at a place for the time being approved under section 1(3) of the principal Act or employed at such a place, or

(*b*) is, or has been at any time within a period of six months previously, associated with a person carrying out treatment for the termination of pregnancy at a place for the time being approved under section 1(3) of the principal Act

he shall withdraw his approval under the said section 1(3).

(2) For the purposes of subsection (1) of this section, a person is associated with another person if—

(*a*) where both persons are bodies corporate

(i) the same person is a controller of both, or a person is a controller of one and persons who are his associates, or he and persons who are his associates, are controllers of the other; or

(ii) a group of two or more persons is a controller of each company, and the groups either consist of the same persons or could be regarded as consisting of the same persons by treating (in one or more cases) a member of either group as replaced by a person of whom he is an associate, or

(*b*) where one of the persons is a body corporate, if the other person is a controller of it or if that person and persons who are his associates together are controllers of it, or

(*c*) an agreement exists between the persons with regard to the referral by one of the other of pregnant women for treatment for termination of pregnancy, or

(*d*) one person has received, or has been promised, a financial inducement in relation to the referral by one to the other of pregnant women for treatment for termination of pregnancy.

(3) The Secretary of State may by order made by statutory instrument amend subsection (2) of this section so as to add further categories but an order under this subsection shall be of no effect unless a draft of the order has been laid before and approved by each House of Parliament.

Offences by bodies corporate.
1861 c. 100.
1929 c. 34.

5. Where an offence under sections 58 and 59 of the Offences against the Person Act 1861, the Infant Life (Preservation) Act 1929, the principal Act, or this Act or against any regulations made under those Acts, which has been committed by a body corporate is proved to have been committed with the consent or connivance of, or to be attributable to any neglect or misrepresentation on the part of any director, manager, secretary or other similar officer of the body corporate or any person who was purporting to act in any such capacity he, as well as the body corporate, shall be guilty of that offence and shall be liable to be proceeded against and punished accordingly.

Time limit for commencement of summary proceedings.
1952 c. 55.

6.—(1) Notwithstanding anything in section 104 of the Magistrates' Courts Act 1952, summary proceedings in England and Wales for an offence under section 2(3) of the principal Act may, subject to subsection (3) below, be commenced at any time within the period of six months beginning with the date on which evidence sufficient in the opinion of the prosecutor to justify the proceedings comes to his knowledge.

(2) Notwithstanding anything in section 331 of the Criminal Procedure (Scotland) Act 1975, summary proceedings in Scotland for any such offence may, subject to subsection (3) below, be commenced at any time—

(*a*) within the period of six months beginning with the date on which evidence sufficient in the opinion of the prosecutor to justify the proceedings comes to his knowledge; or

(*b*) where such evidence was reported to him by the Secretary of State within the period of six months beginning with the date on which it came to the knowledge of the Secretary of State,

and subsection (3) of the said section 331 shall apply for the purposes of this section as it applies for the purpose of that section.

(3) Nothing in this section shall authorise the commencement of proceedings for any offence after the expiration of the period of three years beginning with the date on which the offence was committed.

(4) For the purposes of this section a certificate signed by or on behalf of the prosecutor or, as the case may be, the Secretary of State and stating the date on which such evidence as aforesaid

came to his knowledge shall be conclusive evidence of that fact; and a certificate stating that fact and purporting to be so signed shall be deemed to be so signed unless the contrary is proved.

(5) In relation to offences committed before the coming into force of this section, neither subsection (1) nor subsection (2) above shall apply if the time allowed for taking the proceedings has already expired before this section comes into force.

Interpretation. 1967 c. 87.

7. In this Act unless the context otherwise requires " the principal Act " means the Abortion Act 1967.

Short title, citation, extent and commencement.

8.—(1) This Act may be cited as the Abortion (Amendment) Act 1980, and this Act and the principal Act may be cited together as the Abortion Acts 1967 and 1980.

(2) This Act does not extend to Northern Ireland.

(3) Section 4 of this Act shall come into force at the expiration of six months beginning with the date of the coming into force of the remainder of this Act.

Bibliography

Political

Books

Barker, A. and Rush, M., *The Member of Parliament and his Information,* London, Allen and Unwin, 1970

Blalock, H., *Social Statistics,* New York, McGraw-Hill, 1972

Bromhead, P., *Private Members Bills,* London, Routledge & Kegan Paul, 1956

Hulke, M. (ed.), *Cassell's Parliamentary Directory,* London, Cassells, 1975

Norton, P., *Dissention in the House of Commons 1945-74,* London, Macmillan, 1975

Norton, P., *Dissention in the House of Commons 1974-79,* Oxford, Clarendon Press, 1980

Norton, P., *Conservative Dissents: Dissent within the Parliamentary Conservative party 1970-74,* London, Temple Smith, 1978

Richards, P., *Parliament and Conscience,* London, Allen and Unwin, 1970

Richards, P., 'Private Members Legislation' in S. Walkland (ed.) *The House of Commons in the Twentieth Century,* Oxford, Clarendon Press, 1979

Times Guide to the House of Commons, The, London, Times Books, published after each general election

Valance, E., *Women in Parliament,* London, Athlone Press, 1979

Articles

Dewry, G., 'Legislation' in S. Walkland and M. Ryle, *The Commons in the 70s,* London, Martin Robertson, 1977

Moyser, G., 'Voting Patterns on "Moral" Issues in the British House of Commons, 1964-69', paper delivered at the Political Studies Association Conference, 1980

Abortion

Books

Bourne, A., *A Doctor's Creed,* London, Gollancz, 1962

Dickens, B.M., *Abortion and the Law,* London, MacGibbon & Kee, 1966

Gardiner, G. and Andrew, M., *Law Reform Now,* London, Gollancz, 1963

Greenwood, V. and Young, J., *Abortion in Demand,* London, Pluto Press, 1976

Jenkins, A., *Law for the Rich,* London, Gollancz, 1960; paperback edn., Yellow Riband Books series, Riband Books, 1964

Litchfield, M. and Kentish, S., *Babies for Burning,* London, Serpentine Press, 1974

Simms, M. and Hindell, K., *Abortion Law Reformed,* London, Peter Owen, 1971

St John-Stevas, N., *The Right to Life,* London, Hodder & Stoughton, 1963

Williams, G., *The Sanctity of Life and the Criminal Law,* London, Faber and Faber, 1958

Pamphlets

Abortion and the Right to Live, London, Catholic Information Service, 1980

Abortion, an Ethical Discussion, London, Church Information Office, 1965

Abortion Law Reform London, Church Information Office, 1974/5

A Commentary on the Corrie Bill and What You can Do ..., London, Abortion Law Reform Association, 1979

A Guide to the Abortion (Amendment) Bill 1977 and its Implications, London, Birth Control Trust, 1977

A Guide to the Abortion (Amendment) Bill 1979 and its Implications, London, Birth Control Trust, 1979

Campaign for Corrie, Guidelines for all who want to help Mr John Corrie's Abortion (Amendment) Bill reach the Statute Book, London, LIFE, 1979

Ten Years On, London, Birth Control Trust, 1979

The Select Committee on the Abortion (Amendment) Bill, Extracts from Minutes of Evidence, London, Birth Control Trust, 1976

General

Catholic Directory, The, London, Association Catholic Publications Ltd, annually

Prospects for the Eighties: From a Census of the Churches in 1979; undertaken by the Nationwide Initiative in Evangelism, London, The Bible Society, 1980

Parliamentary Debates on Abortion

John Reeves Bill
HC Debs., 27 February 1953, vol. 511, col. 2506

Kenneth Robinson Bill
HC Debs., 10 February 1961, vol. 643, cols. 853-92

Renée Short Bill
HC Debs., 15 June 1965, vol. 714, cols. 254-9

Simon Wingfield Digby Bill
HC Debs., 26 February 1966, vol. 725, cols. 837-56

Lord Silkin First Bill
HL Debs., 30 November 1965, vol. 270, cols. 1139-242
HL Debs., 1 February 1966, vol. 272, cols. 284-356
HL Debs., 3 February 1966, vol. 272, cols. 491-557
HL Debs., 7 February 1966, vol. 272, cols. 581-601
HL Debs., 22 February 1966, vol. 273, cols. 92-152
HL Debs., 28 February 1966, vol. 273, cols. 520-76
HL Debs., 7 March 1966, vol. 273, cols. 910-20 and 929-46

Lord Silkin Second Bill
HL Debs., 10 May 1966, vol. 274, cols. 577-605
HL Debs., 23 May 1966, vol. 274, cols. 1206-50

David Steel Bill
HC Debs., 22 July 1966, vol. 732, cols. 1067-162
HC Debs., Reports of Standing Committee, Session 1966-67. Vol. X Committee F on Medical Termination of Pregnancy Bill 18 Jan-5 April 1967

HC Debs., 2 June 1967, vol. 747, cols. 448-536
HC Debs., 30 June 1967, vol. 749, cols. 895-1102
HC Debs., 13 July 1967, vol. 750, cols. 1159-386
HC Debs., 25 October 1967, vol. 751, cols. 1737-82
Norman St John-Stevas Bill
HC Debs., 15 July 1969, vol. 787, cols. 411-24
Bryant Godman Irvine Bill
HC Debs., 13 February 1970, vol. 795, cols. 1653-703
John Hunt Bill
HC Debs, 1 December 1971, vol. 827, col. 460
Michael Gryll Bill
HC Debs., 8 May 1974, vol. 873, cols. 403-6 and col. 853
James White Bill
HC Debs., 7 February 1975, vol. 885, cols. 1757-868
William Benyon Bill
HC Debs., 25 February 1977, vol. 926, cols. 1783-896
HC Debs., Reports of Standing Committee C on the Abortion (Amendment) Bill, 22 June-12 July 1977
Sir Bernard Braine Bill
HC Debs., 21 February 1978, vol. 944, cols. 1213-24
John Corrie Bill
HC Debs., 13 July 1979, vol. 970, cols. 891-984
HC Debs., Report on Standing Committee C on the Abortion (Amendment) Bill, 25 July-18 December 1979
HC Debs., 8 February 1980, vol. 978 (Report Stage of John Corrie's Bill) cols. 929-1015
HC Debs., 15 February 1980, vol. 978, cols. 931-2019
HC Debs., 28 February 1980, vol. 979, cols. 1715-810
HC Debs., 14 March 1980, vol. 980, cols. 1745-828
David Alton Bill
HC Debs., 22 April 1980, vol. 983, cols. 221-6

Papers on Abortion

Report on the Committee on the Working of the Abortion Act (The Lane Committee) 3 vols., HMSO 1974, Cmnd 5579, 5579-1 and 5579-11

Special Reports and Minutes of Evidence of the Select Committee on the Abortion (Amendment) Bill Together with the proceedings of the Committee, Session 1974-75, HMSO 692-11, 10 November 1975

First Report from the Select Committee on Abortion Together with the Proceedings of the Committee and Appendices, Session 1975-76, vol. 1: Report, HMSO HC 573-11, 12 July 1976

First Report from the Select Committee on Abortion, Session 1975-76, vol. 11: Minutes of Evidence and Appendices, HMSO HC 573-11, 12 July 1976

Second Report from the Select Committee on Abortion Together with the Proceedings of the Committee, Minutes of Evidence and Appendices, Session 1975-76, HMSO, 737, 22 November 1976

Parliamentary Debates on Homosexuality

HC Debs., 3 July 1967, vol. 749 (Third Reading of Sexual Offences Bill) cols. 1501-26

HC Debs., 22 July 1980, vol. 989, (Amendment to Criminal Justice (Scotland) Bill), cols. 283-322

Parliamentary Debates on Capital Punishment

HC Debs., 13 July 1965, vol. 716 (Murder (Abolition of Death Penalty) Bill, Third Reading) cols. 407-66

HC Debs., 22 November 1966, vol. 736 (Duncan Sandys's motion to reintroduce capital punishment) cols. 1409-18

HC Debs., 24 June 1969, vol. 785 (motion for leave to introduce a Ten-Minute Rule Bill), cols. 1228-38

HC Debs., 13 December 1969, vol. 793 (vote on Government affirmative motion on capital punishment) cols. 1148-298

HC Debs., 11 December 1974, vol. 883 (vote on anti-capital punishment amendment to Government motion on capital punishment) cols. 518-640

HC Debs., 19 July 1979, vol. 970 (vote on Government affirmative motion on capital punishment) cols. 2019-126

Index